The Social Anthropology
of Radcliffe-Brown

The Social Anthropology of Radcliffe-Brown

edited by
Adam Kuper

Routledge & Kegan Paul
London, Henley and Boston

First published in 1977
by Routledge & Kegan Paul Ltd
39 Store Street,
London WC1E 7DD,
Broadway House,
Newtown Road,
Henley-on-Thames,
Oxon RG9 1EN and
9 Park Street,
Boston, Mass. 02108, USA
Set in 11/12pt Garamond
by Weatherby Woolnough
Wellingborough, Northants
and printed in Great Britain by
Lowe & Brydone Printers Ltd
Thetford, Norfolk

British Library Cataloguing in Publication Data

Radcliffe-Brown, Alfred Reginald
The social anthropology of Radcliffe-Brown.
1. Ethnology – Addresses, essays, lectures
I. Title   II. Kuper, Adam
301.1'08   GN325

ISBN 0-7100-8556-7
ISBN 0-7100-8557-5 Pbk

Contents

Sources and acknowledgments

1 From *Structure and Function in Primitive Society,* Cohen & West, 1952; New York, Free Press paperback, 1965, pp. 1-4.
2 From *Journal of the Royal Anthropological Institute,* 70, 1940, pp. 1-12.
3 From *An Appraisal of Anthropology Today,* ed. Sol Tax *et al.,* University of Chicago Press, 1953, p. 109.
4 Sections I and III from *A Natural Science of Society,* Chicago, Free Press, 1957, pp. 85, 124-8; section II from *The Andaman Islanders,* Cambridge University Press, 1933 edition, pp. vii-viii.
5 From *American Anthropologist,* 51 (2), 1949, pp. 320-2.
6 From *Journal of the Royal Anthropological Institute,* 81, 1951, pp. 15-22.
7 From *The Andaman Islanders,* pp. 232-46, 257-9, 264-5, 297-307, 324-8.
8 From *Journal of the Royal Anthropological Institute,* 75, 1945, pp. 33-43.
9 Part I from *Oceania,* 1 (1), 1930, pp. 34-65; part II from ibid., 1 (4), 1931, pp. 444-56.
10 From *Africa,* 13 (3), 1940, pp. 195-210.
11 From *African Systems of Kinship and Marriage,* ed. A. R. Radcliffe-Brown and D. Forde, Oxford University Press, 1950, pp. 3-85.

The editor and the publishers are grateful to Dr Godfrey Lienhardt and the Royal Anthropological Institute for permission to reprint these selections, and to the following editors and publishers: to the RAI for chapters 2, 6 and 8; to the University of Chicago Press for chapter 3; to Macmillan Publishing Co., Inc., New York, for chapter 4; to Cambridge University Press for part of chapter 4, and chapter 7; to the American Anthropological Association for chapter 5; to the editor, *Oceania* Publications, the University of Sydney, NSW, for chapter 9; to the International African Institute for chapters 10 and 11.

Finally, the editor gratefully acknowledges the bibliographical help given by Mrs R. Kennemore of the Australian Institute of Aboriginal Studies.

Preface

I

Radcliffe-Brown has come to stand for a phase of British social anthropology which is currently out of fashion. For a man so ready to dismiss his predecessors, there is perhaps a certain justice in this, but current stereotypes are too crude to be left unchallenged. There are anthropologists who apparently believe that Radcliffe-Brown (despite his student nickname 'Anarchy Brown') wanted societies to be static, perfectly integrated natural systems, and who regard him as a proponent of the archetypal conservative position in the social sciences. Others, who seem to have read some of his programmatic statements but not his specific analyses, ridicule him as a displaced naturalist, grubbing about for non-existent social species and reifying the 'anatomies' and 'physiologies' of societies. Even more crudely, he is sometimes dismissed as the author of a conglomerate and largely imaginary theory vulgarly termed 'functionalism'. (Malinowski regarded Radcliffe-Brown, accurately enough, as the leading opponent of the specific theory which Malinowski himself called 'functionalism'.)

Even fairly recently he was closely read, and particular ideas of his had great influence. His kinship theories provided the direct inspiration for seminal studies by Fred Eggan, Meyer Fortes, Sol Tax, Lloyd Warner and others; and yet by a particularly unfortunate irony his best-known contribution is his badly-flawed early paper, 'The mother's brother in South Africa'. His influence on kinship theory today is largely indirect, except in the special area of Australian kinship studies. In the field of ritual and symbolic systems, he emerged as the hero of Lévi-Strauss's critical monograph, *Totemism,* and strongly influenced Victor Turner and other leading contemporaries. He could even claim to have made pioneering contributions to the then still embryonic science of semiology. (See chapter 7 in this collection.) Yet in this field too he is rarely cited directly any longer. He remains influential, but, increasingly, indirectly.

I am not concerned here to trace his influence on others (even on those who came to oppose him. Evans-Pritchard's later theoretical position was formulated as a direct, almost point for point, contradiction of Radcliffe-Brown). I want only to point the paradox, and to suggest that the profound yet second-hand nature of his influence on modern anthropology may constitute a real difficulty for the contemporary reader who returns to him. A related difficulty is the disproportionate attention given to some of his analyses because they provoked later controversies. These are by no means always his most enduring contributions.

I have edited this book for two basic reasons. In the first place, I think much that he wrote is still intrinsically worth reading, for what it says, and not simply because Radcliffe-Brown is a figure of some historical significance in the development of comparative sociology. He was a leading exponent of a point of view which might be labelled 'structural positivism', an unfashionable but not untenable position, and one still worth serious consideration. Further, many of his particular analyses are still plausible and suggestive, and often even retain a certain novelty; and they are expressed with a clarity and simplicity which make them a pleasure to read. My second reason is that neither of the readily available collections of his work is representative of the full range of what he has to say to contemporary readers, and both contain a considerable amount of dross. Too many students have dipped into *Structure and Function in Primitive Society,* and taken the part for the whole.

This is intended as a 'readers' edition' of Radcliffe-Brown, and while full bibliographical references are provided, I shall keep biographical and critical remarks to a minimum. To the extent that Radcliffe-Brown can be read as a contemporary, they should be unnecessary.

Briefly, then, Radcliffe-Brown, who lived from 1881 to 1955, was one of the first professional social anthropologists. He carried out extended field-studies in the Andaman Islands and among the Australian aborigines before World War I. Following the war, and a brief period of illness and, it seems, insecurity, he occupied a series of chairs in the discipline – most of them foundation chairs in social anthropology – in Cape Town, Sydney, Chicago and Oxford. At an early stage he was converted to a Durkheimian view of sociology (though he was also influenced by the ideas of Herbert Spencer), and after Durkheim's death he was, with Marcel Mauss, the leading exponent of this tradition. Radcliffe-Brown saw his mission as the establishment of what he considered scientific comparative sociology – that is, a structural and sociological anthropology – in the face of the entrenched traditions of ethnology and social evolutionism. He was a pioneer, even a prophet, and although unusually successful he exhibited many of the characteristic traits of rigidity and extreme sensitivity to criticism. His historical role explains a great deal of the emotion which still surrounds his name.

The Durkheimian tradition contains several clear alternatives – or rather, alternatives which have become clear as different scholars have developed the tradition. In the first place, sociological analysis may explore the connections among social institutions and the connections between these connections. Alternatively, it may concentrate upon the relationship between the individual and the group – upon the processes by which communal values are internalized by the individual and generated by the group. These possibilities are logically compatible, but they do tend to lead the analyst in different directions. In his earlier work, Radcliffe-Brown concentrated upon the way in which structurally requisite 'sentiments' were maintained in individuals. This was the guiding concern behind his work on Andaman Island myth and ritual (see chapter 7 of this book). He did investigate the mutual interlocking of Andaman notions, but presented them as psychologically and situationally, rather than logically, connected. His early analyses in the field of kinship were constructed on a similar basis, though here the sentiments were seen as arising from the vital parental functions, which determined the social forms, rather than the social forms imposing a required pattern of sentiments upon mothers, fathers and children. In his later work, 'sentiments' were not the central focus. The emphasis was rather on the mutual connections among institutions, and between institutions and beliefs. The last major papers he published (chapters 6 and 11 in this book), reflect this shift in the study of cosmological beliefs and kinship systems.

Despite such shifts of emphasis, one persistent notion underlies all Radcliffe-Brown's published work. This is that the structures he was investigating were directly observable. They corresponded in a simple way to 'empirical reality'. The starting-point was a set of living human beings involved in a series of social relationships with one another. This 'social network', as he sometimes described it, and as it would be termed today, he called the 'social structure'. But behind

3

the flux of everyday interactions, regularities could be established. The regular forms of social relationships could thus be abstracted. Together these constituted the 'structural form' of the society. This again was empirically real, since it corresponded to the stated norms and customary usages of various kinds of social relationships. Being real in this sense, the structural form could be functionally related to the actual processes of social life. In the paradigmatic case, recurrent social activities maintain the structural form, and are in turn determined by it.

One obvious difficulty with this position is that the stated norms and customary usages are not necessarily a good guide to what people actually do. Indeed there may be a systematic and stable divergence between the rules and the practices – between the statistical norms and the normative norms.[1] It is surely always best to distinguish a normative form, the sum of various conventions, and a statistical form, the sum of observed actions of various kinds. However, the main thrust of Radcliffe-Brown's argument remains undisturbed. This is, that the aim of sociological analysis is to relate the various institutions of a society to each other, exhibiting both their formal inter-relationships (or structural relationships), and the mutual impact of their activities (or functional relationships).

To proceed further demands comparative research. Radcliffe-Brown argued that functional relationships could properly be established only through a series of comparisons, which would enable the analyst to determine which relationships are necessary and which contingent. Ultimately he hoped to establish functional relationships of such generality as to constitute 'laws'. Comparison is thus simply another logical progression – some variables are gently freed from local or temporary accretions; different institutions and functions are, as it were, given different weightings.

Radcliffe-Brown's insistence upon the need to classify structural forms has been much misunderstood. I suggest that the reader carefully considers the characteristics of his 'Kariera' and 'Aranda' types of Australian social systems (see chapter 9). Are these examples of mindless, empiricist butterfly-collecting? Are his statements about these 'types' tautological? I would not like to argue that these 'types' are still, forty years on, the best formulations of the underlying regularities of Australian social systems, but they are very good examples of the kind of generalization which Radcliffe-Brown's structural positivism sought, as a first or second stage at least; and

I would argue that they are very powerful analytical tools. Another fine example of the procedure is his essay (chapter 6 in this book) on the comparative method (cf. p. 277).

It is in the positivism upon which he so insisted that Radcliffe-Brown differs decisively from the later French Durkheimians. Their 'structures' are creations of the anthropologist, not systematized observations, and if they correspond to an external reality it is to a hidden reality, not to the immediately observable empirical facts. This reality may lie at the level of a 'collective unconscious'; but not at the level of what is conventionally understood by Durkheim's notion of the 'collective consciousness'. In the present idealist climate, when even fashionable Marxism is idealist, these assumptions are readily accepted; positivist formulations are disregarded. In Lévi-Strauss's famous statement:[2]

> The term 'social structure' has nothing to do with empirical reality but with models which are built up after it. This should help one to clarify the difference between two concepts which are so close to each other that they have often been confused, namely, those of *social structure* and of *social relations* ... social relations consist of the raw materials out of which the models making up the social structure are built, while social structure can, by no means, be reduced to the ensemble of the social relations to be described in a given society.

Some juggling of terms is necessary in order to translate this statement into Radcliffe-Brown's language. He used the term 'social structure' precisely to mean the raw material, the 'social relations', of Lévi-Strauss. His notion of 'structural form', however, does not correspond to Lévi-Strauss's 'social structure', although it is close to being a blanket term for what Lévi-Strauss distinguished as 'mechanical models' and 'statistical models'. (Not quite—but that is not relevant at the moment.) Radcliffe-Brown operated at the level of the structural form, the stated norms (and he assumed also, the statistical norms). His concern was with the connections between different norms or institutions, and with the mutual impact of institutionalized forms of behaviour and the individual's 'sentiments'.

I have commented at some length on this issue, because this is perhaps the main contemporary stumbling-block to an understanding of what Radcliffe-Brown was saying. He is seldom less than clear in the statement of his views, but the terms he employed, particularly 'social structure', carry today a burden of associations which are foreign to his purpose. Radcliffe-Brown was a positivist, a structural positivist, to use a neologism which would have dismayed him. His notions are not a crude approximation to the notions of those who have come to be known as 'structuralists', *tout court,* any more than they are a version of the point of view which Malinowski dubbed 'functionalist'.

II

Two collections of Radcliffe-Brown's theoretical essays have already been published. *Structure and Function in Primitive Society* appeared in 1952 and included some of his best-known pieces, together with a specially written introduction. After Radcliffe-Brown's death, Professor Srinivas edited a different selection of papers, which was published under the title *Method in Social Anthropology.* This volume included the famous address, 'The comparative method in social anthropology', and a fragment of an uncompleted textbook on social anthropology. As an ethnographer, Radcliffe-Brown published a long monograph on the Andaman Islanders, and a monograph and various uncollected papers on the Australian aborigines. Finally, after his death, Professor Eggan published a transcript of a special seminar given by Radcliffe-Brown at the University of Chicago in 1937, *A Natural Science of Society.*

In keeping with my overall aim, I have tried to avoid papers which simply rehearse discredited theories or reiterate long-dead controversies—the few exceptions have particular points in their favour which I hope will be apparent. The selection is nevertheless fairly representative of Radcliffe-Brown's published writings, as it should be, for in every field which engaged his interest he had something of enduring significance to say.

The material is ordered roughly by content, although the essay on the comparative method, which I include in the section on general theory, is perhaps chiefly notable for the development of Radcliffe-Brown's theory of totemism. This arrangement should make for easier reading than a chronological presentation of extracts, but it has the disadvantage of obscuring the development of his ideas. I have commented on some changes in his approach, and indeed he mentions them in his introduction to *Structure and Function in Primitive*

Society, reprinted as chapter 1 in this volume. None the less, the problem is less serious than it would be for other, more protean, scholars. Although published over a period of more than three decades, Radcliffe-Brown's mature work is remarkably coherent and internally consistent.

Most of the papers included here appear without any alterations, or with only minor excisions in the introductory or concluding paragraphs. However, the sections on Andamanese ritual and on Australian social organization have been quite heavily edited, in the interest of conserving space and maintaining proportion, and, also, in order to exclude material which is of little interest today. For example, I have omitted the whole second part of the monograph on Australian tribes which, as Radcliffe-Brown wrote, 'is really only a systematic catalogue of the various types or varieties' of Australian social organization; and also much of the third part, which consists largely of general observations on kinship systems, better presented in the long introduction to *African Systems of Kinship and Marriage,* reprinted here as 'Systems of kinship and marriage'. In that piece, incidentally, I have retained the comments on essays in the collection to which it served as an introduction. This may cause minor irritation to the reader, but in general the comments were integral to his argument. There is only one section in which I have taken serious liberties. Chapter 4 of this book is made up of various extracts from Radcliffe-Brown's writings collated to form a coherent statement of his ideas about social function, since in my view his paper 'On the concept of function in social science' does less than justice to his use of this notion in his published work as a whole.

Notes

1 This argument was developed at an early stage by Meyer Fortes in his contribution to Radcliffe-Brown's *Festschrift.* See his 'Time and social structure: an Ashanti case-study', in M. Fortes (ed.), *Social Structure,* Clarendon Press, 1949; but see p. 197 ff. below.

2 C. Lévi-Strauss, *Structural Anthropology,* Basic Books, 1963; Allen Lane the Penguin Press, 1968, p. 279. The quotation is from Lévi-Strauss's paper 'Social structure', to which Radcliffe-Brown wrote a reply, published here as chapter 3.

3 References and names of countries, etc., have been left in their original form, although some missing references have been supplied.

Part I Structure and Function

1   Introduction

The papers reprinted here[1] are occasional papers in the fullest sense of the term; each of them was written for a particular occasion. They do, however, have some measure of unity as being written from a particular theoretical point of view.

What is meant by a theory is a scheme of interpretation which is applied, or is thought to be applicable, to the understanding of phenomena of a certain class. A theory consists of a set of analytical concepts, which should be clearly defined in their reference to concrete reality, and which should be logically connected. I propose, therefore, by way of introduction to these miscellaneous papers, to give definitions of certain concepts of which I make use for purposes of analysis of social phenomena. It must be remembered that there is very little agreement amongst anthropologists in the concepts and terms they use, so that this Introduction and the papers that follow are to be taken as an exposition of one particular theory, not of a commonly accepted theory.

History and theory

The difference between the historical study of social institutions and the theoretical study can be easily seen by comparing economic history and theoretical economics, or by comparing the history of law with theoretical jurisprudence. In anthropology, however, there has been and still is a great deal of confusion which is maintained by discussions in which terms such as 'history' and 'science' or 'theory' are used by disputants in very different meanings. These confusions could be to a considerable extent avoided by using the recognised terms of logic and methodology and distinguishing between *idiographic* and *nomothetic* enquiries.

In an idiographic enquiry the purpose is to establish as acceptable certain particular or factual propositions or statements. A nomothetic enquiry, on the contrary, has for its purpose to arrive at acceptable general propositions. We define the nature of an enquiry by the kind of conclusions that are aimed at.

History, as usually understood, is the study of records and monuments for the purpose of providing knowledge about conditions and events of the past, including those investigations that are concerned with the quite recent past. It is clear that history consists primarily of idiographic enquiries. In the last century there was a dispute, the famous *Methodenstreit,* as to whether historians should admit theoretical considerations in their work or deal in generalisations. A great many historians have taken the view that nomothetic enquiries should not be included in historical studies, which should be confined to telling us what happened and how it happened. Theoretical or nomothetic enquiries should be left to sociology. But there are some writers who think that a historian may, or even should, include theoretical interpretations in his account of the past. Controversy on this subject, and on the relation between history and sociology, still continues after sixty years. Certainly there are writings by historians which are to be valued not solely as idiographic accounts of the facts of the past but as containing theoretical (nomothetic) interpretations of those facts. The tradition in French historical studies of Fustel de Coulanges and his followers, such as Gustave Glotz, illustrates this kind of combination. Some modern writers refer to it as sociological history or historical sociology.

In anthropology, meaning by that the study of what are called the primitive or backward peoples, the term ethnography applies to what is specifically a mode of idiographic enquiry, the aim of which is to give acceptable accounts of such people and their social life. Ethnography differs from history in that the ethnographer derives his knowledge, or some major part of it, from direct observation of or contact with the people about whom he writes, and not, like the historian, from written records. Prehistoric archaeology, which is another branch of anthropology, is clearly an idiographic study, aimed at giving us factual knowledge about the prehistoric past.

The theoretical study of social institutions in general is usually referred to as sociology, but as this name can be loosely used for many different kinds of writings about society we can speak more specifically of theoretical or comparative sociology. When Frazer gave his Inaugural Lecture as the first Professor of Social Anthropology in 1908 he defined social anthropology as that branch of sociology that deals with primitive societies.

Certain confusions amongst anthropologists result from the failure to distinguish between *historical explanation* of institutions and *theoretical understanding.* If we ask why it is that a certain institution exists in a particular society the appropriate answer is a historical statement as to its origin. To explain why the United States has a political constitution with a President, two Houses of Congress, a Cabinet, a Supreme Court, we refer to the history of North America. This is historical explanation in the proper sense of the term. The existence of an institution is explained by reference to a complex sequence of events forming a causal chain of which it is a result.

The acceptability of a historical explanation depends on the fullness and reliability of the historical record. In the primitive societies that are studied by social anthropology there are no historical records. We have no knowledge of the development of social institutions among the Australian aborigines for example. Anthropologists, thinking of their study as a kind of historical study, fall back on conjecture and imagination, and invent 'pseudo-historical' or 'pseudo-causal' explanations. We have had, for example, innumerable and sometimes conflicting pseudo-historical accounts of the origin and development of the totemic institutions of the Australian aborigines. In the papers of this volume mention is made of certain pseudo-historical speculations. The view taken here is that such speculations are not merely useless but are worse than useless. This does not in any way imply the rejection of historical explanation but quite the contrary.

Comparative sociology, of which social anthropology is a branch, is here conceived as a theoretical or nomothetic study of which the aim is to provide acceptable generalisations. The theoretical understanding of a particular institution is its interpretation in the light of such generalisations.

Social process

A first question that must be asked if we are to formulate a systematic theory of comparative sociology is: What is the concrete, observable, phenomenal reality with which the theory is to be concerned? Some anthropologists would say that the reality consists of 'societies' conceived as being in some sense or other discrete real entities. Others, however, describe the reality that has to be studied as consisting of 'cultures', each of which is again conceived as some kind of discrete entity. Still others seem to think of the subject as concerned with both kinds of entities, 'societies' and 'cultures', so that the relation of these then presents a problem.

My own view is that the concrete reality with which the social anthropologist is concerned in observation, description, comparison and classification, is not any sort of entity but a process, the process of social life. The unit of investigation is the social life of some particular region of the earth during a certain period of time. The process itself consists of an immense multitude of actions and interactions of human beings, acting as individuals or in combinations or groups. Amidst the diversity of the particular events there are discoverable regularities, so that it is possible to give statements or descriptions of certain *general features* of the social life of a selected region. A statement of such significant general features of the process of social life constitutes a description of what may be called a *form of social life*. My conception of social anthropology is as the comparative theoretical study of forms of social life amongst primitive peoples.

A form of social life amongst a certain collection of human beings may remain approximately the same over a certain period. But over a sufficient length of time the form of social life itself undergoes change or modification. Therefore, while we can regard the events of social life as constituting a process, there is over and above this the process of change in the form of social life. In a *synchronic* description we give an account of a form of social life as it exists at a certain time, abstracting as far as possible from changes that may be taking place in its features. A *diachronic* account, on the other hand, is an account of such changes over a period. In comparative sociology we have to deal theoretically with the continuity of, and with changes in, forms of social life.

Culture

Anthropologists use the word 'culture' in a number of different senses. It seems to me that some of them use it as equivalent to what I call a form of social life. In its ordinary use in English 'culture', which is much the same idea as cultivation, refers to a process, and we can define it as the process by which a person acquires, from contact with other persons or from such things as books or works of art, knowledge, skill, ideas, beliefs, tastes, sentiments. In a particular society we can discover certain processes of *cultural tradition,* using the word tradition in its literal meaning of handing on or handing down. The understanding and use of a language is passed on by a process of cultural tradition in this sense. An Englishman learns by such a process to understand and use the English language, but in some sections of the society he may also learn Latin, or Greek, or French, or Welsh. In complex modern societies there are a great number of separate cultural traditions. By one a person may learn to be a doctor or surgeon, by another he may learn to be an engineer or an architect. In the simplest forms of social life the number of separate cultural traditions may be reduced to two, one for men and the other for women.

If we treat the social reality that we are investigating as being not an entity but a process, then culture and cultural tradition are names for certain recognisable aspects of that process, but not, of course, the whole process. The terms are convenient ways of referring to certain aspects of human social life. It is by reason of the existence of culture and cultural traditions that human social life differs very markedly from the social life of other animal species. The transmission of learnt ways of thinking, feeling and acting constitutes the cultural process, which is a specific feature of human social life. It is, of course, part of that process of interaction amongst persons which is here defined as the social process thought of as the social reality. Continuity and change in the forms of social life being the subjects of investigation of comparative sociology, the continuity of cultural traditions and changes in those traditions are amongst the things that have to be taken into account.

Social system

It was Montesquieu who, in the middle of the eighteenth century, laid the foundations of comparative sociology, and in doing so formulated and used a conception that has been and can be referred to by the use of the term *social system.* His theory, which constituted what Comte later called 'the first law of social statics', was that in a particular form of social life there are relations of interconnection and interdependence, or what Comte called relations of solidarity, amongst the various features. The idea of a natural or phenomenal system is that of a set of relations amongst events, just as a logical system, such as the geometry of Euclid, is a set of relations amongst

15

propositions, or an ethical system a set of relations amongst ethical judgements. When one speaks of the 'banking system' of Great Britain this refers to the fact that there is a considerable number of actions, interactions and transactions, such for example as payments by means of a signed cheque drawn on a bank, which are so connected that they constitute in their totality a process of which we can make an analytical description which will show how they are interconnected and thus form a system. We are dealing, of course, with a process, a complex part of the total social process of social life in Great Britain.

In these essays I have referred to 'kinship systems'. The idea is that in a given society we can isolate conceptually, if not in reality, a certain set of actions and interactions amongst persons which are determined by the relationships by kinship or marriage, and that in a particular society these are interconnected in such a way that we can give a general analytical description of them as constituting a system. The theoretical significance of this idea of systems is that our first step in an attempt to understand a regular feature of a form of social life, such as the use of cheques, or the custom by which a man has to avoid social contact with his wife's mother, is to discover its place in the system of which it is part.

The theory of Montesquieu, however, is what we may call a theory of a total social system, according to which all the features of social life are united into a coherent whole. As a student of jurisprudence Montesquieu was primarily concerned with laws, and he sought to show that the laws of a society are connected with the political constitution, the economic life, the religion, the climate, the size of the population, the manners and customs, and what he called the general spirit (*esprit général*)—what later writers have called the 'ethos' of the society. A theoretical law, such as this 'fundamental law of social statics', is not the same thing as an empirical law, but is a guide to investigation. It gives us reason to think that we can advance our understanding of human societies if we investigate systematically the inter-connections amongst features of social life.

Statics and dynamics

Comte pointed out that in sociology, as in other kinds of science, there are two sets of problems, which he called problems of statics and problems of dynamics. In statics we attempt to discover and

16

define conditions of existence or of co-existence; in dynamics we try to discover conditions of change. The conditions of existence of molecules or of organisms are matters of statics, and similarly the conditions of existence of societies, social systems, or forms of social life are matters for social statics. Whereas the problems of social dynamics deal with the conditions of change of forms of social life.

The basis of science is systematic classification. It is the first task of social statics to make some attempt to compare forms of social life in order to arrive at classifications. But forms of social life cannot be classified into species and genera in the way we classify forms of organic life; the classification has to be not specific but typological, and this is a more complicated kind of investigation. It can only be reached by means of the establishing of typologies for features of social life or the complexes of features that are given in partial social systems. Not only is the task complex but it has been neglected in view of the idea that the method of anthropology should be a historical method.

But though the typological studies are one important part of social statics, there is another task, that of formulating generalisations about the conditions of existence of social systems, or of forms of social life. The so-called first law of social statics is a generalisation affirming that for any form of social life to persist or continue the various features must exhibit some kind and measure of coherence or consistence, but this only defines the problem of social statics, which is to investigate the nature of this coherence.

The study of social dynamics is concerned with establishing generalisations about how social systems change. It is a corollary of the hypothesis of the systematic connection of features of social life that changes in some features are likely to produce changes in other features.

Social evolution

The theory of social evolution was formulated by Herbert Spencer as part of his formulation of the general theory of evolution. According to that theory the development of life on the earth constitutes a single process to which Spencer applied the term 'evolution'. The theory of organic and super-organic (social) evolution can be reduced to two essential propositions: (1) That both in the development of forms of organic life and in the development of forms of human social life there has been a process of diversification by which many different forms of organic life or of social life have been developed out of a very much smaller number of original forms. (2) That there has been a general trend of development by which more complex forms of structure and organisation (organic or social) have arisen from simpler forms. The acceptance of the theory of evolution only requires the acceptance of these propositions as giving us a scheme of interpretation to apply to the study of organic and social life. But it must be remembered that some anthropologists reject the hypothesis of evolution. We can give provisional acceptance to Spencer's fundamental theory, while rejecting the various pseudo-historical speculations which he added to it, and that acceptance gives us certain concepts which may be useful as analytical tools.

Adaptation

This is a key concept of the theory of evolution. It is, or can be, applied both to the study of the forms of organic life and to the forms of social life amongst human beings. A living organism exists and continues in existence only if it is both internally and externally adapted. The internal adaptation depends on the adjustment of the various organs and their activities, so that the various physiological processes constitute a continuing functioning system by which the life of the organism is maintained. The external adaptation is that of the organism to the environment within which it lives. The distinction of external and internal adaptation is merely a way of distinguishing two aspects of the *adaptational system* which is the same for organisms of a single species.

When we come to the social life of animals another feature of adaptation makes its appearance. The existence of a colony of bees depends on a combination of the activities of the individual worker bees in the collection of honey and pollen, the manufacture of wax, the building of the cells, the tending of eggs and larvae and the feeding of the latter, the protection of the store of honey from robbers, the ventilation of the hive by fanning with their wings, the maintenance of temperature in the winter by clustering together. Spencer uses the term 'co-operation' to refer to this feature of social life. Social life and social adaptation therefore involve the adjustment of the behaviour of individual organisms to the requirements of the process by which the social life continues.

When we examine a form of social life amongst human beings as an adaptational system it is useful to distinguish three aspects of the total system. There is the way in which the social life is adjusted to the physical environment, and we can, if we wish, speak of this as the œcological adaptation. Secondly, there are the institutional arrangements by which an orderly social life is maintained, so that what Spencer calls co-operation is provided for and conflict is restrained or regulated. This we might call, if we wished, the institutional aspect of social adaptation. Thirdly, there is the social process by which an individual acquires habits and mental characteristics that fit him for a place in the social life and enable him to participate in its activities. This, if we wish, could be called cultural adaptation, in accordance with the earlier definition of cultural tradition as process. What must be emphasised is that these modes of adaptation are only different aspects from which the total adaptational system can be looked at for convenience of analysis and comparison.

The theory of social evolution therefore makes it a part of our scheme of interpretation of social systems to examine any given system as an adaptational system. The stability of the system, and therefore its continuance over a certain period, depends on the effectiveness of the adaptation.

Social structure

The theory of evolution is one of a trend of development by which more complex types of structure come into existence by derivation from less complex ones. An address on Social Structure is included in this volume, but it was delivered in wartime and was printed in abbreviated form, so that it is not as clear as it might be. When we use the term structure we are referring to some sort of ordered arrangement of parts or components. A musical composition has a structure, and so does a sentence. A building has a structure, so does a molecule or an animal. The components or units of social structure are *persons*, and a person is a human being considered not as an organism but as occupying position in a social structure.

One of the fundamental theoretical problems of sociology is that of the nature of social continuity. Continuity in forms of social life depends on structural continuity, that is, some sort of continuity in the arrangements of persons in relation to one another. At the present day there is an arrangement of persons into nations, and the fact that for seventy years I have belonged to the English nation, although I have lived much of my life in other countries, is a fact of social structure. A nation, a tribe, a clan, a body such as the French Academy, or such as the Roman Church, can continue in existence as an arrangement of persons though the personnel, the units of which each is composed, changes from time to time. There is continuity of the structure, just as a human body, of which the components are molecules, preserves a continuity of structure though the actual molecules, of which the body consists, are continually changing. In the political structure of the United States there must always be a President; at one time it is Herbert Hoover, at another time Franklin Roosevelt, but the structure as an arrangement remains continuous.

The social relationships, of which the continuing network constitute social structure, are not haphazard conjunctions of individuals, but are determined by the social process, and any relationship is one in which the conduct of persons in their interactions with each other is controlled by norms, rules or patterns. So that in any relationship within a social structure a person knows that he is expected to behave according to these norms and is justified in expecting that other persons should do the same. The established norms of conduct of a particular form of social life it is usual to refer to as *institutions*. An institution is an established norm of conduct recognised as such by a distinguishable social group or class of which therefore it is an institution. The institutions refer to a distinguishable type of class or social relationships and interactions. Thus in a given locally defined society we find that there are accepted rules for the way a man is expected to behave towards his wife and children. The relation of institutions to social structure is therefore twofold. On the one side there is the social structure, such as the family in this instance, for the constituent relationships of which the institutions provide the norms; on the other there is the group, the local society in this instance, in which the norm is established by the general recognition of it as defining proper behaviour. Institutions, if that term is used to refer to the ordering by society of the interactions of persons in social relationships, have this double connection with structure, with a group or class of which it can be said to be an institution, and with those relationships within the structural system to which the norms apply. In a social system there may be institutions which set up norms of behaviour for a king, for judges in the fulfilment of the duties of their office, for policemen, for fathers of families, and so on, and also norms of behaviour relating to persons who come into casual contact within the social life.

A brief mention may be made of the term *organisation*. The concept is clearly closely related to the concept of social structure, but it is desirable not to treat the two terms as synonymous. A convenient use, which does not depart from common usage in English, is to define social structure as an arrangement of persons in institutionally controlled or defined relationships, such as the relationship of king and subject, or that of husband and wife, and to use organisation as referring to an arrangement of activities. The organisation of a factory is the arrangement of the various activities of manager, foremen, workmen within the total activity of the factory. The structure of a family household of parents, children and servants is institutionally controlled. The activities of the various members of the persons of the household will probably be subject to some regular arrangement, and the organisation of the life of the household in this sense may be different in different families in the same society. The structure of a modern army consists, in the first place, of an arrangement into groups—regiments, divisions, army corps, etc., and in the second place an arrangement into ranks—generals, colonels, majors, corporals, etc. The organisation of the army consists of the arrangement of the activities of its personnel whether in time of peace or in time of war. Within an organisation each person may be said to have a *role*. Thus we may say that when we are dealing with a structural system we are concerned with a system of social *positions*, while in an organisation we deal with a system of *roles*.

Social function

The term function has a very great number of different meanings in different contexts. In mathematics the word, as introduced by Euler in the eighteenth century, refers to an expression or symbol which can be written on paper, such as 'log x', and has no relation whatever to the same word as used in such a science as physiology. In physiology the concept of function is of fundamental importance as enabling us to deal with the continuing relation of structure and process in organic life. A complex organism, such as a human body, has a structure as an arrangement of organs and tissues and fluids. Even an organism that consists of a single cell has a structure as an arrangement of molecules. An organism also has a life, and by this we refer to a process. The concept of organic function is one that is used to refer to the connection between the structure of an organism and the life process of that organism. The processes that go on within a human body while it is living are dependent on the organic structure. It is the function of the heart to pump blood through the body. The organic structure, as a living structure, depends for its continued existence on the processes that make up the total life processes. If the heart ceases to perform its function the life process comes to an end and the structure as a living structure also comes to an end. Thus process is dependent on structure and continuity of structure is dependent on process.

In reference to social systems and their theoretical understanding one way of using the concept of function is the same as its scientific use in physiology. It can be used to refer to the interconnection between the social structure and the process of social life. It is this use of the word function that seems to me to make it a useful term in comparative sociology. The three concepts of process, structure and function are thus components of a single theory as a scheme of interpretation of human social systems. The three concepts are logically interconnected, since 'function' is used to refer to the relations of process and structure. The theory is one that we can apply to the study both of continuity in forms of social life and also to processes of change in those forms.

If we consider such a feature of social life as the punishment of crime, or in other words the application, by some organised procedure, of penal sanctions for certain kinds of behaviour, and ask what is its social function, we have a fundamental problem of comparative sociology towards which a first contribution was made by Durkheim in his *Division du Travail Social*. A very wide general problem is posed when we ask what is the social function of religion. As it has been pointed out [chapter 8 in the present book], the study of this problem requires the consideration of a large number of more limited problems, such as that of the social function of ancestor worship in those societies in which it is found. But in these more limited investigations, if the theory here outlined is accepted, the procedure has to be the examination of the connection between the structural features of the social life and the corresponding social process as both involved in a continuing system.

The first paper in this collection[2] may serve to illustrate these theoretical ideas. It deals with an institution by which a sister's son is allowed privileged familiarity in his conduct towards his mother's brother. The custom is known in tribes of North America such as the Winnebago and others, in peoples of Oceania, such as the inhabitants of Fiji and Tonga, and in some tribes of Africa. My own observations on this institution were made in Tonga and Fiji, but as the paper was addressed to a South African audience it seemed preferable to refer to a single South African example, since a wider comparative discussion would have called for a much longer essay. The usual way of dealing with this institution, both in Oceania and in Africa, was to offer a pseudo-historical explanation to the effect that it was a survival in a patrilineal society from a former condition of mother-right.

The alternative method of dealing with the institution is to look for a theoretical understanding of it as a part of a kinship system of a certain type, within which it has a discoverable function. We do not yet have a systematic general typology of kinship systems, for the construction of such is a laborious undertaking. I have indicated some partial and provisional results of such an attempt to determine types in a recent publication in the form of an Introduction to a book on African Systems of Kinship and Marriage [see chapter 11]. Amongst the great diversity of kinship systems we can, I think, recognise a type of what we may call father-right, and another of mother-right. In both these types the kinship structure is based on lineages with maximum emphasis on lineage relationships. In mother-right the lineage is matrilineal, a child belonging to the lineage of the mother. Practically all the jural relations of a man are those with his matrilineal lineage and its members, and therefore he is largely dependent on his mother's brothers, who exercise authority and control over him and to whom he looks for protection and for inheritance of property. In a system of father-right, on the other hand, a man is largely dependent on his patrilineal lineage and therefore on his father and father's brothers, who exercise authority and control over him, while it is to them that he has to look for protection and for inheritance. Father-right is represented by the system of *patria potestas* of ancient Rome, and there are systems that approximate more or less closely to the type to be found in Africa and elsewhere. We may regard the BaThonga as so approximating.

23

Mother-right is represented by the systems of the Nayar of Malabar and the Menangkubau Malays, and again there are systems elsewhere that approximate to the type.

The point of the paper on the mother's brother may be said to be to contrast with the explanation by pseudo-history the interpretation of the institution to which it refers as having a function in a kinship system with a certain type of structure. If I were to rewrite the paper after thirty years I should certainly modify and expand it. . . .

Any interest this volume may have will probably be as an exposition of a theory, in the sense in which the word theory is here used as a scheme of interpretation thought to be applicable to the understanding of a class of phenomena. The theory can be stated by means of the three fundamental and connected concepts of 'process', 'structure' and 'function'. It is derived from such earlier writers as Montesquieu, Comte, Spencer, Durkheim and thus belongs to a cultural tradition of two hundred years. This introduction contains a reformulation in which certain terms are used differently from the way they were used in the early papers here reprinted. For example, in the earliest papers written twenty or more years ago the word 'culture' is used in the accepted meaning of that time as a general term for the way of life, including the way of thought, of a particular locally defined social group.

Notes

1 This Introduction was written for *Structure and Function in Primitive Society,* 1952; a selection of his papers.
2 Radcliffe-Brown, 1924, not reprinted here; but see pp. 180-2 and 226 ff. below.

2   On social structure[1]

It has been suggested to me by some of my friends that I should use this occasion to offer some remarks about my own point of view in social anthropology; and since in my teaching, beginning at Cambridge and at the London School of Economics thirty years ago, I have consistently emphasised the importance of the study of social structure, the suggestion made to me was that I should say something on that subject.

I hope you will pardon me if I begin with a note of personal explanation. I have been described on more than one occasion as belonging to something called the 'Functional School of Social Anthropology' and even as being its leader, or one of its leaders. This Functional School does not really exist; it is a myth invented by Professor Malinowski. He has explained how, to quote his own words, 'the magnificent title of the Functional School of Anthropology has been bestowed by myself, in a way on myself, and to a large extent out of my own sense of irresponsibility'. Professor Malinowski's irresponsibility has had unfortunate results, since it has spread over anthropology a dense fog of discussion about 'functionalism'. Professor Lowie has announced that the leading, though not the only, exponent of functionalism in the nineteenth century was Professor Franz Boas. I do not think that there is any sense, other than the purely chronological one, in which I can be said to be either the follower of Professor Boas or the predecessor of Professor Malinowski. The statement that I am a 'functionalist' would seem to me to convey no definite meaning.

There is no place in natural science for 'schools' in this sense, and I regard social anthropology as a branch of natural science. Each scientist starts from the work of his predecessors, finds problems which he believes to be significant, and by observation and reasoning endeavours to make some contribution to a growing body of theory. Co-operation amongst scientists results from the fact that they are working on the same or related problems. Such co-operation does not result in the formation of schools, in the sense in which there are schools of philosophy or of painting. There is no place for orthodoxies and heterodoxies in science. Nothing is more pernicious in science than attempts to establish adherence to doctrines. All that a teacher can do is to assist the student in learning to understand and use the scientific method. It is not his business to make disciples.

I conceive of social anthropology as the theoretical natural science of human society, that is, the investigation of social phenomena by methods essentially similar to those used in the physical and biological sciences. I am quite willing to call the subject 'comparative sociology', if anyone so wishes. It is the subject itself, and not the name, that is important. As you know, there are some ethnologists or anthropologists who hold that it is not possible, or at least not profitable, to apply to social phenomena the theoretical methods of natural science. For these persons social anthropology, as I have defined it, is something that does not, and never will, exist. For them, of course, my remarks will have no meaning, or at least not the meaning I intend them to have.

While I have defined social anthropology as the study of human society, there are some who define it as the study of culture. It might perhaps be thought that this difference of definition is of minor importance. Actually it leads to two different kinds of study, between which it is hardly possible to obtain agreement in the formulation of problems.

For a preliminary definition of social phenomena it seems sufficiently clear that what we have to deal with are relations of association between individual organisms. In a hive of bees there are the relations of association of the queen, the workers and the drones. There is the association of animals in a herd, of a mother-cat and her kittens. These are social phenomena; I do not suppose that anyone will call them cultural phenomena. In anthropology, of course, we are only concerned with human beings, and in social anthropology, as I define it, what we have to investigate are the forms of association to be found amongst human beings.

Let us consider what are the concrete, observable facts with which the social anthropologist is concerned. If we set out to study, for example, the aboriginal inhabitants of a part of Australia, we find a certain number of individual human beings in a certain natural environment. We can observe the acts of behaviour of these individuals, including, of course, their acts of speech, and the material products of past actions. We do not observe a 'culture', since that word denotes, not any concrete reality, but an abstraction, and as it is commonly used a vague abstraction. But direct observation does reveal to us that these human beings are connected by a complex network of social relations. I use the term 'social structure' to denote this network of actually existing relations. It is this that I regard it as my business to study if I am working, not as an ethnologist or psychologist, but as a social anthropologist. I do not mean that the study of social structure is the whole of social anthropology, but I do regard it as being in a very important sense the most fundamental part of the science.

My view of natural science is that it is the systematic investigation of the structure of the universe as it is revealed to us through our senses. There are certain important separate branches of science, each of which deals with a certain class or kind of structures, the aim being to discover the characteristics of all structures of that kind. So atomic physics deals with the structure of atoms, chemistry with the structure of molecules, crystallography and colloidal chemistry with the structure of crystals and colloids, and anatomy and physiology with the structures of organisms. There is, therefore, I suggest, place for a branch of natural science which will have for its task the discovery of the general characteristics of those social structures of which the component units are human beings.

Social phenomena constitute a distinct class of natural phenomena. They are all, in one way or another, connected with the existence of social structures, either being implied in or resulting from them. Social structures are just as real as are individual organisms. A complex organism is a collection of living cells and interstitial fluids arranged in a certain structure; and a living cell is similarly a structural arrangement of complex molecules. The physiological and psychological phenomena that we observe in the lives of organisms are not simply the result of the nature of the constituent molecules or atoms of which the organism is built up, but are the result of the structure in which they are united. So also the social phenomena which we observe in any human society are not the immediate result of the nature of individual human beings, but are the result of the social structure by which they are united.

It should be noted that to say we are studying social structures is not exactly the same thing as saying that we study social relations, which is how some sociologists define their subject. A particular social relation between two persons (unless they be Adam and Eve in the Garden of Eden) exists only as part of a wide network of social relations, involving many other persons, and it is this network which I regard as the object of our investigations.

I am aware, of course, that the term 'social structure' is used in a number of different senses, some of them very vague. This is unfortunately true of many other terms commonly used by anthropologists. The choice of terms and their definitions is a matter of scientific convenience, but one of the characteristics of a science as soon as it has passed the first formative period is the existence of technical terms which are used in the same precise meaning by all the students of that science. By this test, I regret to say, social anthropology reveals itself as not yet a formed science. One has therefore to select for oneself, for certain terms, definitions which seem to be the most convenient for the purpose of scientific analysis.

There are some anthropologists who use the term social structure to refer only to persistent social groups, such as nations, tribes and clans, which retain their continuity, their identity as individual groups, in spite of changes in their membership. Dr Evans-Pritchard, in his recent admirable book on the Nuer,[2] prefers to use the term social structure in this sense. Certainly the existence of such persistent social groups is an exceedingly important aspect of structure. But I find it more useful to include under the term social structure a good deal more than this.

In the first place, I regard as a part of the social structure all social relations of person to person. For example, the kinship structure of any society consists of a number of such dyadic relations, as between a father and son, or a mother's brother and his sister's son. In an Australian tribe the whole social structure is based on a network of such relations of person to person, established through genealogical connections.

Secondly, I include under social structure the differentiation of individuals and of classes by their social role. The differential social positions of men and women, of chiefs and commoners, of employers and employees, are just as much determinants of social relations as belonging to different clans or different nations.

In the study of social structure the concrete reality with which we are concerned is the set of actually existing relations, at a given moment of time, which link together certain human beings. It is on this that we can make direct observations. But it is not this that we attempt to describe in its particularity. Science (as distinguished from history or biography) is not concerned with the particular, the unique, but only with the general, with kinds, with events which recur. The actual relations of Tom, Dick and Harry or the behaviour of Jack and Jill may go down in our field note-books and may provide illustrations for a general description. But what we need for scientific purposes is an account of the form of the structure. For example, if in an Australian tribe I observe in a number of instances the behaviour towards one another of persons who stand in the relation of mother's brother and sister's son, it is in order that I may be able to record as precisely as possible the general or normal form of this relationship, abstracted from the variations of particular instances, though taking account of those variations.

This important distinction, between structure as an actually existing concrete reality, to be directly observed, and structural form, as what the field-worker describes, may be made clearer perhaps by a consideration of the continuity of social structure through time, a continuity which is not static like that of a building, but a dynamic continuity, like that of the organic structure of a living body. Throughout the life of an organism its structure is being constantly renewed; and similarly the social life constantly renews the social structure. Thus the actual relations of persons and groups of persons change from year to year, or even from day to day. New members come into a community by birth or immigration; others go out of it by death or emigration. There are marriages and divorces. Friends may become enemies, or enemies may make peace and become friends. But while the actual structure changes in this way, the general structural form may remain relatively constant over a longer or shorter period of time. Thus if I visit a relatively stable community and revisit it after an interval of ten years, I shall find that many of its members have died and others have been born; the members who still survive are now ten years older and their relations to one another may have changed in many ways. Yet I may find that the kinds of relations that I can observe are very little different from those observed ten years before. The structural form has changed little.

But, on the other hand, the structural form may change, sometimes gradually, sometimes with relative suddenness, as in revolutions and military conquests. But even in the most revolutionary changes some continuity of structure is maintained.

29

I must say a few words about the spatial aspect of social structure. It is rarely that we find a community that is absolutely isolated, having no outside contact. At the present moment of history, the network of social relations spreads over the whole world, without any absolute solution of continuity anywhere. This gives rise to a difficulty which I do not think that sociologists have really faced, the difficulty of defining what is meant by the term 'a society'. They do commonly talk of societies as if they were distinguishable, discrete entities, as, for example, when we are told that a society is an organism. Is the British Empire a society or a collection of societies? Is a Chinese village a society, or is it merely a fragment of the Republic of China?

If we say that our subject is the study and comparison of human societies, we ought to be able to say what are the unit entities with which we are concerned.

If we take any convenient locality of a suitable size, we can study the structural system as it appears in and from that region, i.e. the network of relations connecting the inhabitants amongst themselves and with the people of other regions. We can thus observe, describe, and compare the systems of social structure of as many localities as we wish. To illustrate what I mean, I may refer to two recent studies from the University of Chicago, one of a Japanese village, Suye Mura, by Dr John Embree, and the other of a French Canadian community, St Denis, by Dr Horace Miner.[2]

Closely connected with this conception of social structure is the conception of 'social personality' as the position occupied by a human being in a social structure, the complex formed by all his social relations with others. Every human being living in society is two things: he is an individual and also a person. As an individual, he is a biological organism, a collection of a vast number of molecules organised in a complex structure, within which, as long as it persists, there occur physiological and psychological actions and reactions, processes and changes. Human beings as individuals are objects of study for physiologists and psychologists. The human being as a person is a complex of social relationships. He is a citizen of England, a husband and a father, a bricklayer, a member of a particular Methodist congregation, a voter in a certain constituency, a member of his trade union, an adherent of the Labour Party, and so on. Note that each of these descriptions refers to a social relationship, or to a place in a social structure. Note also that a social personality is something that changes during the course of the life of the person. As a person, the human being is the object of study for the social anthropologist. We cannot study persons except in terms of social structure, nor can we study social structure except in terms of the persons who are the units of which it is composed.

If you tell me that an individual and a person are after all really the same thing, I would remind you of the Christian creed. God is three persons, but to say that He is three individuals is to be guilty of a heresy for which men have been put to death. Yet the failure to distinguish individual and person is not merely a heresy in religion; it is worse than that; it is a source of confusion in science.

I have now sufficiently defined, I hope, the subject-matter of what I regard as an extremely important branch of social anthropology. The method to be adopted follows immediately from this definition. It must combine with the intensive study of single societies (i.e. of the structural systems observable in particular communities) the systematic comparison of many societies (or structural systems of different types). The use of comparison is indispensable. The study of a single society may provide materials for comparative study, or it may afford occasion for hypotheses, which then need to be tested by reference to other societies; it cannot give demonstrated results.

Our first task, of course, is to learn as much as we can about the varieties, or diversities, of structural systems. This requires field research. Many writers of ethnographical descriptions do not attempt to give us any systematic account of the social structure. But a few social anthropologists, here and in America, do recognise the importance of such data and their work is providing us with a steadily growing body of material for our study. Moreover, their researches are no longer confined to what are called 'primitive' societies, but extend to communities in such regions as Sicily, Ireland, Japan, Canada and the United States.

If we are to have a real comparative morphology of societies, however, we must aim at building up some sort of classification of types of structural systems. That is a complex and difficult task, to which I have myself devoted attention for thirty years. It is the kind of task that needs the co-operation of a number of students and I think I can number on my fingers those who are actively interested in it at the present time. Nevertheless, I believe some progress is being made. Such work, however, does not produce spectacular results and a book on the subject would certainly not be an

31

anthropological best-seller.

We should remember that chemistry and biology did not become fully formed sciences until considerable progress had been made with the systematic classification of the things they were dealing with, substances in the one instance and plants and animals in the other.

Besides the morphological study, consisting in the definition, comparison and classification of diverse structural systems, there is a physiological study. The problem here is: How do structural systems persist? What are the mechanisms which maintain a network of social relations in existence, and how do they work? In using the terms morphology and physiology, I may seem to be returning to the analogy between society and organism which was so popular with medieval philosophers, was taken over and often misused by nineteenth century sociologists, and is completely rejected by many modern writers. But analogies, properly used, are important aids to scientific thinking and there is a real and significant analogy between organic structure and social structure.

In what I am thus calling social physiology we are concerned not only with social structure, but with every kind of social phenomenon. Morals, law, etiquette, religion, government, and education are all parts of the complex mechanism by which a social structure exists and persists. If we take up the structural point of view, we study these things, not in abstraction or isolation, but in their direct and indirect relations to social structure, i.e. with reference to the way in which they depend upon, or affect, the social relations between persons and groups of persons. I cannot do more here than offer a few brief illustrations of what this means.

Let us first consider the study of language. A language is a connected set of speech usages observed within a defined speech-community. The existence of speech-communities and their sizes are features of social structure. There is, therefore, a certain very general relation between social structure and language. But if we consider the special characteristics of a particular language—its phonology, its morphology and even to a great extent its vocabulary—there is no direct connection of either one-sided or mutual determination between these and the special characteristics of the social structure of the community within which the language is spoken. We can easily conceive that two societies might have very similar forms of social structure and very different kinds of language, or vice versa. The coincidence of a particular form of social structure and a particular language in a given community is always the result of historical accident. There may, of course, be certain indirect, remote interactions between social structure and language, but these would seem to be of minor importance. Thus the general comparative study of languages can be profitably carried out as a relatively independent branch of science, in which the language is considered in abstraction from the social structure of the community in which it is spoken.

But, on the other hand, there are certain features of linguistic history which are specifically connected with social structure. As structural phenomena may be instanced the process by which Latin, from being the language of the small region of Latium, became the language of a considerable part of Europe, displacing the other Italic languages, Etruscan, and many Celtic languages; and the subsequent reverse process by which Latin split up into a number of diverse local forms of speech, which ultimately became the various Romance languages of today. —

Thus the spread of language, the unification of a number of separate communities into a single speech-community, and the reverse process of subdivision into different speech-communities, are phenomena of social structure. So also are those instances in which, in societies having a class structure, there are differences of speech usage in different classes.

I have considered language first, because linguistics is, I think, the branch of social anthropology which can be most profitably studied without reference to social structure. There is a reason for this. The set of speech usages which constitute a language does form a system, and systems of this kind can be compared in order to discover their common general, or abstract, characters, the determination of which can give us laws, which will be specifically laws of linguistics.

Let us consider very briefly certain other branches of social anthropology and their relation to the study of social structure. If we take the social life of a local community over a period, let us say a year, we can observe a certain sum total of activities carried out by the persons who compose it. We can also observe a certain apportionment of these activities, one person doing certain things, another doing others. This apportionment of activities, equivalent to what is sometimes called the social division of labour, is an important feature of the social structure. Now activities are carried out because they provide some sort of 'gratification', as I propose to call it, and the characteristic feature of social life is that activities of certain persons

33

provide gratifications for other persons. In a simple instance, when an Australian blackfellow goes hunting, he provides meat, not only for himself, but for his wife and children and also for other relatives to whom it is his duty to give meat when he has it. Thus in any society there is not only an apportionment of activities, but also an apportionment of the gratifications resulting therefrom, and some sort of social machinery, relatively simple or, sometimes, highly complex, by which the system works.

It is this machinery, or certain aspects of it, that constitutes the special subject-matter studied by the economists. They concern themselves with what kinds and quantities of goods are produced, how they are distributed (i.e. their flow from person to person, or region to region), and the way in which they are disposed of. Thus what are called economic institutions are extensively studied in more or less complete abstraction from the rest of the social system. This method does undoubtedly provide useful results, particularly in the study of complex modern societies. Its weaknesses become apparent as soon as we attempt to apply it to the exchange of goods in what are called primitive societies.

The economic machinery of a society appears in quite a new light if it is studied in relation to the social structure. The exchange of goods and services is dependent upon, is the result of, and at the same time is a means of maintaining a certain structure, a network of relations between persons and collections of persons. For the economists and politicians of Canada the potlatch of the Indians of the north-west of America was simply wasteful foolishness and it was therefore forbidden. For the anthropologist it was the machinery for maintaining a social structure of lineages, clans and moieties, with which was combined an arrangement of rank defined by privileges.

Any full understanding of the economic institutions of human societies requires that they should be studied from two angles. From one of these the economic system is viewed as the mechanism by which goods of various kinds and in various quantities are produced, transported and transferred, and utilised. From the other the economic system is a set of relations between persons and groups which maintains, and is maintained by, this exchange or circulation of goods and services. From the latter point of view, the study of the economic life of societies takes its place as part of the general study of social structure.

Social relations are only observed, and can only be described, by reference to the reciprocal behaviour of the persons related. The form of a social structure has therefore to be described by the patterns of behaviour to which individuals and groups conform in their dealings with one another. These patterns are partially formulated in rules which, in our own society, we distinguish as rules of etiquette, of morals and of law. Rules, of course, only exist in their recognition by the members of the society; either in their verbal recognition, when they are stated as rules, or in their observance in behaviour. These two modes of recognition, as every field-worker knows, are not the same thing and both have to be taken into account.

If I say that in any society the rules of etiquette, morals and law are part of the mechanism by which a certain set of social relations is maintained in existence, this statement will, I suppose, be greeted as a truism. But it is one of those truisms which many writers on human society verbally accept and yet ignore in theoretical discussions, or in their descriptive analyses. The point is not that rules exist in every society, but that what we need to know for a scientific understanding is just how these things work in general and in particular instances.

Let us consider, for example, the study of law. If you examine the literature on jurisprudence you will find that legal institutions are studied for the most part in more or less complete abstraction from the rest of the social system of which they are a part. This is doubtless the most convenient method for lawyers in their professional studies. But for any scientific investigation of the nature of law it is insufficient. The data with which a scientist must deal are events which occur and can be observed. In the field of law, the events which the social scientist can observe and thus take as his data are the proceedings that take place in courts of justice. These are the reality, and for the social anthropologist they are the mechanism or process by which certain definable social relations between persons and groups are restored, maintained or modified. Law is a part of the machinery by which a certain social structure is maintained. The system of laws of a particular society can only be fully understood if it is studied in relation to the social structure, and inversely the understanding of the social structure requires, amongst other things, a systematic study of the legal institutions.

I have talked about social relations, but I have not so far offered you a precise definition. A social relation exists between two or more individual organisms when there is some adjustment of their respective interests, by convergence of interest, or by limitation of conflicts that might arise from divergence of interests. I use the term 'interest' here in the widest possible sense, to refer to all behaviour that we regard as purposive. To speak of an interest implies a subject and an object and a relation between them. Whenever we say that a subject has a certain interest in an object we can state the same thing by saying that the object has a certain value for the subject. Interest and value are correlative terms, which refer to the two sides of an asymmetrical relation.

Thus the study of social structure leads immediately to the study of interests or values as the determinants of social relations. A social relation does not result from similarity of interests, but rests either on the mutual interest of persons in one another, or on one or more common interests, or on a combination of both of these. The simplest form of social solidarity is where two persons are both interested in bringing about a certain result and co-operate to that end. When two or more persons have a *common interest* in an object, that object can be said to have a *social value* for the persons thus associated. If, then, practically all the members of a society have an interest in the observance of the laws, we can say that the law has a social value. The study of social values in this sense is therefore a part of the study of social structure.

It was from this point of view that in an early work I approached the study of what can conveniently be called ritual values, i.e. the values expressed in rites and myths. It is perhaps again a truism to say that religion is the cement which holds society together. But for a scientific understanding we need to know just how it does this, and that is a subject for lengthy investigations in many different forms of society.

As a last example let me mention the study of magic and witchcraft, on which there is an extensive anthropological literature. I would point to Dr Evans-Pritchard's work on the Zande[4] as an illuminating example of what can be done when these things are systematically investigated in terms of the part they play in the social relations of the members of a community.

From the point of view that I have attempted briefly to describe, social institutions, in the sense of standardised modes of behaviour, constitute the machinery by which a social structure, a network of social relations, maintains its existence and its continuity. I hesitate to use the term 'function', which in recent years had been so much used and misused in a multitude of meanings, many of them very vague. Instead of being used, as scientific terms ought to be, to assist in making distinctions, it is now used to confuse things that ought to be distinguished. For it is often employed in place of the more ordinary words 'use', 'purpose', and 'meaning'. It seems to me more convenient and sensible, as well as more scholarly, to speak of the use or uses of an axe or digging stick, the meaning of a word or symbol, the purpose of an act of legislation, rather than to use the word function for these various things. 'Function' has been a very useful technical term in physiology and by analogy with its use in that science it would be a very convenient means of expressing an important concept in social science. As I have been accustomed to use the word, following Durkheim and others, I would define the social function of a socially standardised mode of activity, or mode of thought, as its relation to the social structure to the existence and continuity of which it makes some contribution. Analogously in a living organism, the physiological function of the beating of the heart, or the secretion of gastric juices, is its relation to the organic structure to the existence or continuity of which it makes its contribution. It is in this sense that I am interested in such things as the social function of the punishment of crime, or the social function of the totemic rites of Australian tribes, or of the funeral rites of the Andaman Islanders. But this is not what either Professor Malinowski or Professor Lowie means by functional anthropology.

Besides these two divisions of the study of social structure, which I have called social morphology and social physiology, there is a third, the investigation of the processes by which social structures change, of how new forms of structures come into existence. Studies of social change in the non-literate societies have necessarily been almost entirely confined to one special kind of process of change, the modification of the social life under the influence or domination of European invaders or conquerors.

It has recently become the fashion amongst some anthropologists to treat changes of this kind in terms of what is called 'culture contact'. By that term we can understand the one-sided or two-sided effects of interaction between two societies, groups, classes or regions having different forms of social life, different institutions, usages and ideas. Thus in the eighteenth century there was an important exchange of ideas between France and Great Britain, and in the nineteenth century there was a marked influence of German thought on both France and England. Such interactions are, of course, a constant feature of social life, but they need not necessarily involve any marked change of social structure.

The changes that are taking place in the non-literate peoples of Africa are of a very different kind. Let us consider an African colony or possession of a European nation. There is a region that was formerly inhabited by Africans with their own social structure. Europeans, by peaceful or forceful means, establish control over the region, under what we call a 'colonial' régime. A new social structure comes into existence and then undergoes development. The population now includes a certain number of Europeans—government officials, missionaries, traders and in some instances settlers. The social life of the region is no longer simply a process depending on the relations and interactions of the native peoples. There grows up a new political and economic structure in which the Europeans, even though few in numbers, exercise dominating influence. Europeans and Africans constitute different classes within the new structure, with different languages, different customs and modes of life, and different sets of ideas and values. A convenient term for societies of this kind would be 'composite' societies; the term 'plural' societies has also been suggested. A complex example of a composite society is provided by the Union of South Africa with its single political and economic structure and a population including English-speaking and Afrikaans-speaking peoples of European descent, the so-called 'coloured people' of the Cape Province, progeny of Dutch and Hottentots, the remaining Hottentots, the 'Malays' of Cape Town, descendants of persons from the Malay Archipelago, Hindus and Mohammedans from India and their descendants, and a number of Bantu tribes who constitute the majority of the population of the Union taken as a whole.

The study of composite societies, the description and analysis of the processes of change in them, is a complex and difficult task. The attempt to simplify it by considering the process as being one in which two or more 'cultures' interact, which is the method suggested by Malinowski in his Introduction to Memorandum XV of the International Institute of African Language and Culture on 'Methods of Study of Culture Contact in Africa' (1938), is simply a way of avoiding the reality. For what is happening in South Africa, for example, is not the interaction of British culture, and Afrikander (or Boer) culture, Hottentot culture, various Bantu cultures and Indian culture, but the interaction of individuals and groups within an established social structure which is itself in process of change. What is happening in a Transkeian tribe, for example, can only be described by recognising that the tribe has been incorporated into a wide political and economic structural system.

For the scientific study of primitive societies in conditions in which they are free from the domination by more advanced societies which result in these composite societies, we have unfortunately an almost complete lack of authentic historical data. We cannot study, but can only speculate about, the processes of change that took place in the past of which we have no record. Anthropologists speculate about former changes in the societies of the Australian aborigines, or the inhabitants of Melanesia, but such speculations are not history and can be of no use in science. For the study of social change in societies other than the composite societies to which reference has been made we have to rely on the work of historians dealing with authentic records.

You are aware that in certain anthropological circles the term 'evolutionary anthropologist' is almost a term of abuse. It is applied, however, without much discrimination. Thus Lewis Morgan is called an evolutionist, although he rejected the theory of organic evolution and in relation to society believed, not in evolution, but in progress, which he conceived as the steady material and moral improvement of mankind from crude stone implements and sexual promiscuity to the steam engines and monogamous marriage of Rochester, N.Y. But even such anti-evolutionists as Boas believe in progress.

It is convenient, I think, to use the term 'progress' for the process by which human beings attain to greater control over the physical environment through the increase of knowledge and improvement of technique by inventions and discoveries. The way in which we are now able to destroy considerable portions of cities from the air is one of the latest striking results of progress. Progress is not the same thing as social evolution, but it is very closely connected with it.

Evolution, as I understand the term, refers specifically to a process of emergence of new forms of structure. Organic evolution has two important features: (1) in the course of it a small number of kinds of organisms have given rise to a very much larger number of kinds; (2) more complex forms of organic structure have come into existence by development out of simpler forms. While I am unable to attach any definite meaning to such phrases as the evolution of

39

culture or the evolution of language, I think that social evolution is a reality which the social anthropologist should recognise and study. Like organic evolution, it can be defined by two features. There has been a process by which, from a small number of forms of social structure, many different forms have arisen in the course of history; that is, there has been a process of diversification. Secondly, throughout this process more complex forms of social structures have developed out of, or replaced, simpler forms.

Just how structural systems are to be classified with reference to their greater or less complexity is a problem requiring investigation. But there is evidence of a fairly close correlation between complexity and another feature of structural systems, namely, the extent of the field of social relations. In a structural system with a narrow total social field, an average or typical person is brought into direct and indirect social relations with only a small number of other persons. In systems of this type we may find that the linguistic community —the body of persons who speak one language—numbers from 250 to 500, while the political community is even smaller, and economic relations by the exchange of goods and services extend only over a very narrow range. Apart from the differentiation by sex and age, there is very little differentiation of social role between persons or classes. We can contrast with this the systems of social structure that we observe today in England or the United States. Thus the process of human history to which I think the term social evolution may be appropriately applied might be defined as the process by which wide-range systems of social structure have grown out of, or replaced, narrow-range systems. Whether this view is acceptable or not, I suggest that the concept of social evolution is one which requires to be defined in terms of social structure.

There is no time on this occasion to discuss the relation of the study of social structure to the study of culture. For an interesting attempt to bring the two kinds of study together I would refer you to Mr Gregory Bateson's book *Naven*.[5] I have made no attempt to deal with social anthropology as a whole and with all its various branches and divisions. I have endeavoured only to give you a very general idea of the kind of study to which I have found it scientifically profitable to devote a considerable and steadily increasing proportion of my time and energy. The only reward that I have sought I think I have in some measure found—something of the kind of insight into the nature of the world of which we are part that only the patient pursuit of the method of natural science can afford.

Notes

1 Presidential Address to the Royal Anthropological Institute.
2 Clarendon Press, 1940.
3 John Embree, *A Japanese Village: Suye Mura,* Cambridge University Press and Chicago University Press, 1940; Horace Miner, *St Denis: a French-Canadian Parish,* Chicago University Press, 1939.
4 *Witchcraft, Oracles and Magic among the Azande,* Clarendon Press, 1937.
5 Cambridge University Press, 1936.

3   Letter to Lévi-Strauss[1]

As you have recognized, I use the term 'social structure' in a sense so different from yours as to make discussion so difficult as to be unlikely to be profitable. While for you, social structure has nothing to do with reality but with models that are built up, I regard the social structure as a reality. When I pick up a particular sea shell on the beach, I recognize it as having a particular structure. I may find other shells of the same species which have a similar structure, so that I can say there is a form of structure characteristic of the species. By examining a number of different species, I may be able to recognize a certain general structural form or principle, that of a helix, which could be expressed by means of logarithmic equation. I take it that the equation is what you mean by 'model.' I examine a local group of Australian aborigines and find an arrangement of persons in a certain number of families. This, I call the social structure of that particular group at that moment of time. Another local group has a structure that is in important ways similar to that of the first. By examining a representative sample of local groups in one region, I can describe a certain form of structure.

I am not sure whether by 'model' you mean the structural form itself or my description of it. The structural form itself may be discovered by observation, including statistical observation, but cannot be experimented on.

You will see that your paper leaves me extremely puzzled as to your meaning. In dealing with Australian kinship systems, I am really only concerned with arriving at correct descriptions of particular systems and arranging them in a valid typological classification. I regard any genetic hypothesis as being of very little importance, since it cannot be more than a hypothesis or conjecture.

Note

1 Written in response to Lévi-Strauss's paper, 'On social structure', published in A. L. Kroeber (ed.), *Anthropology Today,* University of Chicago Press, 1953, pp. 524-53.

4   'Function', 'meaning' and 'functional consistency'

I Function

Function may be defined as the total set of relations that a single social activity or usage or belief has to the total social system. One of the most important things that people sometimes forget is that, as is perfectly obvious, one can never define all of the functions of an activity, usage, or belief, not if one wrote twenty volumes on the given society. For scientific purposes we do not need a complete description of the function, in this sense, of anything. If we take a particular custom, X, which occurs in one form in one society, and in a somewhat different form, X_2, in another society, the problem of science is to discover what common function there is for this custom in the two or more societies in which its exists. The scientific question then will be, 'What are the significant aspects of this functional relation?' and to determine what is significant, we have to have some sort of hypothesis about human society in general.

II Function and meaning

Just in the sense that words have meanings, so do some other things in culture—customary gestures, ritual actions and abstentions, symbolic objects, myths—they are expressive signs. The meaning of a word, a gesture, a rite, lies in what it expresses, and this is determined by its associations within a system of ideas, sentiments and mental attitudes. Ethnological field-workers have often been content to record myths and describe ceremonies without concerning themselves with the meanings, with what these things express. The excuse for this procedure is that meanings are difficult to discover and that there is no standardized technique for their discovery. There is a danger that the ethnologist may interpret the beliefs of a native people not by a reference to *their* mental life but by reference to his own. My investigations led me to the conclusion that this was what Mr Man had done in his interpretation of some of the Andamanese myths. I did not question his records of what the natives told him but only the meanings that he attached to their statements. It therefore seemed to me necessary for ethnology to provide itself with a method of determining meanings as effective and free from 'personal equation' as the methods by which a linguist determines the meanings of words or morphemes in a newly studied language. Ethnology is faced with the dilemma that it must either give up for ever all hope of understanding such things as myth or ritual, or it must develop proper methods for determining as accurately as can be what meanings they have for the people to whose culture they belong.

The notion of function in ethnology rests on the conception of culture as an adaptive mechanism by which a certain number of human beings are enabled to live a social life as an ordered community in a given environment, Adaptation has two aspects, external and internal. The external aspect is seen in the relation of the society to its geographical environment. The internal aspect is seen in the controlled relations of individuals within the social unity. It is convenient to use the term 'social integration' to cover all the phenomena of internal adaptation. One of the fundamental problems of a science of culture or of human society is therefore the problem of the nature of social integration. This problem can only be approached by the study of a number of different cultures from this specific point of view, by an intensive investigation of each culture as an adaptive and integrative mechanism and a comparison one with another of as many variant types as possible.

The discovery of the integrative function of an institution, usage, or belief is to be made through the observation of its effects, and these are obviously in the first place effects on individuals, or their life, their thoughts, their emotions. Not all such effects are significant, or at least equally so. Nor is it the immediate effects with which we are finally concerned, but the more remote effects upon the social cohesion and continuity.

Thus 'meaning' and 'function' are two different but related things. We cannot discuss the social function of mythology or ritual without an understanding of the meanings of particular myths and ritual actions.

Strictly speaking the solution of any important functional problem requires the use of a comparative method, not however the juxtaposition of superficially similar particular usages or beliefs from two

potlatch. The social structure itself is what supports the potlatch, and the potlatch vitalizes the social structure. There is a relation of reciprocal action between the two. The maintenance of the structure requires the performance of the potlatch at given intervals. We can tie up exchange of goods with the clan system, with relationship, with rank. We can demonstrate the interaction by considering kinship alone, which here is dependent on cross-cousin marriage, that is, marriage between people of this side and of that. A child from the chief's house on this side must marry with a child from the chief's house on that. Children of the marriage will be given their rank by a potlatch of this house and of that house. These people give those a lot of property, and vice versa. Whereas the two bodies compete with each other in giving away goods, each serves to uphold the rank of the other in the total system of ranking families.

If you turn to the system of beliefs, sentiments, and ideas, you see that the potlatch is involved, among other things, with a whole series of myths. Certain ones have no meaning until tied up with the potlatch, and certain features of the potlatch remain meaningless until tied up with the mythology.

Here there is a typical example of something characteristic of society in general. The system primarily concerned is that of the exchange of goods. If you analyse it out, however, you find that before you have finished the analysis, you have studied the complete social structure and made a complete study of the ideas and beliefs of these people. The potlatch enters even into the juridical procedure in certain obscure ways. It has its part to play when offences are committed, by groups of people, who can make restitution either by becoming the objects of retaliation or by a potlatch.

One might offer a hundred other illustrations of the interaction of the traits of a society. Analysing a society as a whole with respect to one aspect, you find everything tying up with that one aspect. The best illustration is from Malinowski. He said, 'Let's take this society and trace the effects on it of sex', i.e., sexual cohabitation. He found that to cover the field thoroughly was to cover the whole Trobriand society. Audrey Richards, one of his students, said, 'Let's follow food through the society and see where it takes us', and again, food took one through the whole society; it is by food also that everything is tied together.

The point I am arguing is that a society is a system in this sense, that in any description we could make of the society, or of what

47

constitutes the culture, all characteristics to a greater or lesser extent function together consistently. The degree of consistency varies from society to society. The lowest order, the absence of all conflict, is an order to which I think a number of simpler societies approximate. Then there is that order in which the parts of the structure, including the cosmology characteristic of that society, work closely together to reinforce each other and maintain the structure. In that latter sense I spoke of the Tlingit as having a system.

But the Tlingit system is similar to that of the Haida south of them. Our analysis will be made more complete by considering the Haida also. The social usages of the Haida vary in certain respects from those of the Tlingit. If we analyse the Haida also, compare the two systems, and eliminate the variations, we can define a system of which the Tlingit and Haida are two examples.

Clearly, we have made an abstraction. The Tlingit and Haida systems are each a highly complex one, and for purposes of comparison it was necessary to break each down into a large number of abstracted characteristics. But the first sense in which the word 'system' is applied to a society of this sort is not the sense of the totality of these abstracted characteristics but is the sense which assumes there is something which we call functional consistency characteristic of the totality of traits of a given society.

5   Functionalism: a protest

The paper by Dorothy Gregg and Elgin Williams in the *American Anthropologist* for October–December 1948 calls for protest. The authors arbitrarily apply the label 'functionalist' to certain writers on anthropology and sociology. By selecting from these writers detached quotations, to which they sometimes attach meanings that they did not have in the minds of the writers, they build up an imaginary picture of something they call 'functionalism,' which they then present as a body of views held by all the persons they have decided to call functionalists. All the canons of scholarly integrity are ignored.

Malinowski has explained that he is the inventor of functionalism, to which he gave its name. His definition of it is clear; it is the theory or doctrine that every feature of culture of any people past or present is to be explained by reference to seven biological needs of individual human beings. I cannot speak for the other writers to whom the label functionalist is applied by the authors, though I very much doubt if Redfield or Linton accept this doctrine. As for myself I reject it entirely, regarding it as useless and worse. As a consistent opponent of Malinowski's functionalism I may be called an anti-functionalist.

Malinowski's view of society is rooted in utilitarianism, and his theory is one of a series of theories of one general kind. There was the theory of Lester Ward that 'desires of associated men' act as 'social forces' and produce the institutions which constitute the social order. He was followed by Albion Small, who proposed to explain the features of social life as the product of six basic interests—health, wealth, sociability, knowledge, beauty, rightness. Sumner sought to explain social evolution as the result of four basic motives—hunger, sex passion, vanity and fear. Malinowski produced a variant, in which culture is substituted for society, and seven 'basic biological needs' are substituted for the desires, interests and motives of the earlier writers.

One thesis of the paper referred to, and apparently the major thesis, is that 'both economists and functionalists derive behaviour from biological sources and as a result view all customs as reasonable and necessary.' After pointing out that every one knows that the 'wants' of human beings in any society are socially determined, the authors continue, 'Nevertheless functionalists, like economists, do take wants and needs as individual, inborn physical mechanisms. They do derive cultural necessities and imperatives from physiological sources. The outcome of this procedure is apparently that all social institutions appear right and good by definition. Behaviour stems from needs; it follows that the institutional manifestations of these needs are reasonable, necessary and just.'

So far as I am concerned, and I can only speak for myself, the statement that I take wants and needs as individual, inborn physical mechanisms is a falsehood invented by the authors for some reason of their own. I generally avoid any use of the word 'need' since it is tainted with ambiguity. As to wants, could anyone in the world believe that my wants, for certain kinds of books, for certain kinds of music, or for a typewriter, are inborn physical mechanisms? This is what the readers of this journal are told that I believe.

In the passage quoted above there is an omitted step in the argument, namely, the proposition that all modes of behaviour that are derived from biological sources, or 'stem from needs,' are right and good; reasonable, necessary and just. What is not clear is whether the authors themselves think this, or whether they are asserting that all functionalists hold this view. For the latter, they do not produce a single scrap of evidence. I find it impossible to believe that Malinowski or any other person has ever entertained it. In any case the anthropologist is not concerned, as an anthropologist, with whether such things as slavery or cannibalism, or the institutions of the United States or Russia, are or are not right, good, reasonable or just. Among the Malays there is an institution known as *amok;* in certain circumstances a man runs *amok* and kills as many persons as he can before he himself is killed; the authors say that all so-called functionalists think that this institution is right, good, reasonable and just. Is this absurdity the sort of thing that deserves to be put before the readers of the *American Anthropologist?*

I have no wish to follow further the irresponsible extravagances of the authors. They certainly do not deserve to be taken seriously. I only ask to be permitted to register a personal protest against a procedure, for which they can find no possible justification or excuse, by which, having applied to me the label 'functionalist,' they attribute to me, first, acceptance of the Malinowskian theory of culture, which I reject, and second, the quite impossible view that all customs and institutions of any society are right and good, and I suppose they might add that all socially accepted beliefs are true.

It is true that I make use of the concept of function, and I did so in my lectures at Cambridge and the London School of Economics before the time when Malinowski began to study anthropology. All physiologists make use of the same concept, but they are not called functionalists. The concept, as I use it, is one that enables us to study the interrelations of a structure and an associated process. An organism has a structure of organs and tissues and fluids. What we call the life of an organism is a process. The structure determines the process; life consists of the actions and interactions of organs. The process determines the structure, by renewing it and keeping it alive. This mutual relation between structure and process in an organism is what is referred to when we speak of function in physiology.

For me, as for many others, there is such a thing as social structure. The theory of social evolution depends on this concept, since that theory is that in human life there has been a development of different types of structual systems by divergence or variation, and a development of more complex systems from simpler ones. A social structure is an arrangement of persons in relationships defined and regulated by institutions; and an institution is an established pattern of conduct, or a set of patterns, relating to some feature of social life. The process that is connected with social structure is social life, the interactions and joint actions of persons who are brought into relation by the structure. The concept of function, as I employ it, is used to describe the discoverable interconnections of the social structure and the processes of social life. The social life is determined by the structure; the structure is maintained in existence by the social life, or undergoes modification through the events of the social life (such as a war, for example). The function of an institution, custom or belief, or of some regular social activity, such as a funeral ceremony, or the trial and punishment of a criminal, lies in the effects it has in the complex whole of social structure and the process of social life.

This theory of society in terms of structure and process, interconnected by function, has nothing in common with the theory of culture as derived from individual biological needs. Why should the authors of the paper referred to pretend that they are the same thing? What do they think they can get out of this attempt to introduce utter confusion?

It is worth while to point out that names ending in *-ism* do not apply to scientific theories, but do apply to philosophical doctrines. There are such things as socialism and utilitarianism, and also Platonism, Hegelianism and Marxism. Chemists work on the basis of the atomic theory, but no one calls their theory 'atomism' though this may be an appropriate name for the philosophy of Democritus. By calling his doctrine 'functionalism' Malinowski seems to have wished to emphasize that it was the product of one mind, like any philosophical doctrine, not, like a scientific theory, the product of the co-operative thinking of a succession of scientists. Might it not prevent confusion if it were renamed Malinowskianism?

6   The comparative method in social anthropology[1]

What is meant when one speaks of 'the comparative method' in anthropology is the method used by such a writer as Frazer in his *Golden Bough*. But comparisons of particular features of social life can be made for either of two very different purposes, which correspond to the distinction now commonly made in England between ethnology and social anthropology. The existence of similar institutions, customs or beliefs in two or more societies may in certain instances be taken by the ethnologist as pointing to some historical connection. What is aimed at is some sort of reconstruction of the history of a society or people or region. In comparative sociology or social anthropology the purpose of comparison is different, the aim being to explore the varieties of forms of social life as a basis for the theoretical study of human social phenomena.

Franz Boas, writing in 1888 and 1896, pointed out that in anthropology there are two tasks to be undertaken. One kind of task is to 'reconstruct' the history of particular regions or peoples, and this he spoke of as being 'the first task'. The second task he describes as follows:

A comparison of the social life of different peoples proves that the foundations of their cultural development are remarkably uniform. It follows from this that there are laws to which this development is subject. Their discovery is the second, perhaps the more important aim of our science ... In the pursuit of these studies we find that the same custom, the same idea, occurs among peoples for whom we cannot establish any historical connection, so that a common historical origin cannot be assumed and it becomes necessary to decide whether there are laws that result in the same, or at least similar, phenomena independently of historical causes. Thus develops the second important task of ethnology, the investigation of the laws governing social life.

The frequent occurrence of similar phenomena in cultural areas that have no historical contact suggests that important results may be obtained from their study, for it shows that the human mind develops everywhere according to the same laws.

Boas included these two tasks in the single discipline which he called sometimes 'anthropology', sometimes 'ethnology'. To some of us in this country it seems more convenient to refer to those investigations that are concerned with the reconstruction of history as belonging to ethnology and to keep the term social anthropology for the study of discoverable regularities in the development of human society in so far as these can be illustrated or demonstrated by the study of primitive peoples.

Thus, the comparative method in social anthropology is the method of those who have been called 'arm-chair anthropologists' since they work in libraries. Their first task is to look for what used to be called 'parallels', similar social features appearing in different societies, in the present or in the past. At Cambridge sixty years ago Frazer represented armchair anthropology using the comparative method, while Haddon urged the need of 'intensive' studies of particular societies by systematic field studies of competent observers. The development of field studies has led to a relative neglect of studies making use of the comparative method. This is both understandable and excusable, but it does have some regrettable effects. The student is told that he must consider any feature of social life in its context, in its relation to the other features of the particular social system in which it is found. But he is often not taught to look at it in the wider context of human societies in general. The teaching of the Cambridge school of anthropology forty-five years ago was not that arm-chair anthropology was to be abandoned but that it must be combined with intensive studies of particular primitive societies in which any particular institution, custom, or belief of the society should be examined in relation to the total social system of which it was a part or item. Without systematic comparative studies anthropology will become only historiography and ethnography. Sociological theory must be based on, and continually tested by, systematic comparison.

The only really satisfactory way of explaining a method is by means of illustration. Let us therefore consider how the method can be applied in a particular instance. We may take our start with a particular feature of some tribes in the interior of New South Wales. In these tribes there is a division of the population into two parts, which are named after the eaglehawk and the crow (Kilpara and Makwara). There is a rule by which a man should only take a wife from the division other than his own, and that the children will belong to the same division as their mother. The system is described in technical terms as one of totemically represented exogamous matrilineal moieties.

One way of explaining why a particular society has the features that it does have is by its history. As we have no authentic history of these or other Australian tribes the historical anthropologists are reduced to offering us imaginary histories. Thus the Rev. John Mathew would explain these divisions and their names by supposing that two different peoples, one called Eaglehawks and the other Crows, met in this part of Australia and fought with each other. Ultimately they decided to make peace and agreed that in future Eaglehawk men would only marry Crow women and *vice versa*.

Let us begin looking for parallels. There is a very close parallel to be found amongst the Haida of north-west America, who also have a division into two exogamous matrilineal moieties which are named after the eagle and the raven, two species which correspond very closely indeed to the eaglehawk and crow of Australia. The Haida have a legend that in the beginning only the eagle possessed fresh water which he kept in a basket. The raven discovered this and succeeded in stealing the water from the eagle. But as he flew with the basket over Queen Charlotte Island the water was spilled from the heavy basket and formed the lakes and rivers from which all birds can now drink; and salmon made their way into the streams and now furnish food for men.

In some parts of Australia there are similar legends about the eaglehawk and the crow. One is to the effect that in the beginning only the eaglehawk possessed a supply of fresh water, which he kept under a large stone. The crow, spying on him, saw him lift the stone and take a drink, then replace the stone. The crow proceeded to lift the stone, and after he had taken a drink of fresh water scratched the lice from his head into the water and did not replace the stone. The result was that the water escaped and formed the rivers of eastern Australia in which the lice became the Murray cod that were an important item of food for the aborigines just as salmon are in north-west America. If we accept the criteria formulated by the

55

diffusionists, such as Graebner, we have here what they would say is evidence of a historical connection between Australia and the Pacific coast of North America.

Once we begin looking for parallels to the eaglehawk-crow division of Australia we find many instances of exogamous moieties, in some instances matrilineal, in others patrilineal, in the rest of Australia, and frequently the divisions are named after or represented by birds. In Victoria we find black cockatoo and white cockatoo, in Western Australia white cockatoo and crow. In New Ireland there is a similar system in which the moieties are associated with the sea-eagle and the fish-hawk. At this point we may feel inclined to ask why these social divisions should be identified by reference to two species of birds.

In Eastern Australia the division of the population into two sexes is represented by what is called sex totemism. In tribes of New South Wales the men have for their 'brother' the bat, and the women have for their 'sister' the night owl in some tribes and the owlet nightjar in others. In the northern part of New South Wales the totems are the bat for men and the tree-creeper for women. (It must be remembered that the Australian aborigines classify the bat as a 'bird'). So we find another dichotomy of society in which the divisions are represented by birds.

Throughout most of Australia there is a very important social division into two alternating generation divisions or endogamous moieties. One division consists of all the persons of a single generation together with those of the generation of their grand-parents and the generation of their grandchildren, while the other division includes all those of the generation of their parents and the generation of their children. These divisions are rarely given names but in some tribes may be referred to by terms, one of which a man applies to his own division and its members while the other is applied to the other division. But in one part of Western Australia these endogamous moieties are named after the kingfisher and the bee-eater, while in another part they are named after a little red bird and a little black bird.

Our question 'Why all these birds?' is thus widened in its scope. It is not only the exogamous moieties, but also dual divisions of other kinds that are identified by connection with a pair of birds. It is, however, not always a question of birds. In Australia the moieties may be associated with other pairs of animals, with two species of kangaroo in one part, with two species of bee in another. In California one moiety is associated with the coyote and the other with the wild cat.

Our collection of parallels could be extended to other instances in which a social group or division is given an identity and distinguished from others by association with a natural species. The Australian moieties are merely one instance of a widely spread social phenomenon. From the particular phenomenon we are led, by the comparative method, to a much more general problem — How can we understand the customs by which social groups and divisions are distinguished by associating a particular group or division with a particular natural species? This is the general problem of totemism, as it has been designated. I do not offer you a solution of this problem, as it seems to me to be the resultant of two other problems. One is the problem of the way in which in a particular society the relation of human beings to natural species is represented, and as a contribution to this problem I have offered an analysis of the non-totemic Andaman Islanders. The other is the problem of how social groups come to be identified by connection with some emblem, symbol, or object having symbolic or emblematic reference. A nation identified by its flag, a family identified by its coat of arms, a particular congregation of a church identified by its relation to a particular saint, a clan identified by its relation to a totemic species: these are all so many examples of a single class of phenomena for which we have to look for a general theory.

The problem to which it is desired to draw your attention here is a different one. Granted that it is for some reason appropriate to identify social divisions by association with natural species, what is the principle by which such pairs as eaglehawk and crow, eagle and raven, coyote and wild cat are chosen as representing the moieties of a dual division? The reason for asking this question is not idle curiosity. We may, it can be held, suppose that an understanding of the principle in question will give us an important insight into the way in which the natives themselves think about the dual division as a part of their social structure. In other words, instead of asking 'Why all these birds?' we can ask 'Why particularly eaglehawk and crow, and other pairs?'

I have collected many tales about Eaglehawk and Crow in different parts of Australia, and in all of them the two are represented as opponents in some sort of conflict. A single example must suffice and

57

it comes from Western Australia. Eaglehawk was the mother's brother of Crow. In these tribes a man marries the daughter of a mother's brother so that Eaglehawk was the possible father-in-law of Crow, to whom therefore he owed obligations such as that of providing him with food. Eaglehawk told his nephew to go and hunt wallaby. Crow, having killed a wallaby, ate it himself, an extremely reprehensible action in terms of native morality. On his return to the camp his uncle asked him what he had brought, and Crow, being a liar, said that he had succeeded in getting nothing. Eaglehawk then said, 'But what is in your belly, since your hunger-belt is no longer tight?' Crow replied that to stay the pangs of hunger he had filled his belly with the gum from the acacia. The uncle replied that he did not believe him and would tickle him until he vomited. (This incident is given in the legend in the form of a song of Eaglehawk—*Balmanangabalu ngabarina, kidji-kidji malidyala.*) The crow vomited the wallaby that he had eaten. Thereupon Eaglehawk seized him and rolled him in the fire; his eyes became red with the fire, he was blackened by the charcoal, and he called out in pain, 'Wa! Wa! Wa!' Eaglehawk pronounced what was to be the law, 'You will never be a hunter, but you will for ever be a thief.' And that is how things now are.

To interpret this tale we have to consider how these birds appear to the aborigines. In the first place they are two chief meat-eating birds and the Australian aborigine thinks of himself as a meat-eater. One method of hunting in this region is for a number of men and women to come together at an appropriate season for a collective hunt. A fire across a stretch of country is started in such a way that it will be spread by the wind. The men advance in front of the fire killing with spear or throwing stick the animals that are fleeing from it, while the women follow the fire to dig out such animals as bandicoots that have taken refuge underground. When such a hunt has been started it will not be long before first one and then another eaglehawk makes its appearance to join in the hunting of the animals in flight from the advancing flames. Eaglehawk is the hunter.

The crow does not join in this or any other kind of hunt, but when a camp fire is started it is rarely very long before a crow makes his appearance to settle in a tree out of reach of a throwing stick and wait for the chance of thieving a piece of meat for his dinner.

Amongst the tales told by the Australians about animals we can find an immense number of parallels to this tale of Eaglehawk and

Crow. Here, as an example, is one about the wombat and the kangaroo from the region where South Australia adjoins Victoria. In this region the wombat and the kangaroo are the two largest meat animals. In the beginning Wombat and Kangaroo lived together as friends. One day Wombat began to make a 'house' for himself. (The wombat lives in a burrow in the ground.) Kangaroo jeered at him and thus annoyed him. Then one day it rained. (It is to be remembered that in these tales whatever happens is thought of as happening for the first time in the history of the world.) Wombat went into his 'house' out of the rain. Kangaroo asked Wombat to make room for him, but the latter explained that there was only room for one. Thus Wombat and Kangaroo quarrelled and fought. Kangaroo hit Wombat on the head with a big stone, flattening his skull; Wombat threw a spear at Kangaroo which fixed itself at the base of the backbone. The wombat has a flattened skull to this day and the kangaroo has a tail; the former lives in a burrow while the kangaroo lives in the open; they are no longer friends.

This is, of course, a 'just-so' story which you may think is childish. It amuses the listeners when it is told with the suitable dramatic expressions. But if we examine some dozens of these tales we find that they have a single theme. The resemblances and differences of animal species are translated into terms of friendship and conflict, solidarity and opposition. In other words the world of animal life is represented in terms of social relations similar to those of human society.

One may find legends which relate not to particular species or pairs of species but to animals in general. There is a legend in New South Wales according to which in the beginning all the animals formed a single society. Then the bat was responsible for introducing death into the world by killing his two wives. His brothers-in-law called all the animals to a corroborree, and catching the bat unawares threw him into the fire. This started a general fight in which the animals attacked each other with fire, and of this fight all the animals now show the marks. The various species no longer form one society of friends.

There is a very similar tale in the Andaman Islands. The various species of animals originally formed a single society. At a meeting one of them brought fire. There was a general quarrel in which they all threw fire at each other. Some fled into the sea and became fishes, others escaped into the trees and became birds, and birds and fishes still show the marks of the burns they suffered.

A comparative study therefore reveals to us the fact that the Australian ideas about the eaglehawk and the crow are only a particular instance of a widespread phenomenon. First, these tales interpret the resemblances and differences of animal species in terms of social relationships of friendship and antagonism as they are known in the social life of human beings. Secondly, natural species are placed in pairs of opposites. They can only be so regarded if there is some respect in which they resemble each other. Thus eaglehawk and crow resemble each other in being the two prominent meat-eating birds. When I first investigated the sex totems of New South Wales I supposed, quite wrongly, that what was the basic resemblance of the bat and night owl or nightjar was that they both fly about at night. But the tree-creeper does not fly at night and is the totem of the women in the northern part of New South Wales. As I was sitting in the region of the Macleay River with a native a tree-creeper made its appearance, and I asked him to tell me about it. 'That is the bird that taught women how to climb trees,' he told me. After some conversation I asked, 'What resemblance is there between the bat and the tree-creeper?' and with an expression on his face that showed surprise that I should ask such a question he replied, 'But of course they both live in holes in trees.' I realised that the night owl and the nightjar also live in trees. The fact that certain animals eat meat constitutes a sort of social similarity, as of eaglehawk and crow or dingo and wild cat. Similarly the habit of living in holes in trees.

We can now answer the question 'Why eaglehawk and crow?' by saying that these are selected as representing a certain kind of relationship which we may call one of 'opposition'.

The Australian idea of what is here called 'opposition' is a particular application of that association by contrariety that is a universal feature of human thinking, so that we think by pairs of contraries, upwards and downwards, strong and weak, black and white. But the Australian conception of 'opposition' combines the idea of a pair of contraries with that of a pair of opponents. In the tales about eaglehawk and crow the two birds are opponents in the sense of being antagonists. They are also contraries by reason of their difference of character, Eaglehawk the hunter, Crow the thief. Black cockatoo and white cockatoo which represent the moieties in Western Victoria are another example of contrariety, the birds being essentially similar except for the contrast of colour. In America the moieties are referred to by other pairs of contraries, Heaven and Earth, war and peace, up-stream and down-stream, red and white. After a lengthy comparative study I think I am fully justified in stating a general law, that wherever, in Australia, Melanesia or America, there exists a social structure of exogamous moieties, the moieties are thought of as being in a relation of what is here called 'opposition'.

Obviously the next step in a comparative study is to attempt to discover what are the various forms that the opposition between the moieties of a dual division takes in actual social life. In the literature there are occasional references to a certain hostility between the two divisions described as existing or reported to have existed in the past. All the available evidence is that there is no real hostility in the proper sense of the term but only a conventional attitude which finds expression in some customary mode of behaviour. Certainly in Australia, although in some instances where there is a dispute it is possible to observe the members of the two patrilineal moieties forming separate 'sides', real hostility, of the kind that may lead to violent action is not between the moieties but between local groups, and two local groups of the same patrilineal moiety seem to be just as frequently in conflict as two groups belonging to different moieties. Indeed, since a common source of actual conflict is the taking by one man of a woman married to or betrothed to another the two antagonists or groups of antagonists in such instances will both belong to the same patrilineal moiety.

The expression of opposition between the moieties may take various forms. One is the institution to which anthropologists have given the not very satisfactory name of 'the joking relationship'. Members of opposite divisions are permitted or expected to indulge in teasing each other, in verbal abuse or in exchange of insults. Kroeber (*Handbook of Indians of California*) writes that amongst the Cupeño 'a sort of good natured opposition is recognized between the moieties, whose members frequently taunt each other with being unsteady and slow-witted, respectively'. Strong (*Aboriginal Society in Southern California*) reports the same thing:

A good-natured antagonism between the moieties exhibits itself in joking between persons of the one and the other. The coyote people taunt the wild cat people with being slow-witted and lazy like their animal representative and the wild cat people retaliate by accusing their opponents with being unsteady. There are indications that this teasing of one moiety by another entered into their serious ceremonies. There were songs of a satirical kind that could be sung by one moiety against the other. However, the opposition between the moieties seems to have been much less strong than between certain pairs of clans, sometimes belonging to the same moiety, which were traditionally 'enemies'. These clans, on certain occasions would sing 'enemy songs' against each other.

This institution, for which it is to be hoped that some one will find a better name than 'joking relationship', is found in a variety of forms in a number of different societies, and calls for systematic comparative study. It has for its function to maintain a continuous relationship between two persons, or two groups, of apparent but factitious hostility or antagonism. I have offered a suggestion towards a comparative study of this institution in a paper published in the journal *Africa*. [See chapter 10.]

Another significant custom in which is expressed the relation of opposition between the two moieties is that by which, in some tribes of Australia and in some of North America the moieties provide the 'sides' in games such as football. Competitive games provide a social occasion on which two persons or two groups of persons are opponents. Two continuing groups in a social structure can be maintained in a relation in which they are regularly opponents. An example is provided by the two universities of Oxford and Cambridge.

There are other customs in which the opposition of moieties is expressed. For example, in the Omaha tribe of North America the camp circle was divided into semi-circles, and when a boy of the one half crossed into the other he took companions with him and there was a fight with the boys of the other moiety. We need not and can not here examine these various customs.

Let us consider briefly the institution of moiety exogamy, by which every marriage, where the rule is observed, is between persons belonging to opposite moieties. There are innumerable customs which show that in many primitive societies the taking of a woman in marriage is represented symbolically as an act of hostility against her family or group. Every anthropologist is familiar with the custom by which it is represented that the bride is captured or taken by force from her kinsfolk. A first collection of instances of this custom was made by McLennan, who interpreted them historically as being survivals from the earliest condition of human society in which the only way to obtain a wife was to steal or capture a woman from another tribe.

An illuminating example of this kind of custom is provided by the people of the Marquesas. When a marriage has been arranged the kinsmen of the bridgroom take the gifts which are to be offered to the kinsfolk of the bride and proceed towards the bride's home. On the way they are ambushed and attacked by the bride's kin who seize by force the goods that they are conveying. The first act of violence comes from the kin of the bride. By the Polynesian principle of *utu* those who suffer an injury are entitled to retaliate by inflicting an injury. So the bridegroom's kinsmen exercise this right by carrying off the bride. No example could better illustrate the fact that these customary actions are symbolic.

Viewed in relation to social structure the meaning or symbolic reference of these customs ought to be obvious. The solidarity of a group requires that the loss of one of its members shall be recognized as an injury to the group. Some expression of this is therefore called for. The taking of a woman in marriage is represented as in some sense an act of hostility against her kin. This is what is meant by the saying of the Gusii of East Africa, 'Those whom we marry are those whom we fight.'

It is in the light of this that we must interpret the custom of marriage by exchange. The group or kin of a woman lose her when she marries; they are compensated for their loss if they receive another who will become the wife of one of them. In Australian tribes, with a few exceptions, the custom is that when a man takes a wife he should give a sister to replace her. In the Yaralde tribe of South Australia, which did not have a system of moieties, when a man married a woman of another local clan, his own clan was expected to provide a wife for some member of the clan from which the bride came. Otherwise the marriage was regarded as irregular, improper, or we might almost say illegal. It has been reported from the tribes of the eastern part of Victoria (Gippsland) that the only proper form of marriage was by exchange. The system of exogamous moieties provides a system of generalization of marriage by exchange, since every marriage is one incident in the continual process by which the men of one moiety get their wives from the other.

A comparative study shows that in many primitive societies the relation established between two groups of kin by a marriage between a man of one group and a woman of the other is one which is expressed by customs of avoidance and by the joking relationship. In many societies a man is required to avoid any close social contact with the mother of his wife, frequently also with her father, and with other persons of that generation amongst his wife's kin. With this custom there is frequently associated the custom called the 'joking relationship' by which a man is permitted or even required to use insulting behaviour to some of his wife's kin of his own generation. I have elsewhere suggested that these customs can be understood as being the conventional means by which a relationship of a peculiar kind, which can be described as a compound of friendship or solidarity with hostility or opposition is established and maintained.

In a complete study there are other features of the dual organization that would need to be taken into consideration. There are instances in which there are regular exchanges of goods or services between the two moieties. In that competitive exchange of food and valuables known as 'potlatch' in North America, the moieties may be significant. Amongst the Tlingit, for example, it is members of one moiety who potlatch against members of the other moiety. The two moieties provide the 'sides' for what is a sort of competitive game in which men 'fight with property.'

Our comparative study enables us to see the eaglehawk-crow division of the Darling River tribes as one particular example of a widespread type of the application of a certain structural principle. The relation between the two divisions, which has here been spoken of by the term 'opposition' is one which separates and also unites, and which therefore gives us a rather special kind of social integration which deserves systematic study. But the term 'opposition' which I have been obliged to use because I cannot find a better, is not wholly appropriate, for it stresses too much what is only one side of the relationship, that of separation and difference. The more correct description would be to say that the kind of structure with which we are concerned is one of the union of opposites.

The idea of a unity of contraries was one of the leading ideas of the philosophy of Heraclitus. It is summed up in his statement, 'Polemos is king, rules all things.' The Greek word *polemos* is sometimes translated as 'strife', but the appropriate translation would be 'opposition' in the sense in which that word has been used in this lecture. Heraclitus uses as one example the mortise and the tenon; these are not at strife; they are contraries or opposites which combine to make a unity when they are joined together.

There is some evidence that this idea of the union of opposites was derived by Heraclitus and the Pythagoreans from the East. At any rate the most complete elaboration of the idea is to be found in the Yin-Yang philosophy of ancient China. The phrase in which this is summed up is '*Yi yin yi yang wei tze tao.*' One yin and one yang make an order. Yin is the feminine principle, Yang the masculine. The word 'tao' can here by best translated as 'an ordered whole'. One man (yang) and his wife (yin) constitute the unity of a married couple. One day (yang) and one night (yin) make a unified whole or unity of time. Similarly one summer (yang) and one winter (yin) make up the unity we call a year. Activity is yang and passivity is yin and a relation of two entities or persons of which one is active and the other passive is also conceived as a unity of opposites. In this ancient Chinese philosophy this idea of the unity of opposites is given the widest possible extension. The whole universe including human society is interpreted as an 'order' based on this.

There is historical evidence that this philosophy was developed many centuries ago in the region of the Yellow River, the 'Middle Kingdom'. There is also evidence that the social organization of this region was one of paired intermarrying clans, the two clans meeting together at the Spring and Autumn Festivals and competing in the singing of odes, so that the men of the one clan could find wives amongst the daughters of the other. The evidence is that the system of marriage was one where a man married his mother's brother's daughter, or a woman of the appropriate generation of his mother's clan. According to my information this kind of organization, which apparently existed forty centuries ago in that region, still survived there in 1935, but the investigation of it that I had planned to be carried out by Li Yu I was unfortunately prevented by the Japanese attack on China. It may still not be too late for this to be done; it would enable us to evaluate more exactly the historical reconstruction of Marcel Granet.

This Yin-Yang philosophy of ancient China is the systematic elaboration of the principle that can be used to define the social structure of moieties in Australian tribes, for the structure of moieties is, as may be seen from the brief account here given, one of a unity of opposing groups, in the double sense that the two groups are friendly opponents, and that they are represented as being in some sense opposites, in the way in which eaglehawk and crow or black and white are opposites.

Light can be thrown on this by the consideration of another instance of opposition in Australian societies. An Australian camp includes men of a certain local clan and their wives who, by the rule of exogamy, have come from other clans. In New South Wales there is a system of sex totemism, by which one animal species is the 'brother' of the men, and another species is the 'sister' of the women. Occasionally there arises within a native camp a condition of tension between the sexes. What is then likely to happen, according to the accounts of the aborigines, is that the women will go out and kill a bat, the 'brother' or sex totem of the men, and leave it lying in the camp for the men to see. The men then retaliate by killing the bird which in that tribe is the sex totem of the women. The women then utter abuse against the men and this leads to a fight with sticks (digging sticks for the women, throwing sticks for the men) between the two sex groups in which a good many bruises are inflicted. After the fight peace is restored and the tension is eliminated. The Australian aborigines have the idea that where there is a quarrel between two persons or two groups which is likely to smoulder the thing to do is for them to fight it out and then make friends. The symbolic use of the totem is very significant. This custom shows us that the idea of the opposition of groups, and the union of opposites is not confined to the exogamous moieties. The two sex groups provide a structure of a similar kind; so sometimes do the two groups formed by the alternating generation divisions. The group of the fathers, and the group of their sons are in a relation of opposition, not dissimilar from the relation between husbands and their wives.

We can say that in the relatively simple social structure of Australian tribes we can recognize three principal types of relationship between persons or groups. There is the relationship of enmity and strife; at the other extreme there is the relationship of simple solidarity, and in the Australian system this ought to exist between brothers, and between persons of the same generation in the local group; such persons may not fight, though in certain circumstances it is thought to be legitimate for one person to 'growl' against the other, to express in the camp a complaint against the action of the other. There is thirdly the relationship of opposition, which is not at all the same thing as strife or enmity, but is a combination of agreement and disagreement, of solidarity and difference.

We began with a particular feature of a particular region in Australia, the existence of exogamous moieties named after the eaglehawk and the crow. By making comparisons amongst other societies, some of them not Australian, we are enabled to see that this is not something particular or peculiar to one region, but is one instance of certain widespread general tendencies in human societies. We thus substitute for a particular problem of the kind that calls for a historical explanation, certain general problems. There is, for example, the problem of totemism as a social phenomenon in which there is a special association of a social group with a natural species. Another, and perhaps more important, problem that has been raised, is that of the nature and functioning of social relationships and social structures based on what has here been called 'opposition'. This is a much more general problem than that of totemism for it is the problem of how opposition can be used as a mode of social integration. The comparative method is therefore one by which we pass from the particular to the general, from the general to the more general, with the end in view that we may in this way arrive at the universal, at characteristics which can be found in different forms in all human societies.

But the comparative method does not only formulate problems, though the formulation of the right problems is extremely important in any science; it also provides material by which the first steps may be made towards the solution. A study of the system of moieties in Australia can give us results that should have considerable value for the theory of human society.

At the beginning of this lecture I quoted Franz Boas as having distinguished two tasks with which an anthropologist can concern himself in the study of primitive society, and these two tasks call for two different methods. One is the 'historical' method, by which the existence of a particular feature in a particular society is 'explained' as the result of a particular sequence of events. The other is the comparative method by which we seek, not to 'explain', but to understand a particular feature of a particular society by first seeing it as a particular instance of a general kind or class of social phenomena, and then by relating it to a certain general, or preferably a universal, tendency in human societies. Such a tendency is what is called in certain instances a law. Anthropology as the study of primitive society includes both methods, and I have myself consistently used both in the teaching of ethnology and social anthropology in a number of universities. But there must be discrimination. The historical method will give us particular propositions, only the comparative method can give us general propositions. In primitive societies historical evidence is always lacking or inadequate. There is no historical evidence as to how the eaglehawk-crow division in Australia came into existence, and guesses about it seem to me of no significance whatever. How the Australian aborigines arrived at their present social systems is, and forever must be, entirely unknown. The supposition that by the comparative method we might arrive at valid conclusions about the 'origins' of those systems shows a complete disregard for the nature of historical evidence. Anthropology, as the study of primitive societies, includes both historical (ethnographical and ethnological) studies and also the generalizing study known as social anthropology which is a special branch of comparative sociology. It is desirable that the aims and methods should be distinguished. History, in the proper sense of the term, as an authentic account of the succession of events in a particular region over a particular period of time, cannot give us generalizations. The comparative method as a generalizing study of the features of human societies cannot give us particular histories. The two studies can only be combined and adjusted when their difference is properly recognized and it is for this reason that thirty years ago I urged that there should be a clear distinction between ethnology as the historical study of primitive societies and social anthropology as that branch of comparative sociology that concerns itself specially with the societies we call primitive. We can leave all questions of historical reconstruction to ethnology. For social anthropology the task is to formulate and validate statements about the conditions of existence of social systems (laws of social statics) and the regularities that are observable in social change (laws of social dynamics). This can only be done by the systematic use of the comparative method, and the only justification of that method is the expectation that it will provide us with results of this kind, or, as Boas stated it, will provide us with knowledge of the laws of social development. It will be only in an integrated and organized study in which historical studies and sociological studies are combined that we shall be able to reach a real understanding of the development of human society, and this we do not yet have.

Note

1 Huxley Memorial Lecture for 1951.

Part II Rites and Values

The interpretation of Andaman Island ceremonies

I Method: marriage, mourning, peace-making and weeping

Any attempt to explain or interpret the particular beliefs and customs of a savage people is necessarily based on some general psychological hypothesis as to the real nature of the phenomena to be explained. The sound rule of method is therefore to formulate clearly and explicitly the working hypothesis on which the interpretation is based. It is only in this way that its value can be properly tested.

The hypothesis that seems to be most usually adopted by English writers on anthropology is that the beliefs of savage peoples are due to attempts on the part of primitive man to explain to himself the phenomena of life and nature. The student of human customs, examining his own mind, finds that one of the motives most constantly present in his consciousness is the desire to understand, to explain—in other words what we call scientific curiosity. He concludes that his motive is equally insistent in the mind of primitive man. Thus he supposes that primitive man, wishing to explain the phenomena of death and of sleep and dreams, framed a hypothesis that every man possesses a soul or spiritual double.[1] The hypothesis, once formulated, is supposed to have been accepted and believed because it satisfied this need of comprehension. On this view the belief in a soul (animism) is exactly similar in character to the scientific belief in atoms, let us say. The same general hypothesis appears in the explanation of totemism as having arisen as a theory invented by primitive man in order to explain the phenomena of pregnancy and childbirth.[2]

On this hypothesis the beliefs are primary, arising first merely as beliefs and then acquiring the power to influence action and so giving rise to all sorts of ceremonies and customs. Thus these customs are only to be explained by showing that they depend on particular beliefs. This hypothesis, which we may call the intellectualist hypothesis, has never, so far as I am aware, been very clearly formulated or defended, but it does seem to underlie many of the explanations of the customs of primitive man to be found in works on ethnology.

A second hypothesis explains the beliefs of primitive man as being due to emotions of surprise and terror,[3] or of awe and wonder[4] aroused by the contemplation of the phenomena of nature.

Both these hypotheses may be held together, one being used to explain some primitive beliefs and the other to explain others.[5]

Doubtless there are other psychological hypotheses underlying the many attempts that have been made to explain the customs of primitive peoples, but these two seem to be the most important and the most widespread. They are mentioned here, not in order to criticise them, but in order to contrast them with the hypothesis to be formulated in the present chapter.[6]

Stated as briefly as possible the working hypothesis here adopted is as follows. (1) A society depends for its existence on the presence in the minds of its members of a certain system of sentiments[7] by which the conduct of the individual is regulated in conformity with the needs of society. (2) Every feature of the social system itself and every event or object that in any way affects the well-being or the cohesion of the society becomes an object of this system of sentiments. (3) In human society the sentiments in question are not innate but are developed in the individual by the action of the society upon him. (4) The ceremonial customs of a society are a means by which the sentiments in question are given collective expression on appropriate occasions. (5) The ceremonial (i.e. collective) expression of any sentiment serves both to maintain it at the requisite degree of intensity in the mind of the individual and to transmit it from one generation to another. Without such expression the sentiments involved could not exist.

Using the term 'social function' to denote the effects of an institution (custom or belief) in so far as they concern the society and its solidarity or cohesion, the hypothesis of this chapter may be more briefly resumed in the statement that the social function of the ceremonial customs of the Andaman Islanders is to maintain and to transmit from one generation to another the emotional dispositions on which the society (as it is constituted) depends for its existence.

The present chapter contains an attempt to apply this hypothesis to the ceremonial customs of the Andaman Islanders. An attempt will be made to show that there is a correspondence between the customs and beliefs of the Andamanese and a certain system of social sentiments, and that there is also a correspondence between these sentiments and the manner in which the society is constituted. It is an attempt to discover necessary connections between the different characters of a society as they exist in the present. No attempt will be made to discover or imagine the historical process by which these customs have come into existence.

For the clearer understanding of the argument it is necessary to draw attention to a few rules of method that will be observed. (1) In explaining any given custom it is necessary to take into account the explanation given by the natives themselves. Although these explanations are not of the same kind as the scientific explanations that are the objects of our search yet they are of great importance as data. Like the civilised man of Western Europe the savage of the Andamans seeks to rationalise his behaviour; being impelled to certain actions by mental dispositions of whose origin and real nature he is unaware, he seeks to formulate reasons for his conduct, or even if he does not so when left to himself he is compelled to when the enquiring ethnologist attacks him with questions. Such a reason as is produced by this process of rationalisation is rarely if ever identical with the psychological cause of the action that it justifies, yet it will nearly always help us in our search for the cause. At any rate the reason given as explaining an action is so intimately connected with the action itself that we cannot regard any hypothesis as to the meaning of a custom as being satisfactory unless it explains not only the custom but also the reasons that the natives give for following it. (2) The assumption is made that when the same or a similar custom is practised on different occasions it has the same or a similar meaning in all of them. For example, there are different occasions on which a personal name is avoided; it is assumed that there is something in common to all these occasions and that the meaning of the custom is to be discovered by ascertaining what that common element is. (3) It is assumed that when different customs are practised together on one and the same occasion there is a common element in the customs. This rule is the inverse of the last. As an example may be mentioned the different customs observed by mourners, which may be assumed to be all related to one another. The discovery of what is common to them all will explain the meaning of each. (4) I have avoided, as being misleading as well as unnecessary, any comparison of Andamanese customs with similar customs of other races. Only in one or two instances have I broken this rule, and in those I believe I am justified by special considerations.

We can conveniently begin by considering the Andamanese marriage ceremony, which is one of the simplest and most easily understood. The main feature of it is that the bride and bridegroom are required publicly to embrace each other. In the North Andaman the embrace is made gradually, by stages as it were, each stage being more intimate than the preceding. At first the two sit side by side, then their arms are placed around each other, and finally the bridegroom is made to sit on the bride's lap.

Everywhere in human life the embrace is employed as an expression of such feelings as love, affection, friendship, i.e. of feelings of attachment between persons. There is no need to enquire into the psycho-physical basis of this expression. It is probably intimately related to the nursing of the infant by the mother, and is certainly very closely connected with the development of the sex instinct. It is sufficient for our purpose to satisfy ourselves that the embrace in all its forms does always express feelings of one generic kind. Nor is it necessary for us to consider the peculiar form of the Andamanese embrace, in which one person sits down and extends his or her legs, while the other person sits on the lap so formed and the two wrap their arms round one another's necks and shoulders.

The meaning of the marriage ceremony is readily seen. By marriage the man and woman are brought into a special and intimate relation to one another; they are, as we say, united. The social union is symbolised or expressed by the physical union of the embrace. The ceremony brings vividly to the minds of the young couple and also to those of the spectators the consciousness that the two are entering upon a new social relation of which the essential feature is the affection in which they must hold one another.

The rite has two aspects according as we regard it from the standpoint of the witnesses or from that of the couple themselves. The witnesses, by their presence, give their sanction to the union that is thus enacted before them. The man who conducts the ceremony is merely the active representative of the community; in what he does and says he acts as a deputy and not as a private individual. Thus the ceremony serves to make it clear that the marriage is a matter which concerns not only those who are entering into it, but the whole community, and its occasional performance serves to keep alive this sentiment with regard to marriage in general. The existence of the sentiment is shown in the reprobation felt and often expressed at an irregular marriage, in which the couple unite without a ceremony: such a union showing a contemptuous or careless thrusting aside of an important social principle.

For the witnesses, then, the ceremony serves to awaken to activity and to express this sentiment; but it also serves as a recognition on their part of the change of status of the marrying pair. It makes them realise that henceforward the young couple must be treated no longer as children but as responsible adults, and it is thus the occasion of a change of sentiment towards those whose social position is being changed. For in the society of the Andamans there is a very marked division between married and unmarried persons in the way in which they are regarded by others, and in respect of their place in the community.

The married couple are made to realise, in a different way and with a much greater intensity of feeling, these same two things; first, that their union in marriage is a matter that concerns the whole community, and second, that they are entering a new condition, with new privileges but also with new duties and obligations. For them, indeed, the ceremony is a sort of ordeal from which they would only too gladly escape, and which, by the powerful emotions it evokes in them very vividly impresses upon them what their marriage means.

The wedding gifts that are bestowed upon the young couple are an expression of the general good-will towards them. The giving of presents is a common method of expressing friendship in the Andamans. Thus when two friends meet after separation, the first thing they do after having embraced and wept together, is to give one another presents. In most instances the giving is reciprocal, and is therefore really an exchange. If a present be given as a sign of good-will the giver expects to receive a present of about equal value in return. The reason for this is obvious; the one has expressed his good-will towards the other, and if the feeling is reciprocated a return present must be given in order to express it. So also it would be an insult to refuse a present offered, for to do so would be equivalent to rejecting the good-will it represents. At marriage the giving is one-sided, no return being expected, for it is an expression not of personal friendship on the part of the givers, but of the general social good-will and approval. It is for this reason that it is the duty of everybody who is present to make some gift to the newly-married pair.

In another simple ceremony, the peace-making ceremony of the North Andaman, the meaning is again easily discovered; the symbolism of the dance being indeed at once obvious to a witness, though perhaps not quite so obvious from the description given. The dancers are divided into two parties. The actions of the one party throughout are expressions of their aggressive feelings towards the other. This is clear enough in the shouting, the threatening gestures, and the way in which each member of the 'attacking' party gives a good shaking to each member of the other party. On the other side what is expressed may be described as complete passivity; the performers stand quite still throughout the whole dance, taking care to show neither fear nor resentment at the treatment to which they have to submit. Thus those of the one side give collective expression to their collective anger, which is thereby appeased. The others, by passively submitting to this, humbling themselves before the just wrath of their enemies, expiate their wrongs. Anger appeased dies down; wrongs expiated are forgiven and forgotten; the enmity is at an end.

The screen of fibre against which the passive participants in the ceremony stand has a peculiar symbolic meaning that will be explained later . . . The only other elements of the ceremony are the weeping together, which will be dealt with very soon, and the exchange of weapons, which is simply a special form of the rite of exchanging presents as an expression of good-will. The special form is particularly appropriate as it would seem to ensure at least some months of friendship, for you cannot go out to fight a man with his weapons while he has yours.

The purpose of the ceremony is clearly to produce a change in the feelings of the two parties towards one another, feelings of enmity being replaced through it by feelings of friendship and solidarity. It depends for its effect on the fact that anger and similar aggressive feelings may be appeased by being freely expressed. Its social function is to restore the condition of solidarity between two local groups that has been destroyed by some act of offence.

The marriage ceremony and the peace-making dance both afford examples of the custom which the Andamanese have of weeping together under certain circumstances. The principal occasions of this ceremonial weeping are as follows: (1) when two friends or relatives meet after having been for some time parted, they embrace each other and weep together; (2) at the peace-making ceremony the two parties of former enemies weep together, embracing each other; (3) at the end of the period of mourning the friends of the mourners (who have not themselves been mourning) weep with the latter: (4) after a death the relatives and friends embrace the corpse and weep over it; (5) when the bones of a dead man or woman are recovered from the grave they are wept over; (6) on the occasion of a marriage the relatives of each weep over the bride and bridegroom; (7) at various stages of the initiation ceremonies the female relatives of a youth or girl weep over him or her.

First of all it is necessary to note that not in any of the above-mentioned instances is the weeping simply a spontaneous expression of feeling. It is always a rite the proper performance of which is demanded by custom. (As mentioned in an earlier chapter, the Andamanese are able to sit down and shed tears at will.) Nor can we explain the weeping as being an expression of sorrow. It is true that some of the occasions are such as to produce sorrowful feelings (4 and 5, for example), but there are others on which there would seem to be no reason for sorrow but rather for joy. The Andamanese do weep for sorrow and spontaneously. A child cries when he is scolded or hurt; a widow weeps thinking of her recently dead husband. Men rarely weep spontaneously for any reason, though they shed tears abundantly when taking part in the rite. The weeping on the occasions enumerated is therefore not a spontaneous expression of individual emotion but is an example of what I have called ceremonial customs. In certain circumstances men and women are required by custom to embrace one another and weep, and if they neglected to do so it would be an offence condemned by all right-thinking persons.

According to the postulate of method laid down at the beginning of the chapter we have to seek such an explanation of this custom as will account for all the different occasions on which the rite is performed, since we must assume that one and the same rite has the same meaning in whatever circumstances it may take place. It must be noted, however, that there are two varieties of the rite. In the first three instances enumerated above the rite is reciprocal, i.e. two persons or two distinct groups of persons weep together and embrace each other, both parties to the rite being active. In the other four instances it is one-sided; a person or group of persons weeps over another person (or the relics of a person) who has only a passive part in the ceremony. Any explanation, to be satisfactory, must take account of the difference between these two varieties.

I would explain the rite as being an expression of that feeling of attachment between persons which is of such importance in the almost domestic life of the Andaman society. In other words the purpose of the rite is to affirm the existence of a social bond between two or more persons.

There are two elements in the ceremony, the embrace and the weeping. We have already seen that the embrace is an expression, in the Andamans as elsewhere, of the feeling of attachment, i.e. the feeling of which love, friendship, affection are varieties. Turning to the second element of the ceremony, we are accustomed to think of weeping as more particularly an expression of sorrow. We are familiar, however, with tears of joy, and I have myself observed tears that were the result neither of joy nor of sorrow but of a sudden overwhelming feeling of affection. I believe that we may describe weeping as being a means by which the mind obtains relief from a condition of emotional tension, and that it is because such conditions of tension are most common in feelings of grief and pain that weeping comes to be associated with painful feelings. It is impossible here to discuss this subject, and I am therefore compelled to assume without proof this proposition on which my explanation of the rite is based.[8] My own conclusion, based on careful observation, is that in this rite the weeping is an expression of what has been called the tender emotion.[9] Without doubt, on some of the occasions of the rite, as when weeping over a dead friend, the participants are suffering a painful emotion, but this is evidently not so on all occasions. It is true, however, as I shall show, that on every occasion of the rite there is a condition of emotional tension due to the sudden calling into activity of the sentiment of personal attachment.

When two friends or relatives meet after having been separated, the social relation between them that has been interrupted is about to be renewed. This social relation implies or depends upon the existence of a specific bond of solidarity between them. The weeping rite (together with the subsequent exchange of presents) is the affirmation of this bond. The rite, which, it must be remembered, is obligatory, compels the two participants to act as though they felt certain emotions, and thereby does, to some extent, produce those emotions in them. When the two friends meet their first feeling seems to be one of shyness mingled with pleasure at seeing each other again. This is according to the statements of the natives as well as my own observation. Now this shyness (the Andamanese use the same word as they do for 'shame') is itself a condition of emotional tension, which has to be relieved in some way. The embrace awakens to full activity that feeling of affection or friendship that has been dormant and which it is the business of the rite to renew. The weeping gives relief to the emotional tension just noted, and also reinforces the effect of the embrace. This it does owing to the fact that a strong feeling of personal attachment is always produced when two persons join together in sharing and simultaneously expressing one and the same emotion.[10] The little ceremony thus serves to dispel the initial feeling of shyness and to reinstate the condition of intimacy and affection that existed before the separation.

In the peace-making ceremony the purpose of the whole rite is to abolish a condition of enmity and replace it by one of friendship. The once friendly relations between the two groups have been interrupted by a longer or shorter period of antagonism. We have seen that the effect of the dance is to dispel the wrath of the one group by giving it free expression. The weeping that follows is the renewal of the friendship. The rite is here exactly parallel to that on the meeting of two friends, except that not two individuals but two groups are concerned, and that owing to the number of persons involved the emotional condition is one of much greater intensity.[11] Here therefore also we see that the rite is an affirmation of solidarity or social union, in this instance between the groups, and that the rule is in its nature such as to make the participants feel that they are bound to each other by ties of friendship.

We now come to a more difficult example of the rite, that at the end of mourning ... during the period of mourning the mourners are cut off from the ordinary life of the community. By reason of the ties that still bind them to the dead person they are placed, as it were, outside the society and the bonds that unite them to their group are temporarily loosened. At the end of the mourning period they re-enter the society and take up once more their place in the social life. Their return to the community is the occasion on which they and their friends weep together. In this instance also, therefore, the rite may be explained as having for its purpose the renewal of the social relations that have been interrupted. This explanation will seem more convincing when we have considered in detail the customs of mourning. If it be accepted, then it may be seen that in the first three instances of the rite of weeping (those in which the action is reciprocal) we have conditions in which social relations that have been interrupted are about to be renewed, and the rite serves as a ceremony of aggregation.

Let us now consider the second variety of the rite, and first of all its meaning as part of the ceremony of marriage. By marriage the social bonds that have to that time united the bride and bridegroom to their respective relatives, particularly their female relatives such as mother, mother's sister, father's sister and adopted mother, are modified. The unmarried youth or girl is in a position of dependence upon his or her older relatives, and by the marriage this dependence is partly abolished. Whereas the principal duties of the bride were formerly those towards her mother and older female relatives, henceforth her chief duties in life will be towards her husband. The position of the bridegroom is similar, and it must be noted that his social relations with his male relatives are less affected by his marriage than those with his female relatives. Yet, though the ties that have bound the bride and bridegroom to their relatives are about to be modified or partially destroyed by the new ties of marriage with its new duties and rights they will still continue to exist in a weakened and changed condition. The rite of weeping is the expression of this. It serves to make real (by feeling), in those taking part in it, the presence of the social ties that are being modified.

When the mother of the bride or bridegroom weeps at a marriage she feels that her son or daughter is being taken from her care. She has the sorrow of a partial separation and she consoles herself by expressing in the rite her continued feeling of tenderness and affection towards him in the new condition that he is entering upon. For her the chief result of the rite is to make her feel that her child is still an object of her affection, still bound to her by close ties, in spite of the fact that he or she is being taken from her care.

Exactly the same explanation holds with regard to the weeping at the initiation ceremonies. By these ceremonies the youth (or girl) is gradually withdrawn from a condition of dependence on his mother and older female relatives and is made an independent member of the community. The initiation is a long process that is only completed by marriage. At every stage of the lengthy ceremonies therefore, the social ties that unite the initiate to these relatives are modified or weakened, and the rite of weeping is the means by which the significance of the change is impressed upon those taking part in it. For the mother the weeping expresses her resignation at her necessary loss, and acts as a consolation by making her feel that her son is still hers, though now being withdrawn from her care. For the boy the rite has a different meaning. He realises that he is no longer merely a child, dependent upon his mother, but is now entering upon manhood. His former feelings towards his mother must be modified. That he is being separated from her is, for him, the most important aspect of the matter, and therefore while she weeps he must give no sign of tenderness in return but must sit passive and silent. So also in the marriage ceremony, the rite serves to impress upon the young man and woman that they are, by reason of the new ties that they are forming with one another, severing their ties with their families.

When a person dies the social bonds that unite him to the survivors are profoundly modified. They are not in an instant utterly destroyed, as we shall see better when we deal with the funeral and mourning customs, for the friends and relatives still feel towards the dead person that affection in which they held him when alive, and this has now become a source of deep grief. It is this affection still binding them to him that they express in the rite of weeping over the corpse. Here rite and natural expression of emotion coincide, but it must be noted that the weeping is obligatory, a matter of duty. In this instance, then, the rite is similar to that at marriage and initiation. The man is by death cut off from the society to which he belonged, and from association with his friends, but the latter still feel towards him that attachment that bound them together while he lived, and it is this attachment that they express when they embrace the lifeless corpse and weep over it.

There remains only one more instance of the rite to be considered. When the period of mourning for a dead person is over and the bones are recovered the modification in the relations between the dead and the living, which begins at death, and is, as we shall see, carried out by the mourning customs and ceremonies, is finally accomplished. The dead person is now entirely cut off from the world of the living, save that his bones are to be treasured as relics and amulets. The weeping over the bones must be taken, I think, as a rite of aggregation whereby the bones as representative of the dead person (all that is left of him) are received back into the society henceforth to fill a special place in the social life. It really constitutes a renewal of social relations with the dead person, after a period during which all active social relations have been interrupted owing to the danger in all contact between the living and the dead. By the rite the affection that was once felt towards the dead person is revived and is now directed to the skeletal relics of the man or woman that once was their object. If this explanation seems unsatisfactory, I would ask the reader to suspend his judgment until the funeral customs of the Andamans have been discussed, and then to return to this point.

The proffered explanation of the rite of weeping should now be plain. I regard it as being the affirmation of a bond of social solidarity between those taking part in it, and as producing in them a realisation of that bond by arousing the sentiment of attachment. In some instances the rite therefore serves to renew social relations when they have been interrupted, and in such instances the rite is reciprocal. In others it serves to show the continued existence of the social bond when it is being weakened or modified, as by marriage, initiation or death. In all instances we may say that the purpose of the rite is to bring about a new state of the affective dispositions that regulate the conduct of persons to one another, either by reviving sentiments that have lain dormant, or producing a recognition of a change in the condition of personal relations.

The study of these simple ceremonies has shown us several things of importance. (1) In every instance the ceremony is the expression of an affective state of mind shared by two or more persons. Thus the weeping rite expresses feelings of solidarity, the exchange of presents expresses good-will. (2) But the ceremonies are not spontaneous expressions of feeling; they are all customary actions to which the sentiment of obligation attaches, which it is the duty of persons to perform on certain definite occasions. It is the duty of everyone in a community to give presents at a wedding; it is the duty of relatives to weep together when they meet. (3) In every instance the ceremony is to be explained by reference to fundamental laws regulating the affective life of human beings. It is not our business here to analyse these phenomena but only to satisfy ourselves that they are real. That weeping is an outlet for emotional excitement, that the free expression of aggressive feelings causes them to die out instead of smouldering on, that an embrace is an expression of feelings of attachment between persons: these are the psychological generalisations upon which are based the explanations given above of various ceremonies of the Andamanese. (4) Finally, we have seen that each of the ceremonies serves to renew or to modify in the minds of those taking part in it some one or more of the social sentiments. The peace-making ceremony is a method by which feelings of enmity are exchanged for feelings of friendship. The marriage rite serves to arouse in the minds of the marrying pair a sense of their obligations as married folk, and to bring about in the minds of the witnesses a change of feeling towards the young people such as should properly accompany their change of social status. The weeping and exchange of presents when friends come together is a means of renewing their feelings of attachment to one another. The weeping at marriage, at initiation, and on the occasion of a death is a reaction of defence or compensation when feelings of solidarity are attacked by a partial breaking of the social ties that bind persons to one another.

II Protective powers: fire and bow and arrow

In such a primitive society as that of the Andamans one of the most powerful means of maintaining the cohesion of the society and of enforcing that conformity to custom and tradition without which social life is impossible, is the recognition by the individual that for his security and well-being he depends entirely upon the society. Now for the Andaman Islander the society is not sufficiently concrete and particular to act as the object of such a sentiment, and he therefore feels his dependence upon the society not directly but in a number of indirect ways. The particular way with which we are now concerned is that the individual experiences this feeling of dependence towards every important possession of the society, towards every object which for the society had constant and important uses.

The most prominent example of such an object is fire. It may be said to be the one object on which the society most of all depends for its well-being. It provides warmth on cold nights; it is the means whereby they prepare their food, for they eat nothing raw save a few fruits; it is a possession that has to be constantly guarded, for they have no means of producing it, and must therefore take care to keep it always alight; it is the first thing they think of carrying with them when they go on a journey by land or sea; it is the centre around which the social life moves, the family hearth being the centre of the family life, while the communal cooking place is the centre round which the men often gather after the day's hunting is over. To the mind of the Andaman Islander, therefore, the social life of which his own life is a fragment, the social well-being which is the source of his own happiness, depend upon the possession of fire, without which the society could not exist. In this way it comes about that his dependence on the society appears in his consciousness as a sense of dependence upon fire and a belief that it possesses power to protect him from dangers of all kinds.

The belief in the protective power of fire is very strong. A man would never move even a few yards out of camp at night without a fire-stick. More than any other object fire is believed to keep away the spirits that cause disease and death. This belief, it is here maintained, is one of the ways in which the individual is made to feel his dependence upon the society.

Now this hypothesis is capable of being very strictly tested by the facts, for if it is true we must expect to find that the same protective power is attributed to every object on which the social life depends. An examination of the Andamanese beliefs shows that this is so, and thereby confirms the hypothesis.

In their daily life the Andamanese depend on the instrinsic qualities of the materials they use for their bows and arrows and harpoons and other hunting implements, and it can be shown that they do attribute to these implements and to the materials from which they are made powers of protection against evil. Moreover it is even possible to apply a quantitative test and show that the more important the place a thing occupies in the social life the greater is the degree of protective power attributed to it. Finally I shall be able to show that as different materials are used for special purposes so they are supposed to have certain special powers of protection against certain sorts of danger. Thus the hypothesis I have stated is capable of being as nearly demonstrated as is possible in such psychological enquiries as the one we are engaged in.

A man carrying his bow and arrows is supposed to be less likely to fall a victim to the spirits than one who has no weapons with him. One way of stopping a violent storm is to go into the sea (storms being supposed to be due to the spirits of the sea) and swish the water about with arrows. The natives sometimes wear a necklace formed of short lengths of the bamboo shaft of a fish-arrow. All the examples of such necklaces that I met with had been made from an old arrow. I asked a native to make one for me, and although he could readily have made one from bamboo that had never served as an arrow he did not do so, but used the shaft of one of his arrows. Such a necklace may therefore be described as an arrow in such a form that it can be worn round the neck and thus carried continually without trouble. The protective power of the bow is at first sight not quite so evident, but the material used for the string is regarded as possessing protective power. . . .

[There follows a passage discussing the various vegetable fibres used by the people, to which protective powers are also attributed.]

To conclude the present argument, it would seem that the function of the belief in the protective power of such things as fire and the materials from which weapons are made is to maintain in the mind of the individual the feeling of his dependence upon the society; but viewed from another aspect the beliefs in question may be regarded as expressing the social value of the things to which they relate. This term—social value—will be used repeatedly in the later part of this chapter, and it is therefore necessary to give an exact definition. By the social value of anything I mean the way in which that thing affects or is capable of affecting the social life. Value may be either positive or negative, positive value being possessed by any thing that contributes to the well-being of the society, negative value by anything that can adversely affect that well-being.

The social value of a thing (such as fire) is a matter of immediate experience to every member of the society, but the individual does not of necessity consciously and directly realise that value. He is made to realise it indirectly through the belief, impressed upon him by tradition, that the thing in question affords protection against danger. A belief or sentiment which finds regular outlet in action is a very different thing from a belief which rarely or never influences conduct. Thus, though the Andaman Islander might have a vague realisation of the value of *Hibiscus,* for example, that would be something very different from the result on the mind of the individual of the regular use of the leaves of that tree in initiation ceremonies as a protection against unseen dangers. So that the protective uses of such things are really rites or ceremonies by means of which the individual is made to realise (1) his own dependence on the society and its possessions, and (2) the social value of the things in question.

I have had to postpone to the later parts of the chapter the consideration of some of the objects possessing protective power, but

I venture to state here three propositions some part of the evidence for which has already been examined [and which will be sufficiently demonstrated, I hope, before the end of the chapter]. They are as follows: (1) any object that contributes to the well-being of the society is believed to afford protection against evil; (2) the degree of protective power it is believed to possess depends on the importance of the services it actually renders to the society; (3) the kind of special protection it is supposed to afford is often related to the kind of special service that it does actually render.

III The spirits

It is now possible for us to understand the Andamanese beliefs about the spirits. The basis of these beliefs, I wish to maintain, is the fact that at the death of an individual his social personality ... is not annihilated, but is suddenly changed. This continuance after death is a fact of immediate experience to the Andaman Islanders and not in any way a deduction. The person has not ceased to exist. For one thing his body is still there. But above all he is still the object of the social sentiments of the survivors, and thereby he continues to act upon the society. The removal of a member of the group is felt not as something negative but as the positive cause of great social disturbance.

The spirits are feared or regarded as dangerous. The basis of this fear is the fact that the spirit (i.e. the social personality of a person recently dead) is obviously a source of weakness and disruption to the community, affecting the survivors through their attachment to him, and producing a condition of dysphoria, of diminished social activity. The natural impulse of the Andaman Islander or of any other human being, would be, I believe, not to shun the dead body of a loved one, but to remain near it as long as possible. It is the society, acting under a quite different set of impulses, that compels the relatives to separate themselves from the remains of the one they loved. The death of a small child has very little influence on the general activity of the community, and the motive for severing connection with the dead that is present in the case of an adult, either does not exist or is so weak as to be overruled by the private feelings of affection, and so the child is buried in the hut of the parents, that they may continue to keep it near them. This affords a good test of the hypothesis, and gives strong support to the view that the fear of the dead man (his body and his spirit) is a collective feeling induced in the society by the fact that by death he has become the object of a dysphoric condition of the collective consciousness.

If the Andamanese are asked what they fear from the spirit of a dead man they reply that they fear sickness or death, and that if the burial and mourning customs are not properly observed the relatives of the dead person will fall sick and perhaps die.

The basis of this notion of the spirits is that the near relatives of the deceased, being bound to him by close social ties, are influenced by everything that happens to him, and share in his good or evil fortune. So that when by sickness and resulting death he is removed from the community, they are as it were drawn after him. For this reason they are, during the period of mourning, between life and death, being still attached to the dead man. Contact with the world of the dead is therefore regarded as dangerous for the living because it is believed that they may be drawn completely into that world. Death is a process by which a person leaves the living world and enters the world of the spirits, and since no one dies willingly he is conceived as being under a compulsive force acting from the world of spirits. Now sickness is a condition that often ends in death, a first stage of the way leading to the world of spirits. Hence sickness is conceived by the Andamanese as a condition of partial contact with that world. This is what is meant by the statement that sickness and death come from the spirits.

The way the Andamanese think about the spirits is shown in the *Akar-Bale* legend of the origin of death. *Yaramurud,* having died through an accident, self-caused, becomes a spirit, but he does so only under the compulsion exercised upon him by his mother, who, now that he is dead, insists that he must go away from the world of the living and become a spirit. The spirit then comes back to see his brother and by this contact causes the brother's death. The story implies that it was not because *Yaramurud* was evilly disposed towards his brother that he killed him, but on the contrary it was his attachment to his relative that caused him to return to visit him, and death followed as a result of this contact of the living man with the spirit. Since that time deaths have continued to occur in the same way. Thus it appears that the Andamanese conceive that the spirits do not cause death and sickness through evil intention, but through their mere proximity, and, as the legend very clearly shows, the burial customs are intended to cut off the unwilling spirit from contact with the living. This explains also why during the period of mourning the relatives of a dead person are thought to be in danger of sickness, and have more to fear from the spirit than others, for since it is they who were most attached to him during life it is they who are most likely to suffer from contact with him after he is dead. It was *Yaramurud's* brother who was the first to die through the influence of the spirits.

The feelings of the living towards the spirits of the dead are therefore ambivalent, compounded of affection and fear, and this must be clearly recognised if we are to understand all the Andamanese beliefs and customs. We may compare the relation between the society of the living and the society of the dead to that between two hostile communities having occasional friendly relations. That the Andamanese themselves look upon it in some such way is shown by the belief that the ceremony by which a dead man is initiated into the world of spirits resembles the peace-making ceremony. The dead man, up to the time of his death, has been living in a state of enmity with the spirits, and before he can enter their community and share their life he has to make peace with them in the same way that men make peace with one another after they have been at war.

This notion of hostility between the society and the world of spirits is found in other primitive societies, and seems everywhere to have a definite social function. The removal of a member of the community either by death or otherwise is a direct attack on the social solidarity and produces in primitive societies an emotional reaction of the same general character as anger. This collective anger, if freely expressed, serves as a compensating mechanism, satisfying and restoring the damaged sentiment.[12] But this can only happen if there is some object against which the anger can be directed. In the instance of homicide the social anger is directed against the person responsible for the death and against the social group to which he belongs. In the instance of death from sickness some other object has to be found, and amongst primitive peoples there are two chief ways in which this is done. An example of one method is afforded by the tribes of Australia, amongst whom there is a strong and constant hostility between neighbouring local groups, with a result that the anger at a death from sickness directs itself against some community with which the group of the dead man is at enmity and it is believed that some member of that community has caused the death by magic. The Andamans afford an example of the second method.

Amongst them it would seem that the enmity between different local groups (except as concerns the *Jarawa* in the South Andaman) was never very strong and the belief in evil magic was not highly developed, so that the anger at a death is directed against the spirits, and sometimes finds expression in violent railings against them, accompanied by all the bodily manifestations of extreme rage and hatred.

Now though the Andamanese regard the spirits with fear and hatred, and believe that all contact with them is dangerous for living men, yet they do not look on them as essentially evil, for that would conflict with their own feelings of attachment to their dead friends.

I gathered a few hints that they even believe that at times the spirits can and will help them. Thus a man will call on the sea-spirits of his own country to send plenty of turtle (over which the spirits seem to be assumed to have power) when he is going hunting. A very important fact in this connection is the different way in which a native regards the spirits of his own country and of other parts, the latter being thought to be much more dangerous than the former because presumably they are the spirits not of relatives and friends but of strangers at the best or enemies at the worst.

There is other evidence that the Andamanese do not regard the power that is possessed by the spirits as being essentially evil. This power, whereby the spirits are able to cause sickness, seems to be shared by the bones of dead men. Indeed the Andamanese call such bones 'spirit-bones' (*lau-toi, čauga-ta*). Now this power in the bones (though it may at times be supposed to cause sickness) is more commonly made use of in order to prevent or cure it.

The most conclusive evidence that the power of the spirits is not intrinsically evil, but may be used to produce both good and evil is afforded by the beliefs about medicine-men or dreamers (*oko-jumu*). There are three ways in which a man can become a medicine-man. The first is (as the natives put it) by dying and coming back to life. Now when a man dies he becomes a spirit and therefore acquires the peculiar powers and qualities of a spirit, which he retains if he returns to life. Secondly, if a man straying in the jungle by himself be affronted by the spirits, and if he show no fear (for if he is afraid they will kill him) they may keep him with them for a time and then let him go. Such a man, on his return, is regarded as being a medicine-man, and possessing all the powers of medicine-men. I was told of one man who became a medicine-man in this way within living memory, and it was stated that when he returned from the forest where he had been kept by the spirits for two or three days he was decorated with *koro* fibre. [We have seen that] this fibre is used by the spirits in the ceremony by which they initiate dead men, and its presence on the returned warrior was perhaps accepted by his friends as evidence that he had been initiated by the spirits. The third and last way in which a man may become a medicine-man is by having intercourse with the spirits in his dreams. [This is a point to which it will be necessary to return later.] For the present it is sufficient to note that in every instance the power of the medicine-man is believed to be derived from his contact with the spirits in one of the three possible ways.

We are justified in concluding that the special power of the medicine-man, by which he is distinguished from his fellows, is simply the same power that is possessed by the spirits, from contact with whom he has obtained it. The medicine-man is believed be be able both to cause and to cure sickness, to arouse and to dispel storms. In other words he has power for both good and evil, and we must conclude that the spirits have the same. Moreover, it is commonly said that the medicine-man is able to produce the effects he does, whether they be harmful or beneficial to his fellows, by communicating with the spirits in dreams and enlisting their aid. This would seem to prove the point that I am here concerned with, that the power possessed by the spirits, though contact with it is always dangerous, may yet in certain circumstances be of benefit to the society, and is therefore not essentially evil in nature.

The Andamanese believe that a medicine-man communicates with the spirits in sleep, and this is not the only evidence that they believe sleep to be a condition in which contact with the world of spirits is easier than in waking life. It is believed that sickness is more likely to begin during sleep than when awake. During the initiation ceremonies the initiate is required to abstain from sleep after eating pork or turtle, and this would seem to be because sleep is regarded as generally dangerous and therefore to be avoided on such occasions as this when every precaution needs to be taken.

The explanation of this belief seems to lie in the fact that sleep is a condition of diminished social activity, in which the individual is withdrawn from active social life, and is therefore also withdrawn from the protection of the society. After eating turtle the initiate is in urgent need of the protection of the society, which would be lost to him if he were permitted to sleep. After a death, when the corpse remains in the camp all night the people remain awake, and since there is no other common activity in which they can join, they sing, and thus protect themselves from the spirits that are present as the cause of the death.

This explanation implies that all conditions of diminished social activity on the part of an individual are dangerous. One example of such a condition is sickness, in which the sick person is unable to pursue his ordinary occupations. Other examples are afforded by a mother, and to a certain extent a father during the period preceding and following the birth of a child, and by a woman during the menstrual period. All these, as various customs show, are believed by the Andamanese to be conditions of danger in which it is necessary to take ritual or magical precautions. A better example for our purpose is that of an adolescent during the period covered by the initiation ceremonies, when, as we have seen, he is as it were cut off from the society, and there is abundant evidence that the Andamanese believe this to be a state of danger. Another example is the condition of a homicide during the period of his isolation. Lastly, we have seen that a mourner is cut off from the ordinary social life, and it may now be noted that the native explanation of the restrictions observed in that state is that if things were not done thus the mourner would be ill; in other words the condition of mourning is one of danger, and the ritual referring to it is the means by which the danger (from the spirit world) is avoided. This explanation does not conflict with the one previously given but on the contrary we can now see that the notion that the mourner is in a position partly withdrawn from active participation in social life necessarily involves the belief that he is in a condition of danger.

We may conclude that every condition in which the individual is withdrawn from full participation in active social life is regarded as dangerous for him, and that this is at least one of the reasons why sleep is so regarded. We have already noted that all conditions of danger tend to be thought of as due to contact with the spirits, and sleep is therefore supposed to be a state in which such contact is easier than in waking life. Now sleep is visited by dreams and it comes about that the dream-life, by reason of its contrast with waking-life, is seized upon by the Andamanese as a means by which the nature of the spirit world may be represented to the imagination.

The Andaman Islander seems to regard the dream-world as a

world of shadows or reflections, for he uses the same word to denote a shadow, a reflection in a mirror, and a dream (the stem *-jumu* in *Aka-Jeru*). Now when a man enters this shadow-world in sleep he is, as we have seen, conceived as coming into partial contact with the world of spirits. Hence the Andaman Islander believes that in dreams he may communicate with the spirits, that dreams may be a cause of sickness, and that in dreams a medicine-man can cause or cure sickness in his fellows. In this shadow-world the man himself becomes as it were a shadow, a mere reflection of himself; it is not he that lives and acts in his dreams but his *ot-jumulo,* his double, his shadow-self, or, as we might say, his soul. It is but a step from this to the representation of the spirit-world as a similar world of shadows and dream-shapes, and to the conclusion that when a man dies it is his *ot-jumulo* that becomes the spirit.

To summarise the argument, the belief in the world of spirits rests on the actual fact that a dead person continues to affect the society. As the effect is one of disorganisation, whereby the social sentiments are wounded, the dead are avoided and the spirits are regarded with fear. But as a recently dead person is still regarded with feelings of attachment by his friends, the resulting final attitude towards the spirits is ambivalent. By a simple step the spirits come to be regarded as the cause of sickness and death, and therefore as hostile to living men. Yet, as the beliefs about medicine-men show, it is possible for exceptional individuals to be on terms of friendship with the spirits. Finally, the dream-life affords a means by which the spirit-world may be represented in a simple and concrete manner. This last feature (the association of the spirits with dreams) I believe to be a secondary elaboration of the primary or fundamental belief which shows itself in the ritual of death and mourning, serving only to rationalise it and make it more concrete. This need of concrete representation of the spirit-world shows itself in other beliefs, in which may be seen the tendency to become self-contradictory that is often the mark of ideas that arise as the result of attempts to rationalise conative and affective impulses. The spirits are, on the one hand, as it were shadows or images of living men, and yet, since they are feared and disliked, they are often represented as being repulsive and inhuman, with long legs and short bodies, with long beards and ugly faces.[13] The spirits must be thought of as somewhere, but there is no consistency in the statements as to where that somewhere is; one man will say that they live in the sky, another that they are under the earth, a third will point to a particular island as their home; at the same time it is evident from other statements that they vaguely conceive them as being everywhere, in the forest and the sea.

We are now in a position to understand what the Andaman Islander means when he says that the danger he fears from food is from the spirits. The greatest evil that can happen to the community is the sickness or death of its members, and these are believed to be the work of the spirits. The sense of the social value of food takes the form of a belief that food is dangerous, and inevitably the danger comes to be conceived as that of sickness or death, and is therefore associated in their minds with the spirits.

But there is a more fundamental reason than this. I have tried to show that it is because food has such important effects for good and evil on the social life that it is believed to be endued with a peculiar power which makes it necessary to approach it with ritual precautions. If this thesis be valid it should be capable of generalisation, and we should find the same power attributed to every object or being that is capable of affecting in important ways the well-being of the society. We should expect that the Andamanese would attribute this power not only to the more important things used for food but also to such things as the weather and dead men (i.e., the spirits). Now this, if the argument has been correct, is exactly what we do find, and we have here the reason why the Andaman Islander, when asked what he fears from eating dangerous foods, replies that he fears sickness or the spirits of the dead.

We may formulate in precise language the beliefs that underlie the ceremonial, remembering always that the Andaman Islanders themselves are quite incapable of expressing these beliefs in words and are probably only vaguely conscious of them. (1) There is a power or force in all objects or beings that in any way affect the social life. (2) It is by virtue of this power that such things are able to aid or harm the society. (3) The power, no matter what may be the object or being in which it is present, is never either essentially good or essentially evil, but is able to produce both good and evil results. (4) Any contact with the power is dangerous, but the danger is avoided by ritual precautions. (5) The degree of power possessed by anything is directly proportioned to the importance of the effects that it has on the social life. (6) The power in one thing may be used to counteract the danger due to contact with the power in some other thing.

We have studied this power in the animals and plants used for food and the things used as materials. It is this that makes turtle dangerous to eat and *Anadendron* fibre dangerous to prepare, and it is this also that makes animal bones or the leaves of *Hibiscus* available for protection. We have now seen that the same power is present in dead men, in their bodies, their bones, and in the spirit-world to which dead men go. All contact with the world of the dead is highly dangerous, and yet we have seen that human bones may be used for protection and that even the spirits may be induced to heal sickness or allay storms. We have also seen that the same power is present in the *oko-jumu,* and we have made the important discovery that it is through contact with the spirits that he acquires the power. This reveals another important principle. (7) If an individual comes into contact with the power in any thing and successfully avoids the danger of such contact, he becomes himself endowed with power of the same kind as that with which he is in contact. Now although the *oko-jumu* possesses a very special social value, yet every man and woman has some social value, some of that power which makes any being capable of affecting the society for good or ill, and we can now see that the initiation ceremonies are the means by which the individual is endowed with power (or, as the natives say, made strong) by being brought into contact with the special power present in each of the important kinds of food. The initiation of the ordinary man or woman is parallel to the initiation of the *oko-jumu* save that in one instance it is the power in foods and in the other that in the spirits with which the initiation is concerned.

It has been held in this chapter that the society or the social life itself is the chief source of protection against danger for the individual. If this be so then the society itself possesses this same power with which we are dealing, and we must expect to find that contact with this power is also dangerous for the individual. Now the occasion on which the individual comes into contact with the power in the society is in the dance, and I found evidence that the natives believe that dancing is dangerous in exactly the same way as eating food. (. . .)

It would seem that for the Andaman Islander the social life is a process of complex interaction of powers or forces present in the society itself, in each individual, in animals and plants and the phenomena of nature, and in the world of spirits, and on these powers the well-being of the society and its members depends. By the action of the principle of opposition the society—the world of the living—comes to be opposed to the spirits—the world of the dead. The society itself is the chief source of protection to the individual; the spirits are the chief source of danger. Hence all protection tends to be referred to the society and all danger to the spirits. In the initiation ceremonies it is the society that protects the initiate against the dangers of food, and those dangers are referred, generally if not quite consistently, to the spirits, with which at first sight they would seem to have nothing to do.

IV Conclusion

It is time to bring the argument to a conclusion. It should now, I hope, be evident that the ceremonial customs of the Andaman Islands form a closely connected system, and that we cannot understand their meaning if we only consider each one by itself, but must study the whole system to arrive at an interpretation. This in itself I regard as a most important conclusion, for it justifies the contention that we must substitute for the old method of dealing with the customs of primitive people,—the comparative method by which isolated customs from different social types were brought together and conclusions drawn from their similarity—a new method by which all the institutions of one society or social type are studied together so as to exhibit their intimate relations as parts of an organic system.

I have tried to show that the ceremonial customs are the means by which the society acts upon its individual members and keeps alive in their minds a certain system of sentiments. Without the ceremonial those sentiments would not exist, and without them the social organisation in its actual form could not exist. There is great difficulty, however, in finding a suitable method of describing these sentiments. In attempting to put into precise words the vague *feelings* of the Andaman Islander there is always the danger that we may attribute to him *conceptions* that he does not possess. For he is not himself capable of thinking about his own sentiments.

In the attempt to exhibit the meaning of the ceremonial I have shown that it implies a complex system of beliefs about what I have called power, and have stated those beliefs in more or less precise terms. But the Andaman Islander is of course quite incapable of making similar statements or even of understanding them. In his

97

consciousness appear only the very vaguest conceptions, such as those associated with the word *kimil* or with odours. We, in order to understand his customs must substitute for such vague notions others capable of precise statement, must formulate in words the beliefs that are revealed in his actions, but we must be careful not to fall into the error of attributing to him the conceptions by which we make clear to ourselves his indefinite sentiments and notions and the ceremonies in which they are expressed.

With this qualification, then, the ceremonial of the Andaman Islands may be said to involve the assumption of a power of a peculiar kind, and we have been able to formulate certain principles which, although the native is quite incapable of stating them as principles, are revealed in the ceremonial. This power, though in itself neither good nor evil, is the source of all good and all evil in human life. It is present in the society itself and in everything that can affect in important ways the social life. All occasions of special contact with it are dangerous, i.e., are subject to ritual precautions.

It should already, from the course of the argument, be plain that this power or force, the interaction of whose different manifestations constitutes the process of social life, is not imaginary, is not even something the existence of which is surmised as the result of intellectual processes, but is real, an object of actual experience. It is, in a few words, the moral power of the society acting upon the individual directly or indirectly and felt by him in innumerable ways throughout the whole course of his life.[14]

One of the most important ways in which the individual experiences the moral force of the society of which he is a member is through the feeling of moral obligation, which gives him the experience of a power compelling him to subordinate his egoistic desires to the demands of social custom. The individual feels this force acting upon him both from outside and from inside himself. For he recognises that it is the society with its traditions and customs that constrains him through the force of public opinion, and yet the conflict between customary duty and selfish inclination takes place in his own mind and is experienced as the clash of antagonistic mental forces. The moral sense within impels towards the same end as the social opinion without.

This force of moral obligation is felt not only in relation to right and wrong conduct towards other persons, but is also felt in all ritual, whether negative or positive.

The moral force of the society is also felt, in a quite different way, in all states of intense collective emotion, of which the dance affords a good example. [I have shown how] in the dance the individual feels the society acting upon him, constraining him to join in the common activity and regulate his actions to conform with those of others, and, when he so acts in harmony with them, giving him the experience of a grat increase of his own personal force or energy. All ceremonies in which the whole community takes part give the individual the experience of the moral force of the society acting upon him in somewhat the same way as the dance.

Thus in these and other ways the individual does experience the action of the society upon himself as a sort of force, not however as a physical force, but as a moral force, acting directly in his own mind and yet clearly felt as something outside his own self, and with which that self may be in conflict.

How is it, then, that this force comes to be projected into the world of nature? The answer to that question, which can only be very briefly indicated here, is to be found in the conclusions at which we have arrived with regard to social values. The moral force of the society is experienced by the individual not only directly but also as acting upon him indirectly through every object that has social value. The best example of this process is found in the things used for food. Thus, in the Andamans, food is very closely connected with the feeling of moral obligation, as we have seen. Further, food is one of the principal sources of those alternations of social euphoria and dysphoria in which, through the action of the collective emotion, the individual experiences the action of the society upon his own well-being. When food is plentiful happiness spreads through the community and the time is spent in dancing and feasting so that the individual feels a great increase in his own personal force coming to him from the society or from the food. On the other hand, when food is scarce and hunting unsuccessful the community feels itself thwarted and restrained and experiences a sense of weakness, which collective feeling has for its immediate object the food the lack of which is its origin.

Similarly with the phenomena of the weather and all other objects that have social value, they are all associated in the mind of the individual with his experience of the action of the society upon himself, so that the moral force of the society is actually felt as acting through them.

99

But it is really through the ceremonial that this is mainly brought about. It is in the initiation ceremonies that the moral force of the society acting through foods is chiefly felt, and the same experience is repeated in a less intense form in the rite of painting the body after food. It is similarly through the protective use of the materials used for weapons and through the various ritual prohibitions connected with them that the moral force of the society acting through them is chiefly felt. The argument has been that it is by means of the ceremonial that the individual is made to feel the social value of the various things with which the ceremonial is concerned. Putting this in other words we can now define the ceremonial as the means by which the individual is made to feel the moral force of the society acting upon him either directly, or in some instances indirectly through those things that have important effects on the social life. By its action upon the individual the ceremonial develops and maintains in existence in his mind an organised system of dispositions by which the social life, in the particular form it takes in the Andamans, is made possible, using for the purpose of maintaining the social cohesion all the instinctive tendencies of human nature, modifying and combining them according to its needs.

As an example of such modification of primary instincts let us briefly consider that of fear, to which, from the time of Petronius[15] to the present day, so much importance has been attributed in relation to the origin of religion. In childhood any fear of danger makes the child run to its mother or father for protection, and thus the instinct of fear becomes an important component of that feeling of dependence that the child has towards its parents. The primitive society uses the fear instinct in much the same way. The Andaman Islander, through the ceremonies and customs of his people, is made to feel that he is in a world full of unseen dangers—dangers from the foods he eats, from the sea, the weather, the forest and its animals, but above all from the spirits of the dead,—which can only be avoided by the help of the society and by conformity with social custom. As men press close to one another in danger, the belief in and fear of the spirit-world make the Andaman Islander cling more firmly to his fellows, and make him feel more intensely his own dependence on the society to which he belongs, just as the fear of danger makes the child feel its dependence upon its parents. So the belief in the spirit-world serves directly to increase the cohesion of the society through its action on the mind of the individual. An important law of sociology is that the solidarity of a group is increased when the group as a whole finds itself opposed to some other group; so, enmity between two tribes or nations increases the solidarity of each; and so also, the antagonism between the society of the living and the world of the dead increases the solidarity of the former.

Notes

1 Tylor, *Primitive Culture,* 1, 387.

2 Frazer, *Totemism and Exogamy*, vol. 4.

3 Max Müller, *Physical Religion,* p. 119.

4 Marett, *Threshold of Religion.*

5 McDougall, *Introduction to Social Psychology,* chap. XIII, seems to combine the two hypotheses.

6 For a criticism of the hypotheses of animism and naturism as explanations of primitive religion see Durkheim, *Elementary Forms of the Religious Life,* Book I, chapters 2 and 3.

7 Sentiment—an organised system of emotional tendencies centred upon some object.

8 In a few words the psycho-physical theory here assumed is that weeping is a substitute for motor activity when the kinetic system of the body (motor centres, thyroid, suprarenals, etc.) is stimulated but no effective action in direct response to the stimulus is possible at the moment. When a sentiment is stimulated and action to which it might lead is frustrated, the resultant emotional state is usually painful, and hence weeping is commonly associated with painful states.

9 McDougall, *Social Psychology.*

10 Active sympathy, the habitual sharing of joyful and painful emotions, is of the utmost importance in the formation of sentiments of personal attachment.

11 It is a commonplace of psychology that a collective emotion, i.e. one felt and expressed at the same moment by a number of persons, is felt much more intensely than an unshared emotion of the same kind.

12 The psychological function of individual anger is to restore to their normal condition the wounded self-regarding sentiments. The function of collective anger is similarly to restore the collective sentiments on which the solidarity of the society depends.

13 I once drew a few grotesque figures for the amusement of some Andamanese children, and they at once pronounced them to be 'spirits'.

14 The exposition of this important thesis can only be given here in the most abbreviated form. The thesis itself, as applied to primitive ritual in general, owes its origin to Professor Émile Durkheim, and has been

101

expounded by him (more particularly in his work *Elementary Forms . . .*) and by Messieurs H. Hubert and M. Mauss.

15 Primus in orbe deos fecit timor.

8   Religion and society[1]

The Royal Anthropological Institute has honoured me with an invitation to deliver the Henry Myers Lecture on the rôle of religion in the development of human society. That is an important and complex subject, about which it is not possible to say very much in a single lecture, but as it is hoped that this may be only the first of a continuing series of lectures, in which different lecturers will each offer some contribution, I think that the most useful thing I can do is to indicate certain lines along which I believe that an enquiry into this problem can be profitably pursued.

The usual way of looking at religions is to regard all of them, or all except one, as bodies of erroneous beliefs and illusory practices. There is no doubt that the history of religions has been in great part a history of error and illusion. In all ages men have hoped that by the proper performance of religious actions or observances they would obtain some specific benefit: health and long life, children to carry on their line, material well-being, success in hunting, rain, the growth of crops and the multiplication of cattle, victory in war, admission of their souls after death to a paradise, or inversely, release by the extinction of personality from the round of reincarnation. We do not believe that the rain-making rites of savage tribes really produce rain. Nor do we believe that the initiates of the ancient mysteries did actually attain through their initiation an immortality denied to other men.

When we regard the religions of other peoples, or at least those of what are called primitive peoples, as systems of erroneous and illusory beliefs, we are confronted with the problem of how these beliefs came to be formulated and accepted. It is to this problem that anthropologists have given most attention. My personal opinion is that this method of approach, even though it may seem the most direct, is not the one most likely to lead to a real understanding of the nature of religions.

There is another way in which we may approach the study of

103

religions. We may entertain as at least a possibility the theory that any religion is an important or even essential part of the social machinery, as are morality and law, part of the complex system by which human beings are enabled to live together in an orderly arrangement of social relations. From this point of view we deal not with the origins but with the social function of religions, i.e. the contribution that they make to the formation and maintenance of a social order. There are many persons who would say that it is only *true* religion (i.e. one's own) that can provide the foundation of an orderly social life. The hypothesis we are considering is that the social function of a religion is independent of its truth or falsity, that religions which we think to be erroneous or even absurd and repulsive, such as those of some savage tribes, may be important and effective parts of the social machinery, and that without these 'false' religions social evolution and the development of modern civilisation would have been impossible.

The hypothesis, therefore, is that in what we regard as false religions, though the performance of religious rites does not actually produce the effects that are expected or hoped for by those who perform or take part in them, they have other effects, some at least of which may be socially valuable.

How are we to set to work to test this hypothesis? It is of no use thinking in terms of religion in general, in the abstract, and society in the abstract. Nor is it adequate to consider some one religion, particularly if it is the one in which we have been brought up and about which we are likely to be prejudiced one way or another. The only method is the experimental method of social anthropology, and that means that we must study in the light of our hypothesis a sufficient number of diverse particular religions or religious cults in their relation to the particular societies in which they are found. This is a task not for one person but for a number.

Anthropologists and others have discussed at length the question of the proper definition of religion. I do not intend to deal with that controversial subject on this occasion. But there are some points that must be considered. I shall assume that any religion or any religious cult normally involves certain ideas or beliefs on the one hand, and on the other certain observances. These observances, positive and negative, i.e. actions and abstentions, I shall speak of as rites.

In European countries, and more particularly since the Reformation, religion has come to be considered as primarily a matter of belief. This is itself a phenomenon which needs to be explained, I think, in terms of social development. We are concerned here only with its effects on the thinking of anthropologists. Among many of them there is a tendency to treat belief as primary: rites are considered as the results of beliefs. They therefore concentrate their attention on trying to explain the beliefs by hypotheses as to how they may have been formed and adopted.

To my mind this is the product of false psychology. For example, it is sometimes held that funeral and mourning rites are the result of a belief in a soul surviving death. If we must talk in terms of cause and effect, I would rather hold the view that the belief in a surviving soul is not the cause but the effect of the rites. Actually the cause-effect analysis is misleading. What really happens is that the rites and the justifying or rationalising beliefs develop together as parts of a coherent whole. But in this development it is action or the need of action that controls or determines belief rather than the other way about. The actions themselves are symbolic expressions of sentiments.

My suggestion is that in attempting to understand a religion it is on the rites rather than on the beliefs that we should first concentrate our attention. Much the same view is taken by Loisy, who justifies his selection of sacrificial rites as the subject of his analysis of religion by saying that rites are in all religions the most stable and lasting element, and consequently that in which we can best discover the spirit of ancient cults.[2]

That great pioneer of the science of religion, Robertson Smith, took this view. He wrote as follows:[3]

> In connection with every religion, whether ancient or modern, we find on the one hand certain beliefs, and on the other certain institutions, ritual practices and rules of conduct. Our modern habit is to look at religion from the side of belief rather than that of practice; for, down to comparatively recent times, almost the only forms of religion seriously studied in Europe have been those of the various Christian Churches, and all parts of Christendom are agreed that ritual is important only in connection with its interpretation. Thus the study of religion has meant mainly the study of Christian beliefs, and instruction in religion has habitually begun with the creed, religious duties being presented to the learner as flowing from the dogmatic

truths he is taught to accept. All this seems to us so much a matter of course that, when we approach some strange or antique religion, we naturally assume that here also our first business is to search for a creed, and find in it the key to ritual and practice. But the antique religions had for the most part no creed; they consisted entirely of institutions and practices. No doubt men will not habitually follow certain practices without attaching a meaning to them; but as a rule we find that while the practice was rigorously fixed, the meaning attached to it was extremely vague, and the same rite was explained by different people in different ways, without any question of orthodoxy or heterodoxy arising in consequence. In ancient Greece, for example, certain things were done at a temple, and people were agreed that it would be impious not to do them. But if you asked why they were done you would probably have had several mutually contradictory explanations from different persons, and no one would have thought it a matter of the least religious importance which of these you chose to adopt. Indeed, the explanations offered would not have been of a kind to stir any strong feeling; for in most cases they would have been merely different stories as to the circumstances under which the rite first came to be established, by the command or by the direct example of the god. The rite, in short, was connected not with dogma but with a myth.

... It is of the first importance to realise clearly from the outset that ritual and practical usage were, strictly speaking, the sum-total of ancient religions. Religion in primitive times was not a system of belief with practical applications; it was a body of fixed traditional practices to which every member of society conformed as a matter of course. Men would not be men if they agreed to do certain things without having a reason for their action; but in ancient religion the reason was not first formulated as a doctrine and then expressed in practice, but conversely, practice preceded doctrinal theory. Men form general rules of conduct before they begin to express general principles in words; political institutions are older than political theories, and in like manner religious institutions are older than religious theories. This analogy is not arbitrarily chosen, for in fact the parallelism in ancient society between religious and political institutions is complete. In each sphere great importance was attached to form and precedent, but the explanation why the precedent was followed consisted merely of a legend as to its first establishment. That the precedent, once established, was authoritative did not appear to require any proof. The rules of society were based on precedent, and the continued existence of the society was sufficient reason why a precedent once set should continue to be followed.

The relative stability of rites and the variability of doctrines can be illustrated from the Christian religions. The two essential rites of all Christian religions are baptism and the eucharist, and we know that the latter solemn sacrament is interpreted differently in the Orthodox Church, the Roman Church and the Anglican Church. The modern emphasis on the exact formulation of beliefs connected with the rites rather than on the rites themselves is demonstrated in the way in which Christians have fought with and killed one another over differences of doctrine.

Thirty-seven years ago (1908), in a fellowship thesis on the Andaman Islanders (which did not appear in print till 1922), I formulated briefly a general theory of the social function of rites and ceremonies. It is the same theory that underlies the remarks I shall offer on this occasion. Stated in the simplest possible terms the theory is that an orderly social life amongst human beings depends upon the presence in the minds of the members of a society of certain sentiments, which control the behaviour of the individual in his relation to others. Rites can be seen to be the regulated symbolic expressions of certain sentiments. Rites can therefore be shown to have a specific social function when, and to the extent that, they have for their effect to regulate, maintain and transmit from one generation to another sentiments on which the constitution of the society depends. I ventured to suggest as a general formula that religion is everywhere an expression in one form or another of a sense of dependence on a power outside ourselves, a power which we may speak of as a spiritual or moral power.

This theory is by no means new. It is to be found in the writings of the philosophers of ancient China. It is most explicit in the teachings of Hsün Tzŭ who lived in the third century B.C., and in the *Book of Rites* (the *Li Chi*), which was compiled some time later. The Chinese writers do not write about religion. I am doubtful if there is in Chinese any word which will convey just what we understand by the word religion. They write about *li,* and the word is variously translated as ceremonial, customary morality, rites, rules of good manners, propriety. But the character by which this word is written consists of two parts, of which one refers to spirits, sacrifice and prayer, and the other originally meant a vessel used in performing sacrifices. We may therefore appropriately translate *li* as 'ritual'. In any case what the ancient philosophers are chiefly concerned with are the rites of mourning and sacrificial rites.

There is no doubt that in China, as elsewhere, it was thought that many or all of the religious rites were efficacious in the sense of averting evils and bringing blessings. It was believed that the seasons would not follow one another in due order unless the Emperor, the Son of Heaven, performed the established rites at the appropriate times. Even under the Republic a reluctant magistrate of a *hsien* may be compelled by public opinion to take the leading part in a ceremony to bring rain. But there developed among the scholars an attitude which might perhaps be called rationalistic and agnostic. For the most part the question of the efficacy of rites was not considered. What was thought important was the social function of the rites, i.e. their effects in producing and maintaining an orderly human society.

In a text that is earlier than Confucius we read that 'sacrifice is that through which one can show one's filial piety and give peace to the people, pacify the country and make the people settled. . . . It is through the sacrifices that the unity of the people is strengthened' (*Ch'u Yü,* II, 2).

You know that one of the major points of the teaching of Confucius was the importance of the proper performance of rites. But it is said of Confucius that he would not discuss the supernatural.[4] In the Confucian philosophy, music and ritual are considered as means for the establishment and preservation of social order, and regarded as superior to laws and punishments as means to this end. We take a very different view of music, but I may remind you that Plato held somewhat similar ideas, and I suggest that an anthropological study of the relations between music (and dancing) and religious rituals would provide some interesting results. In the *Book of Rites* one section (the *Yüeh Chi*) is concerned with music. The third paragraph reads:[5]

The ancient kings were watchful in regard to the things by which the mind was affected. And so they instituted ceremonies to direct men's aims aright; music to give harmony to their voices; laws to unify their conduct; and punishments to guard against their tendencies to evil. The end to which ceremonies, music, punishments and laws conduct is one; they are the instruments by which the minds of the people are assimilated, and good order in government is made to appear.

The view of religion that we are here concerned with might be summed up in the following sentence from the *Book of Rites,* 'Ceremonies are the bond that holds the multitudes together, and if the bond be removed, those multitudes fall into confusion.'

The later Confucian philosophers, beginning with Hsün Tzŭ, paid attention to the ways in which rites, particularly the mourning and sacrificial rites, performed their function of maintaining social order. The chief point of their theory is that the rites serve to 'regulate' and 'refine' human feelings. Hsün Tzŭ says:[6]

Sacrificial rites are the expressions of man's affectionate longings. They represent the height of altruism, faithfulness, love and reverence. They represent the completion of propriety and refinement.

Of the mourning rites Hsün Tzŭ says:

The rites *(li)* consist in being careful about the treatment of life and death. Life is the beginning of man, Death is the end of man. When the end and beginning are both good, the way of humanity is complete. Hence the Superior Man respects the beginning and venerates the end. To make the end and beginning uniform is the practice of the Superior man, and is that in which lies the beauty of *li* and standards of justice *(i)*. For to pay over-attention to the living and belittle the dead would be to respect them when they have knowledge and disrespect them when they have not. . . .

The way of death is this: once dead, a person cannot return again. [It is in realising this that] the minister most completely fulfils the honour due to his ruler, and the son the honour of his parents.

Funeral rites are for the living to give beautified ceremonial to the dead; to send off the dead as if they were living; to render the same service to the dead as to the living; to the absent as to the present; and to make the end be the same as the beginning . . .

Articles used in life are prepared so as to be put into the grave, as if [the deceased] were only moving house. Only a few things are taken, not all of them. They are to give the appearance, but are not for practical use. . . . Hence the things [such as were used] in life are adorned, but not completed, and the 'spiritual utensils'[7] are for appearance but not use.

Hence the funeral rites are for no other purpose than to make clear the meaning of death and life, to send off the dead with sorrow and reverence, and when the end comes, to prepare for storing the body away. . . . Service to the living is beautifying their beginning; sending off the dead is beautifying their end. When the end and the beginning are both attended to, the service of the filial son is ended and the way of the Sage is completed. Slighting the dead and over-emphasising the living is the way of Mo (Tzŭ).[8] Slighting the living and over-attention to the dead is the way of superstition. Killing the living to send off the dead is murder.[9] The method and manner of *li* and standards of justice *(i)* is to send off the dead as if they were alive, so that in death and life, the end and the beginning, there is nothing that is not appropriate and good. The Confucian does this.

The view taken by this school of ancient philosophers was that religious rites have important social functions which are independent of any beliefs that may be held as to the efficacy of the rites. The rites gave regulated expression to certain human feelings and sentiments and so kept these sentiments alive and active. In turn it was these sentiments which, by their control of or influence on the conduct of individuals, made possible the existence and continuance of an orderly social life.

It is this theory that I propose for your consideration. Applied, not to a single society such as ancient China, but to all human societies, it points to the correlation and co-variation of different characteristics or elements of social systems. Societies differ from one another in their structure and constitution and therefore in the customary rules of behaviour of persons one to another. The system of sentiments on which the social constitution depends must therefore vary in correspondence with the difference of constitution. In so far as religion has the kind of social function that the theory suggests, religion must also vary in correspondence with the manner in which the society is constituted. In a social system constituted on the basis of nations which make war on one another, or stand ready to do so, a well-developed sentiment of patriotism in its members is essential to maintain a strong nation. In such circumstances patriotism or national feeling may be given support by religion. Thus the Children of Israel, when they invaded the land of Canaan under the leadership of Joshua, were inspired by the religion that had been taught to them by Moses and was centred upon the Holy Tabernacle and its rites.

War or the envisaged possibility of war is an essential element in the constitution of great numbers of human societies, though the warlike spirit varies very much from one to another. It is thus in accordance with our theory that one of the social functions of religion is in connection with war. It can give man faith and confidence and devotion when they go out to do battle, whether they are the aggressors or are resisting aggression. In the recent conflict the German people seem to have prayed to God for victory not less fervently than the people of the allied nations.

It will be evident that to test our theory we must examine many societies to see if there is a demonstrable correspondence of the religion or religions of any one of them and the manner in which that society is constituted. If such a correspondence can be made out, we must then try to discover and as far as possible define the major sentiments that find their expression in the religion and at the same time contribute to the maintenance of stability in the society as constituted.

An important contribution to our study is to be found in a book that is undeservedly neglected by anthropologists, *La Cité antique,* by the historian Fustel de Coulanges. It is true that it was written some time ago (1864) and that in some matters it may need correction in the light of later historical research, but it remains a valuable contribution to the theory of the social function of religion.

The purpose of the book is to show the point-by-point correspondence between religion and the constitution of society in ancient Greece and Rome, and how in the course of history the two changed together. It is true that the author, in conformity with the ideas of the nineteenth century, conceived this correlation between two sets

111

of social features in terms of cause and effect, those of one set being thought of as the cause producing those of the other set. The men of the ancient world, so the argument runs, came to hold certain beliefs about the souls of the dead. As the result of their beliefs they made offerings at their tombs.[10]

> Since the dead had need of food and drink it appeared to be a duty of the living to satisfy this need. The care of supplying the dead with sustenance was not left to the caprice or to the variable sentiments of men; it was obligatory. Thus a complete religion of the dead was established, whose dogmas might soon be effaced, but whose rites endured until the triumph of Christianity.

It was a result of this religion that ancient society came to be constituted on the basis of the family, the agnatic lineage and the gens, with its laws of succession, property, authority and marriage.[11]

> A comparison of beliefs and laws shows that a primitive religion constituted the Greek and Roman family, established marriage and paternal authority, fixed the order of relationship, and consecrated the right of property and the right of inheritance. This same religion, after having enlarged and extended the family, formed a still larger association, the city, and reigned in that as it had reigned in the family. From it came all the institutions, as well as all the private law, of the ancients. It was from this that the city received all its principles, its rules, its usages and its magistracies. But, in the course of time, this ancient religion became modified or effaced, and private law and political institutions were modified with it. Then came a series of revolutions, and social changes regularly followed the development of knowledge.

In his final paragraph the author writes:[12]

> We have written the history of a belief. It was established and human society was constituted. It was modified, and society underwent a series of revolutions. It disappeared and society changed its character.

This idea of the primacy of belief and of a causal relation in which the religion is the cause and the other institutions are the effect is in accordance with a mode of thought that was common in the nineteenth century. We can, as I indeed do, completely reject this theory and yet retain as a valuable and permanent contribution to our subject a great deal of what Fustel de Coulanges wrote. We can say that he has produced evidence that in ancient Greece and Rome the religion on the one side and the many important institutions on the other are closely united as interdependent parts of a coherent and unified system. The religion was an essential part of the constitution of the society. The form of the religion and the form of the social structure correspond one with the other. We cannot, as Fustel de Coulanges says, understand the social, juridical and political institutions of the ancient societies unless we take the religion into account. But it is equally true that we cannot understand the religion except by an examination of its relation to the institutions.

A most important part of the religion of ancient Greece and Rome was the worship of ancestors. We may regard this as one instance of a certain type of religion. A religious cult of the same general kind has existed in China from ancient times to the present day. Cults of the same kind exist today and can be studied in many parts of Africa and Asia. It is therefore possible to make a wide comparative study of this type of religion. In my own experience it is in ancestor-worship that we can most easily discover and demonstrate the social function of a religious cult.

The term 'ancestor-worship' is sometimes used in a wide, loose sense to refer to any sort of rites referring to dead persons. I propose to use it in a more limited and more precisely defined sense. The cult group in this religion consists solely of persons related to one another by descent in one line from the same ancestor or ancestors. In most instances descent is patrilineal, through males. But in some societies, such as the Bakongo in Africa and the Nayar in India, descent is matrilineal, and the cult group consists of descendants of a single ancestress. The rites in which the members of the group, and only they, participate have reference to their own ancestors, and normally they include the making of offerings or sacrifices to them.

A particular lineage consists of three or more generations. A lineage of four or five generations will normally be included as a part in one of six or seven generations. In a well-developed system related lineages are united into a larger body, such as the Roman gens, or

113

what may be called the clan in China. In parts of China we can find a large body of persons, numbering in some instances as much as a thousand, all having the same name and tracing their descent in the male line from a single ancestor, the founder of the clan. The clan itself is divided into lineages.

A lineage, if it is of more than three or four generations, includes both living persons and dead persons. What is called ancestor-worship consists of rites carried out by members of a larger or smaller lineage (i.e. one consisting of more or fewer generations) with reference to the deceased members of the lineage. Such rites include the making of offerings, usually of food and drink, and such offerings are sometimes interpreted as the sharing of a meal by the dead and the living.

In such a society, what gives stability to the social structure is the solidarity and continuity of the lineage, and of the wider group (the clan) composed of related lineages. For the individual, his primary duties are those to his lineage. These include duties to the members now living, but also to those who have died and to those who are not yet born. In the carrying out of these duties he is controlled and inspired by the complex system of sentiments of which we may say that the object on which they are centred is the lineage itself, past, present and future. It is primarily this system of sentiments that is expressed in the rites of the cult of the ancestors. The social function of the rites is obvious: by giving solemn and collective expression to them the rites reaffirm, renew and strengthen those sentiments on which the social solidarity depends.

We have no means of studying how an ancestor-worshipping society comes into existence, but we can study the decay of this type of system in the past and in the present. Fustel de Coulanges deals with this in ancient Greece and Rome. It can be observed at the present time in various parts of the world. The scanty information I have been able to gather suggests that the lineage and joint-family organisation of some parts of India is losing something of its former strength and solidarity and that what we should expect as the inevitable accompaniment of this, a weakening of the cult of ancestors, is also taking place. I can speak with more assurance about some African societies, particularly those of South Africa. The effect of the impact of European culture, including the teaching of the Christian missionaries, is to weaken in some individuals the sentiments that attach them to their lineage. The disintegration of the social structure and the decay of the ancestral cult proceed together.

Thus for one particular type of religion I am ready to affirm that the general theory of the social function of religions can be fully demonstrated.

A most important contribution to our subject is a work of Emile Durkheim published in 1912. The title is *Les Formes élémentaires de la vie religieuse,* but the sub-title reads: *La Système totémique en Australie.* It is worth while mentioning that Durkheim was a pupil of Fustel de Coulanges at the École Normale Supérieure and that he himself said that the most important influence on the development of his ideas about religion was that of Robertson Smith.

Durkheim's aim was to establish a general theory of the nature of religion. Instead of a wide comparative study of many religions, he preferred to take a simple type of society and carry out an intensive and detailed analysis, and for this purpose he selected the aboriginal tribes of Australia. He held the view that these tribes represent the simplest type of society surviving to our own times, but the value of his analysis is in no way affected if we refuse to accept this view, as I do myself.

The value of Durkheim's book is as an exposition of a general theory of religion which had been developed with the collaboration of Henri Hubert and Marcel Mauss, starting from the foundations provided by Robertson Smith. Durkheim's exposition of this theory has often been very much misunderstood. A clear, though very brief, statement of it is to be found in the Introduction written by Henri Hubert in 1904 for the French translation of the *Manuel d'histoire des religions* of Chantepie de la Saussaye. But it is not possible on this occasion to discuss this general theory. I wish only to deal with one part of Durkheim's work, namely his theory that religious ritual is an expression of the unity of society and that its function is to 're-create' the society or the social order by reaffirming and strengthening the sentiments on which the social solidarity and therefore the social order itself depend.[13] This theory he tests by an examination of the totemic ritual of the Australians. For while Frazer regarded the totemic rites of the Australian tribes as being a matter of magic, Durkheim treats them as religious because the rites themselves are sacred and have reference to sacred beings, sacred places and sacred objects.

In 1912 very much less was known about the Australian aborigines than is known at present. Some of the sources used by

Durkheim have proved to be unreliable. The one tribe that was well known, through the writings of Spencer and Gillen and Strehlow—the Aranda—is in some respects atypical. The information that Durkheim could use was therefore decidedly imperfect. Moreover, it cannot be said that his handling of this material was all that it might have been. Consequently there are many points in his exposition which I find unacceptable. Nevertheless, I think that Durkheim's major thesis as to the social function of the totemic rites is valid and only requires revision and correction in the light of the more extensive and more exact knowledge we now have.[14]

The beings to which the Australian cult refers are commonly spoken of as 'totemic ancestors', and I have myself used the term. But it is somewhat misleading, since they are mythical beings and not ancestors in the same sense as the dead persons commemorated in ancestor-worship. In the cosmology of the Australian natives the cosmos, the ordered universe, including both the order of nature and the social order, came into existence at a time in the past which I propose to speak of as the World-Dawn, for this name corresponds to certain ideas that I have found amongst the aborigines of some tribes. This order (of nature and of society) resulted from the doings and adventures of certain sacred beings. These beings, whom I shall call the Dawn Beings, are the totemic ancestors of ethnological literature. The explanations of topographical features, of natural species and their characteristics, and of social laws, customs and usages are given in the form of myths about the happenings of the World-Dawn.

The cosmos is ruled by law. But whereas we think of the laws of nature as statements of what invariably does happen (except, of course, in miracles), and of moral or social laws as what ought to be observed but are sometimes broken, the Australian does not make this distinction. For him men and women ought to observe the rules of behaviour that were fixed for all time by the events of the World-Dawn, and similarly the rain ought to fall in its proper season, plants should grow and produce fruit or seed, and animals should bear young. But there are irregularities in human society and in nature.

In what I shall venture to call the totemic religion of the Australian aborigines, there are two main types of ritual. One of these consists of rites carried out at certain spots which are commonly referred to as 'totem centres'. A totem centre is a spot that is specially connected with some species of object, most commonly with a particular species of animal or plant, or with an aspect of nature such as rain or hot weather. Each centre is associated with one (or occasionally more than one) of the Dawn Beings. Frequently the Being is said to have gone into the ground at this spot. For each totem centre there is a myth connecting it with the events of the World-Dawn. The totem centre, the myth connected with it and the rites that are performed there, belong to the local group that owns the territory within which the totem centre lies. Each totem centre is thought of as containing, in a rock or a tree or a pool of water or a heap of stones, what we may perhaps call the life-spirit or life-force of the totem species.

The rites performed at the totem centre by the members of the local group to which it belongs, or under their leadership and direction, are thought to renew the vitality of this life-spirit of the species. In eastern Australia the totem centre is spoken of as the 'home' or 'dwelling-place' of the species, and the rites are called 'stirring up'. Thus, the rite at a rain totem centre brings the rain in its due season, that at a kangaroo totem centre ensures the supply of kangaroos, and that at the baby totem centre provides for the birth of children in the tribe.

These rites imply a certain conception, which I think we can call specifically a religious conception, of the place of man in the universe. Man is dependent upon what we call nature: on the regular successions of the seasons, on the rain falling when it should, on the growth of plants and the continuance of animal life. But, as I have already said, while for us the order of nature is one thing and the social order another, for the Australian they are two parts of a single order. Well-being, for the individual or for the society, depends on the continuance of this order free from serious disturbance. The Australians believe that they can ensure this continuance, or at least contribute to it, by their actions, including the regular performance of the totemic rites.

In the rites that have been described, each group takes care (if we may so express it) of only a small part of nature, of those few species for which it owns totem centres. The preservation of the natural order as a whole therefore depends on the actions of many different groups.

The social structure of the Australian natives is based on two things: a system of local groups, and a system of kinship based on the family. Each small local group is a closed patrilineal descent group; that is, a man is born into the group of his father and his sons belong to his group. Each group is independent and autonomous. The stability and continuity of the social structure depends on the strong solidarity of the local group.

Where there existed the totemic cult which I have just described (and it existed over a very large part of Australia), each local group was a cult group. The totemic ritual served to express the unity and solidarity of the group and its individuality and separation from other groups by the special relation of the group to its *sacra*: the totem centre or centres, the Dawn Beings associated with them, the myths and songs referring to those Beings, and the totems or species connected with the centres. This aspect of the social function of totemism was emphasised, and I think somewhat over-emphasised, by Durkheim.

There is, however, another aspect, for while the local totemic groups are separate individual and continuing social entities, they are also part of a wider social structure. This wider structure is provided by the kinship system. For an individual in Australian native society, every person with whom he has any social contact is related to him by some bond of kinship, near or distant, and the regulation of social life consists essentially of rules concerning behaviour towards different kinds of kin. For example, a man stands in very close relation to his mother's local group and, in many tribes, in a very close relation to its *sacra*: its totems, totem centres and totemic rites.

While Australian totemism separates the local groups and gives each an individuality of its own, it also links the groups together. For while each group is specially connected with certain parts of the natural order (e.g. with rain, or with kangaroo) and with certain of the Beings of the World-Dawn, the society as a whole is related through the totemic religion to the whole order of nature and to the World-Dawn as a whole. This is best seen in another kind of totemic cult, part of which consists of sacred dramas in which the performers impersonate various Dawn Beings. Such dramatic dances are only performed at those religious meetings at which a number of local groups come together, and it is on these occasions that young men are initiated into manhood and into the religious life of the society.

Australian society is not merely a collection of separate local groups; it is also a body of persons linked together in the kinship system. Australian totemism is a cosmological system by which the phenomena of nature are incorporated in the kinship organisation. When I was beginning my work in Australia in 1910, a native said to me, '*Bungurdi* (kangaroo) [is] my *kadja* (elder brother).' This simple sentence of three words gives the clue to an understanding of Australian totemism. The speaker did not mean that individuals of the kangaroo species are his brothers. He meant that to the kangaroo species, conceived as an entity, he stood in a social relation analogous to that in which a man stands to his elder brother in the kinship system. I am sorry that there is not time on this occasion to expound this thesis more fully.

The account I have just given of Australian totemism differs considerably from that given by Durkheim. But far from contradicting, it confirms Durkheim's fundamental general theory as to the social function of the totemic religion of Australia and its rites. The two kinds of totemic cult are the demonstration, in symbolic action, of the structure of Australian society and its foundations in a mythical and sacred past. In maintaining the social cohesion and equilibrium, the religion plays a most important part. The religion is an intrinsic part of the constitution of society.

I have dwelt, if only cursorily, with two types of religion: ancestor-worship and Australian totemism. In both of them it is possible to demonstrate the close correspondence of the form of religion and form of the social structure. In both it is possible to see how the religious rites reaffirm and strengthen the sentiments on which the social order depends. Here then are results of some significance for our problem. They point to a certain line of investigation. We can and should examine other religions in the light of the results already reached. But to do this we must study religions *in action*; we must try to discover the effects of active participation in a particular cult, first direct efforts on the individual and then the further effects on the society of which these individuals are members. When we have a sufficient number of such studies, it will be possible to establish a general theory of the nature of religions and their rôle in social development.

In elaborating such a general theory it will be necessary to determine by means of comparative studies the relations between religion and morality. There is only time to refer very briefly here to the question of religion and morality. As representing a theory that seems to be widely held, I quote the following passages from Tylor:

One great element of religion, that moral element which among the higher nations forms its most vital part, is indeed little represented in the religion of the lower races.[15]

The comparison of savage and civilised religions bring into view, by the side of a deep-lying resemblance in their philosophy, a deep-lying contrast in their practical action on human life. So far as savage religion can stand as representing natural religion, the popular idea that the moral government of the universe is an essential tenet of natural religion simply falls to the ground. Savage animism is almost devoid of that ethical element which to the educated modern mind is the very mainspring of practical religion. Not, as I have said, that morality is absent from the life of the lower races. Without a code of morals, the very existence of the rudest tribe would be impossible; and indeed the moral standards of even savage races are to no small extent well-defined and praiseworthy. But these ethical laws stand on their ground of tradition and public opinion, comparatively independent of the animistic beliefs and rites which exist beside them. The lower animism is not immoral, it is unmoral. . . . The general problem of the relation of morality to religion is difficult, intricate, and requiring immense array of evidence.[16]

I agree with Tylor that the problem of the relation of morality to religion is difficult and intricate. But I wish to question the validity of the distinction he makes between the religions of savages and those of civilised peoples, and of his statement that the moral element 'is little represented in the religion of the lower races'. I suspect that when this view is held it often means only that in the 'lower races' the religion is not associated with the kind of morality which exists in contemporary Western societies. But societies differ in their systems of morals as in other aspects of the social system, and what we have to examine in any given society is the relation of the religion or religions of that society to their particular system of morality.

Dr R. F. Fortune, in his book on Manus religion, has challenged the dictum of Tylor.[17] The religion of Manus is what may be called a kind of spiritualism, but it is not ancestor-worship in the sense in which I have used the term in this lecture. The Manus code of morals rigidly forbids sexual intercourse except between husband and wife, condemns dishonesty and insists on the conscientious fulfilment of obligations, including economic obligations, towards one's relatives and others. Offences against the moral code bring down on the offender, or on his household, punishment from the spirits, and the remedy is to be found in confession and reparation for wrong.

Let us now reconsider the case of ancestor-worship. In the societies which practise it, the most important part of the moral code is that which concerns the conduct of the individual in relation to his lineage and clan and the individual members thereof. In the more usual form of ancestor-worship, infractions of this code fall under religious or supernatural sanctions, for they are offences against the ancestors, who are believed to send punishment.

Again we may take as an example of the lower races the aborigines of Australia. Since the fundamental social structure is a complex system of widely extended recognition of relations of kinship, the most important part of the moral code consists of the rules of behaviour towards kin of different categories. One of the most immoral actions of which a man can be guilty is having sexual relations with any woman who does not belong to that category of his kinsfolk into which he may legally marry.

The moral law of the tribe is taught to young men in the very sacred ceremonies known as initiation ceremonies. I will deal only with the Bora ceremonies, as they are called, of some of the tribes of New South Wales. These ceremonies were instituted in the time of the World-Dawn by Baiame, who killed his own son Daramulun (sometimes identified with the sacred bull-roarer) and on the third day brought him back to life. As the ceremony is conducted the initiates all 'die' and are brought back to life on the third day.[18]

On the sacred ceremonial ground where these initiations take place there is usually an image of Baiame made of earth, and sometimes one of Baiame's wife. Beside these images sacred rites are shown to the initiates, and sacred myths about Baiame are recounted.

Now Baiame instituted not only the initiation ceremonies, which are, amongst other things, schools of morals for young men, but also the kinship system with its rules about marriage and behaviour towards different categories of kin. To the question, 'Why do you observe these complex rules about marriage?' the usual answer is, 'Because Baiame established them'. Thus Baiame is the divine law-giver, or, by an alternative mode of expression, he is the personification of the tribal laws of morality.

I agree with Andrew Lang and Father Schmidt that Baiame thus closely resembles one aspect of the God of the Hebrews. But Baiame gives no assistance in war as Jehovah did for the children of Israel, nor is Baiame the ruler or controller of nature, of storms and seasons. That position is held by another deity, the Rainbow-Serpent, whose image in earth also appears on the sacred ceremonial ground. The position held by Baiame is that of the Divine Being who established the most important rules of morality and the sacred ceremonies of initiation.

These few examples will perhaps suffice to show that the idea that it is only the higher religions that are specially concerned with morality, and that the moral element is little represented in the religions of the lower races, is decidedly open to question. If there were time I could provide instances from other parts of the world.

What makes these problems complex is the fact that law, morality and religion are three ways of controlling human conduct which in different types of society supplement one another, and are combined, in different ways. For the law there are legal sanctions, for morality there are the sanctions of public opinion and of conscience, for religion there are religious sanctions. A single wrongful deed may fall under two or three sanctions. Blasphemy and sacrilege are sins and so subject to religious sanctions; but they may also sometimes be punished by law as crimes. In our own society murder is immoral; it is also a crime punishable by death; and it is also a sin against God, so that the murderer, after his sudden exit from this life at the hands of the executioner, must face an eternity of torment in the fires of Hell.

Legal sanctions may be brought into action in instances where there is no question of morality or immorality, and the same is true of religious sanctions. It is held by some of the Fathers or doctors of the Christian churches that an upright and virtuous life devoted to good works will not save a man from Hell unless he has attained grace by accepting as true the specific doctrines taught by a church.

There are different kinds of religious sanctions. The penalty for sin may be conceived simply as alienation from God. Or there may be a belief in rewards and punishments in an after-life. But the most widespread form of the religious sanction is the belief that certain actions produce in an individual or in a community a condition of ritual pollution, or uncleanness, from which it is necessary to be purified. Pollution may result from things done unintentionally and unwittingly, as you may see from the fifth chapter of the Book of Leviticus. One who unwittingly has touched any unclean thing, such as the carcass of an unclean beast, is guilty and has sinned and must bear his iniquity. He must make a sacrifice, a trespass offering, by which he may be cleansed from his sin.

Ritual uncleanness does not in itself involve moral condemnation. We read in the twelfth chapter of the same Book of Leviticus that the Lord instructed Moses that a woman who has borne a male child shall be unclean for seven days and her purification must continue for a further three and thirty days, during which she shall touch no hallowed thing, nor come into the sanctuary. If the child she bears is female, the first period of uncleanness is to be two weeks and the period of purification threescore-and-six days. Thus, it is polluting, but no one can suppose that it is immoral, to bear a child, and more polluting if the child is female than if it is male.

The opposite of pollution or sinfulness is holiness. But holiness comes not from leading an honest and upright life, but from religious exercises, prayer and fasting, the performance of penance, meditation and the reading of sacred books. In Hinduism the son of a Brahmin is born holy; the son of a leather-worker is born unclean.

The field covered by morality and that covered by religion are different; but either in primitive or in civilised societies there may be a region in which they overlap.

To return to our main topic, a writer who has dealt with the social function of religions on the basis of a comparative study is Loisy, who devotes to the subject a few pages of the concluding chapter of his valuable *Essai historique sur le sacrifice*.[19] Although he differs from Durkheim in some matters, his fundamental theory is, if not identical, at any rate very similar to that of the earlier writer. Speaking of what he calls the sacred action (*l'action sacrée*), of which the most characteristic form is the rite of sacrifice, he writes:[20]

> We have seen its rôle in human societies, of which it has maintained and strengthened the social bonds, if indeed it has not contributed in a large measure to creating them. It was, in certain respects the expression of them; but man is so made that he becomes more firmly fixed in his sentiments by expressing them. The sacred action was the expression of social life, of social aspirations, it has necessarily been a factor of society. . . .

Before we condemn out of hand the mirage of religion and the apparatus of sacrifice as a simple waste of social resources and forces, it is proper to observe that, religion having been the form of social conscience, and sacrifice the expression of this conscience, the loss was compensated by a gain, and that, so far as purely material losses are concerned, there is really no occasion to dwell on them. Moreover the kind of sacred contribution that was required, without real utility as to the effect that was expected from it, was an intrinsic part of the system of renunciations, of contributions which, in every human society, are the condition of its equilibrium and its conservation.

But besides this definition of the social function in terms of social cohesion and continuity, Loisy seeks for what he calls a general formula (*formule générale*) in which to sum up the part that religion has played in human life. Such a formula is useful so long as we remember that it is only a formula. The one that Loisy offers is that magic and religion have served to give men confidence.

In the most primitive societies it is magic that gives man confidence in face of the difficulties and uncertainties, the real and imaginary dangers with which he is surrounded.[21]

A la merci des éléments, des saisons, de ce que la terre lui donne ou lui refuse, des bonnes ou des mauvaises chances de sa chasse ou de sa pêche, aussi du hasard de ses combats avec ses semblables, il croit trouver le moyen de régulariser par des simulacres d'action ces chances plus ou moins incertaines. Ce qu'il fait ne sert à rien par rapport au put qu'il se propose, mais il prend confiance en ses entreprises et en lui-même, il ose, et c'est en osant que réellement il obtient plus ou moins ce qu'il veut. Confiance rudimentaire, et pour une humble vie; mais c'est le commencement du courage moral.

This is the same theory that was later developed by Malinowski in reference to the magical practices of the Trobriand Islanders.

At a somewhat higher stage of development, 'when the social organism has been perfected, when the tribe has become a people, and this people has its gods, its religion, it is by this religion itself that the strength of the national conscience is measured, and it is in the service of national gods that men find a pledge of security in the present, of prosperity in the future. The gods are as it were the expression of the confidence that the people has in itself; but it is in the cult of the gods that his confidence is nourished.'[22]

At a still higher stage of social development, the religions which give men a promise of immortality give him thereby an assurance which permits him to bear courageously the burdens of his present life and face the most onerous obligations. 'It is a higher and more moral form of confidence in life.'[23]

To me this formula seems unsatisfactory in that it lays stress on what is only one side of the religious (or magical) attitude. I offer as an alternative the formula that religion develops in mankind what may be called a sense of dependence. What I mean by this can best be explained by an example. In an ancestor-worshipping tribe of South Africa, a man feels that he is dependent on his ancestors. From them he has received his life and the cattle that are his inheritance. To them he looks to send him children and to multiply his cattle and in other ways to care for his well-being. This is one side of the matter; on his ancestors he *can* depend. The other side is the belief that the ancestors watch over his conduct, and that if he fails in his duties they will not only cease to send him blessings, but will visit him with sickness or some other misfortune. He cannot stand alone and depend only on his own efforts; on his ancestors he *must* depend.

We may say that the beliefs of the African ancestor-worshipper are illusory and his offerings to his gods really useless; that the dead of his lineage do not really send him either blessings or punishments. But the Confucians have shown us that a religion like ancestor-worship can be rationalised and freed from those illusory beliefs that we call superstition. For in the rites of commemoration of the ancestors it is sufficient that the participants should express their reverential gratitude to those from whom they have received their life, and their sense of duty towards those not yet born, to whom they in due course will stand in the position of revered ancestors. There still remains the sense of dependence. The living depend on those of the past; they have duties to those living in the present and to those of the future who will depend on them.

I suggest to you that what makes and keeps a man a social animal is not some herd instinct, but the sense of dependence in the innumerable forms that it takes. The process of socialisation begins on the first day of an infant's life and it has to learn that it both *can* and *must* depend on its parents. From them it has comfort and succour; but it must submit also to their control. What I am calling the sense of dependence always has these two sides. We can face life and its chances and difficulties with confidence when we know that there are powers, forces and events on which we can rely, but we must submit to the control of our conduct by rules which are imposed. The entirely asocial individual would be one who thought that he could be completely independent, relying only on himself, asking for no help and recognising no duties.

I have tried to present to you a theory of the social function of religion. This theory has been developed by the work of such men as Robertson Smith, Fustel de Coulanges, Durkheim, Loisy. It is the theory that has guided my own studies for nearly forty years. I have thought it worth while to indicate that it existed in embryo in the writings of Chinese philosophers more than twenty centuries ago.

Like any other scientific theory it is provisional, subject to revision and modification in the light of future research. It is offered as providing what seems likely to be a profitable method of investigation. What is needed to test and further elaborate the theory is a number of systematic studies of various types of religion in relation to social systems in which they occur.

I will summarise the suggestions I have made:

1 To understand a particular religion we must study its effects. The religion must therefore be studied *in action*.
2 Since human conduct is in large part controlled or directed by what have been called sentiments, conceived as mental dispositions, it is necessary to discover as far as possible what are the sentiments that are developed in the individual as the result of his participation in a particular religious cult.
3 In the study of any religion we must first of all examine the specifically religious actions, the ceremonies and the collective or individual rites.
4 The emphasis on belief in specific doctrines which characterises some modern religions seems to be the result of certain social developments in societies of complex structure.
5 In some societies there is a direct and immediate relation between the religion and the social structure. This has been illustrated by ancestor-worship and Australian totemism. It is also true of what we may call national religions, such as that of the Hebrews or

those of the city states of Greece and Rome.[24] But where there comes into existence a separate independent religious structure by the formation of different churches or sects or cult-groups within a people, the relation of religion to the total social structure is in many respects indirect and not always easy to trace.

6 As a general formula (for whatever such a formula may be worth) it is suggested that what is expressed in all religions is what I have called the sense of dependence in its double aspect, and that it is by constantly maintaining this sense of dependence that religions perform their social function.

Notes

1 The Henry Myers Lecture, 1945.

2 'Les rites étant dans toutes les religions l'élément le plus consistant et le plus durable, celui, par conséquent, où se découvre le mieux l'esprit des cultes anciens.'—*Essai historique sur le sacrifice*, Paris, 1920, p. 1.

3 W. Robertson Smith, *Lectures on the Religion of the Semites*, 1907, pp. 16–17, 20.

4 *Analects*, VII, 20. Waley translates this passage as: 'The Master never talked of prodigies, feats of strength, disorders or spirits.'

5 Legge's translation. An alternative translation of the last sentence would be: 'Rites, music, punishments, laws have one and the same end, to unite hearts and establish order.'

6 The translations from Hsün Tzŭ are those of Fung Yu Lan and are quoted from his *History of Chinese Philosophy*, Peiping, 1937.

7 Fung Yu Lan translates by the term 'spiritual utensils' the Chinese *ming ch'i*, which Legge in the following passage from the *Book of Rites* translates as 'vessels to the eye of fancy': 'Confucius said, "In dealing with the dead, if we treat them as if they were entirely dead, that would show a want of affection, and should not be done; or, if we treat them as if they were entirely alive, that would show a want of wisdom, and should not be done. On this account the vessels of bamboo [used in connection with the burial of the dead] are not fit for actual use; those of earthenware cannot be used to wash in; those of wood are incapable of being carved; the lutes are strung, but not evenly; the pandean pipes are complete, but not in tune; the bells and musical stones are there, but they have no stands. They are called vessels to the eye of fancy; that is [the dead] are thus treated as if they were spiritual intelligences."' Legge, *The Sacred Books of China*, Part III, The Lî Kî, I–X, Oxford, 1885, p. 148.

8 Mo Tzŭ was a philosopher who criticised the mourning rites as being wasteful.

9 Referring to the ancient practice of human sacrifice at the burial of important persons.

10 *The Ancient City* (trans. Willard Small), p. 23.

11 ibid., p. 12.

12 ibid., p. 529.

13 op. cit., pp. 323, 497 and elsewhere.

14 For a criticism of some points in Durkheim's work, see 'The sociological theory of totemism', *Proceedings of the Fourth Pacific Science Congress,* Java, 1930.

15 Tylor, *Primitive Culture,* 3rd ed., 1891, vol. I, p. 427.

16 ibid., vol. II, p. 360.

17 R. F. Fortune, *Manus Religion,* Philadelphia, 1935, pp. 5, 356. Dr Fortune's book is a useful contribution to the study of the social function of religion and deals with a religion of a very unusual type.

18 The suggestion has been made that we have here the influence of Christianity, but that opinion can be dismissed. The idea of ritual death and rebirth is very widespread in religion, and the three-day period is exemplified every month in every part of the world by the death and resurrection of the moon.

19 pp. 531-40.

20 ibid., pp. 535-7.

21 ibid., p. 533.

22 loc. cit.

23 op. cit., p. 534.

24 'among the ancients what formed the bond of every society was a worship. Just as a domestic altar held the members of a family grouped about it, so the city was the collective group of those who had the same protecting deities, and who performed the religious ceremony at the same altar.' Fustel de Coulanges, op. cit., p. 193.

Part III The Study of Kinship Systems

9 The social organization of Australian tribes

Part I

Since Fison and Howitt published in 1880 their *Kamilaroi and Kurnai*, the social organization of the aboriginal tribes of Australia has received a great deal of attention from anthropologists, and the literature on the subject is now very extensive. That literature has given currency to a number of misconceptions. The present paper is an attempt to indicate as concisely as possible what that organization really is, and to give a summary of the existing knowledge about it. It is intended to serve as an introduction to new researches which are now in progress, and the results of which will be published in due course.

There are many different forms of social organization in Australia, but it will appear, I think, that they can all be regarded as different varieties of a single general type. The easiest way to give a descriptive account is therefore to describe the general type first and then go on to describe, and as far as possible classify, the different varieties. That is the procedure that will be followed here.

The basic elements of social structure in Australia are (1) the family, i.e., the group formed by a man and his wife and their children, and (2) the horde, a small group owning and occupying a definite territory or hunting ground. Together with these there is, of course, a grouping for social purposes on the basis of sex and age. It is on the basis of the family and the horde that the somewhat complex kinship organizations of Australia are built.

It is not easy to give a precise and accurate account of the local organization of Australia. In the first place there are many difficulties in the way of a study of the local organization amongst the natives themselves, which can only be overcome with unlimited patience and ample time, and the use of a strict method of enquiry such as that afforded by the collection of genealogies. Those difficulties are greatly increased when the country has been occupied for some time by the

131

white man, for the local organization is the first part of the social system to be destroyed by the advent of the European and the expropriation of the native owners of the land.

What accounts we have of the Australian local organization are therefore mostly unsatisfactory as being based on incomplete observation. Moreover most of them are so lacking in precision as to be almost useless. This is partly due to the fact that the writers have not made sufficiently searching investigations, and partly to the use of vague or confused terminology, such terms as 'tribe', 'family', etc., being used without exact definition.

It is not easy to reconcile the many different statements that can be found in the literature on Australia, and it is impossible to undertake here a critical examination of those statements. It must therefore suffice here to make the bald statement that a careful comparison of them in the light of the results of the latest research leads to the conclusion that the important local group throughout Australia is what will here be spoken of as the *horde*. The horde is a small group of persons owning a certain area of territory, the boundaries of which are known, and possessing in common proprietary rights over the land and its products—mineral, vegetable and animal. It is the primary land-owning or land-holding group. Membership of a horde is determined in the first place by descent, children belonging to the horde of their father. There is normally, in the tribes about which we have adequate information, no provision by which a man could leave his own horde and be 'adopted' or 'naturalized' in another. Therefore, as a normal thing, male members enter the horde by birth and remain in it till death. In many regions the horde is exogamous. But even where there is not a strict rule against marriage within the horde, the great majority of marriages are outside the horde. The woman, at marriage, leaves her horde and joins that of her husband.

The horde, therefore, as an existing group at any moment, consists of (1) male members of all ages whose fathers and fathers' fathers belonged to the horde, (2) unmarried girls who are the sisters or daughters or son's daughters of the male members, (3) married women, all of whom, in some regions, and most of whom, in others, belonged originally to other hordes, and have become attached to the horde by marriage.

It may be added that normally throughout Australia each horde is independent and autonomous, managing its own affairs and acting as a unit in its relations with other hordes.

Throughout Australia hordes are grouped into larger local or territorial units, which will be spoken of as *tribes*. The primary mark of a tribe is that it consists of persons speaking one language, or dialects of one language. Its unity is primarily linguistic. The name of the tribe and the name of its language are normally the same. So that the easiest way to ascertain to what tribe an individual belongs is usually to ask him what language he speaks. In addition to this unity that comes from a common language there is also a unity of custom throughout the tribe.

It is often difficult, however, to say whether a particular recognized local group is a tribe, or a subdivision of a tribe, or whether another group is a tribe or a larger unit consisting of a number of related tribes. Thus within what might be regarded as a large tribe there may be differences of dialect (and differences of custom) in different parts, so that it is divided into *sub-tribes*. Again, adjoining tribes frequently resemble one another in language and custom. It is therefore sometimes difficult to decide whether we are dealing with a tribe subdivided into sub-tribes or with a group of related tribes.

So far as Australia is concerned, therefore, we have to define a tribe as a body of persons having a certain homogeneity of language and custom sufficient to permit them to be recognized as a group, and to demarcate them as distinct from other and neighbouring groups.

A tribe is commonly spoken of as possessing a certain territory, and is regarded as a land-holding group. So far as Australia is concerned, this is not quite accurate. It is true that each tribe may be regarded as occupying a territory, but this is only because it consists of a certain number of hordes, each of which has its territory. The territory of the tribe is the total of the territories of its component hordes. Moreover, in some instances at least, the boundary between one tribe and another may be indeterminate. Thus in Western Australia a horde lying on the boundary of the Ngaluma and Kariera tribes was declared to me to be 'half Ngaluma, half Kariera', i.e., belonging properly to neither of the two tribes. Similar instances of hordes which occupy an indeterminate position between two adjoining tribes of similar language and custom occur elsewhere in Australia.

A tribe is also sometimes spoken of as a body of kindred. It will be shown later that the kinship organization of Australia spreads over the tribal boundaries. A man may have as many kin in another tribe or in other tribes as he has in his own. It is therefore impossible to define the tribe in terms of kinship.

The Australian tribe has usually, if not always, no political unity. There is no central authority for the tribe as a whole, nor does the tribe act as a unit in warfare. The political unit, if it can be properly called such, and normally the war-making unit, is the horde. A number of hordes may unite together in warfare, but they fight as independent allies.

We see, therefore, that the tribe in Australia consists essentially of a number of neighbouring hordes, which are united by the possession of a common language and common customs. The group is often an indeterminate one because it is difficult to say exactly where one language ends and another begins.

Most of the tribes of Australia have some sort of division into two, four, or eight parts, which, since they were supposed to regulate marriage, have been called 'marriage classes'. This name is for several reasons unsuitable. In sociology it is convenient to reserve the term 'class' as a technical term for social groups marked off from one another by differences of rank or occupation. It will be shown that it is somewhat misleading to call the divisions marriage divisions or exogamic divisions. Further, the four divisions of such a tribe as the Mara are of quite a different character and constitution from the four divisions of the Kamilaroi or the Kariera, yet both are commonly spoken of as classes. I shall therefore avoid the term 'class', and shall attempt to substitute a more systematic terminology.

Where there are two divisions I shall speak of *moieties*. In both western and eastern Australia there are tribes that have a division into matrilineal moieties. Thus in the neighbourhood of Perth the tribe was divided into two parts called Manitjmat and Wardangmat after the crow (*wardang*) and the white cockatoo (*manitj*). A man of one division (moiety) had to take his wife from the other. The children belonged to the moiety of the mother. Other tribes had a division into patrilineal moieties. Thus in Central Victoria the natives were divided into moieties named after the eaglehawk and the crow. A man of the eaglehawk moiety might only marry a crow woman, and the children would be eaglehawk like the father.

A large number of tribes have a division into four parts, which will be spoken of throughout this essay as *sections*.[1] Thus in the Kariera tribe the four sections are named Banaka, Burung, Karimera and Palyeri. A man of one section may only marry a woman of one other particular section. Thus a Banaka man may only marry a Burung woman. The children belong to a section different from that of either the father or the mother. The children of a Banaka man and a Burung woman are Palyeri, and they in their turn may only marry with Karimera. It is convenient to represent the system of marriage and descent by means of a diagram.

$$\begin{pmatrix} \text{Banaka} & = & \text{Burung} \\ \text{Karimera} & = & \text{Palyeri} \end{pmatrix}$$

The sign = connects the two sections that intermarry; the arrow sign connects the section of a mother with that of her child. Substituting letters for the specific names we have as the general scheme for the four section system—

$$\begin{pmatrix} A & = & B \\ C & = & D \end{pmatrix}$$

Reading off the rules from this diagram[2] we have—

A	marries	b,	children are	D and	d
B	„	a,	„ „	C „	c
C	„	d,	„ „	B „	b
D	„	c,	„ „	A „	a

I propose to speak of the two sections that intermarry as forming a *pair*. The two pairs are therefore AB, CD. The sections that contain father and child I shall speak of as a *couple*. The two couples are therefore AD and BC. If a man belongs to one section his children belong to the other section of his own couple. The children of Banaka men are always Palyeri.

It will be readily seen that this system of four sections involves a division of the society into two matrilineal moieties and also a cross division into two patrilineal moieties. Thus in the diagram the sections A and D (Banaka and Palyeri) constitute one patrilineal moiety, and B and C (Burung and Karimera) the other. While A and C constitute one matrilineal moiety and B and D the other. In many of the tribes of eastern Australia there are names for the matrilineal moieties in addition to the names for the sections. It is important to remember that the moieties exist in every section system whether they are named or not.

A still more complex system is that in which the tribe has eight subdivisions. These will be called *subsections,* since they can be shown to be subdivisions of the sections of the four-section system. The following diagram shows the rules of marriage and descent in the system of eight subsections:

$$\left(\left(\begin{array}{ccc} A^1 & = & B^1 \\ A^2 & = & B^2 \\ C^1 & = & D^1 \\ C^2 & = & D^2 \end{array}\right)\right)$$

The sign = connects two intermarrying subsections. I shall speak of two such together as an *intermarrying pair* or simply a *pair*. The lines at the side connect the sub-section of a woman with that of her child, the arrow indicating the direction in which the line is to be followed. Thus, reading the diagram we have

A^1 marries	b^1	and the children are			D^2 and d^2	
A^2	„	b^2	„	„	„	D^1 „ d^1
B^1	„	a^1	„	„	„	C^1 „ c^1
B^2	„	a^2	„	„	„	C^2 „ c^2
C^1	„	d^1	„	„	„	B^1 „ b^1
C^2	„	d^2	„	„	„	B^2 „ b^2
D^1	„	c^1	„	„	„	A^2 „ a^2
D^2	„	c^2	„	„	„	A^1 „ a^1

I shall speak of the subsection of a father and the subsection of his child as together forming a *couple* of subsections. Thus the couples are A^1D^2, A^2D^1, B^1C^1, B^2C^2. If a man belongs to one subsection his child belongs to the other subsection of the same couple.

It will also be convenient to use the term *cycle* to denote the four subsections that constitute a matrilineal moiety. A^1 C^1 A^2 C^2 form one cycle. Thus if a woman is a^1 her daughter is c^1, her daughter's daughter is a^2, her daughter's daughter's daughter is c^2, and her daughter's daughter's daughter's daughter is a^1 like herself. The two cycles are

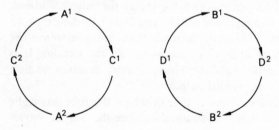

This system of eight subsections extends over a large area, including the greater part of the Northern Territory and part of Western Australia.

There are a few tribes in the region of the Gulf of Carpentaria which really have a system of subsections, but instead of having names for the eight subsections have only names for four divisions, each of which consists of a patrilineal couple of subsections. The subsections exist but are not named. If we consider the diagram of the subsection system we have one division P corresponding to A^1 and D^2 together, Q including A^2 and D^1, R including B^1 and C^1, and S including B^2 and C^2. The rules of marriage and descent can be presented in diagrammatic form as follows:

$$\left(\begin{array}{ccc} P^a & = & R^b \\ Q^a & = & S^b \\ R^c & = & Q^d \\ S^c & = & P^d \end{array}\right)$$

An example of this system is that of the Mara tribe, where the four divisions are named Murungun, Mumbali, Purdal and Kuial. Arranged in the form of the diagram—

Murungun α	=	Purdal β
Mumbali α	=	Kuial β
Purdal γ	=	Mumbali δ
Kuial γ	=	Murungun δ

Murungun and Mumbali together form a patrilineal moiety named Muluri, and Purdal and Kuial constitute the other moiety named Umbana. Since each of these named couples of subsections forms a half of a moiety it will be convenient to refer to them as *semi-moieties*.

That the eight subsections really exist in this system, although they are not named, can be demonstrated by examining the arrangement of marriage. Murungun men may marry either Purdal or Kuial women. Their sons divide into two groups, Murungun α who are the children of Kuial mothers, and Murungun δ who are the children of Purdal mothers. The marriage rule is that a man may not marry a woman of the same semi-moiety as his mother. Those of the first group, Murungun α, sons of Kuial women, may only marry Purdal, and those of the second group, Murungun δ, may only marry Kuial. It can be shown that in this way each of the four semi-moieties consists of two groups which are exactly equivalent to the subsections of other tribes. Spencer and Gillen have demonstrated this also, by showing the relations with respect to kinship and marriage between the tribes with the Mara system and those with eight named subsections.

What at first sight seems a quite anomalous system is found in Western Australia, in the neighbourhood of Southern Cross. Here there are two divisions, named Birangumat and Djuamat, with a rule that a man may only marry a woman of his own division, and the children must belong to the other division. This is really a modification of the system of four sections. The systems exist but are not named. Each of the named divisions is equivalent to one intermarrying pair of sections. The system may therefore be represented thus:

$$\left(\begin{array}{ll} \text{(A) Birangumat} = \text{(B) Birangumat} \\ \text{(C) Djuamat} \quad\;\; = \text{(D) Djuamat} \end{array} \right)$$

There are a few scattered areas in Australia in which there are no divisions of the kinds described above.

With reference to these named divisions we can therefore classify Australian tribes into seven groups:

1 With two matrilineal exogamous moieties.
2 With two patrilineal moieties.
3 With four sections—
    (*a*) with named matrilineal moieties.
    (*b*) ,,   ,,   patrilineal   ,,
    (*c*) without named moieties.
4 With eight subsections.
5 With four named patrilineal semi-moieties.
6 With two endogamous alternating divisions (named pairs of sections).
7 Without named divisions.

Map 1 shows the distribution of these as at present known.

A closer examination of these divisions reveals that they are composed of persons who are or who regard themselves as being related to each other by certain family relationships, and it appears that the named divisions—moieties, sections, subsections, etc.—are in each instance part of a larger whole, which will here be spoken of as the *kinship system* of the tribe. To discover what is the nature and function of the named divisions in any instance it is necessary to study the whole kinship system.

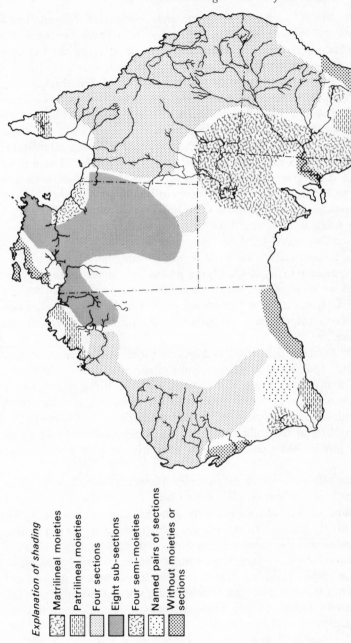

Map 1 Social organization of Australian tribes

Explanation of shading

Matrilineal moieties

Patrilineal moieties

Four sections

Eight sub-sections

Four semi-moieties

Named pairs of sections

Without moieties or
sections

By kinship is here meant genealogical relationship recognized and made the basis of the regulation of social relations between individuals. Genealogical relationships are those set up by the fact that two individuals belong to the same family.

In Western civilization we normally think of genealogical relationships in terms of what are commonly called biological, but may perhaps better be called physiological relationships. There is an obvious physiological relationship between a woman and the child to which she gives birth. For us there is also a physiological relationship between a child and the man who is the genitor. The first of these is recognized by the Australian native, but the second is not recognized. In some tribes it seems to be denied that there is any physiological relationship between genitor and offspring. Even if in any tribes it is definitely recognized it is normally, or probably universally, treated as of no importance.

In modern English the word 'father' is ambiguous. It may be used as equivalent sometimes to Latin *genitor,* sometimes to Latin *pater.* Thus we speak of the 'father' of an illegitimate child. Such a child necessarily has a *genitor* but has no *pater.* On the other hand, when a child is adopted the male parent is his 'father', i.e., *pater* but not *genitor.*

In Australia fatherhood is a purely social thing. *Pater est quem nuptiae demonstrant.* The father and mother of a child are the man and woman who, being husband and wife, i.e., living together in a union recognized by other members of the tribe, look after that child during infancy. Normally, of course, the mother is the woman who gives birth to the child, but even this is not essential as adoption may give a child a second mother who may completely replace the first.

Thus the existence of the family in Australia as elsewhere, involves three kinds of individual relationships (1) that of parents and children, (2) that of children of the same parent or parents (siblings), (3) that of parents of the same children (husband and wife). These are what may be called relationships of the first order. But every person who lives to adult years normally belongs to two families, to one as child and sibling, and to another as parent and spouse, and it is this fact that gives rise to relationships of the second, third and following orders, to the whole system of traceable genealogical relationships.

This system of genealogical relationships is not itself a kinship system, but it affords the basis on which the kinship system is built. Kinship systems vary in different forms of social organization all over the world in respect of three characters; (1) the extent to which genealogical relationships are recognized for social purposes, (2) the way in which relatives are classified and grouped, (3) the particular customs by which the behaviour of relatives, as so recognized, classified and grouped, is regulated in their dealings with each other.

In Australia we have an example of a society in which the very widest possible recognition is given to genealogical relationships. In a tribe that has not been affected by white intrusion, it is easy to collect full pedigrees for the whole tribe. Further, these genealogical relationships are made, in Australia, the basis of an extensive and highly organized system of reciprocal obligations. While amongst ourselves the question of genealogical relationship only affects our relations to a few individuals, our nearest relatives, in native Australian society it regulates more or less definitely the behaviour of an individual to every person with whom he has any social dealings whatever.

In order to study tne way in which kin are classified in any tribe it is essential to study the terms used to denote relatives, for it is by means of those terms that the classification is carried out. The study of kinship terminology, tedious as it may sometimes seem, is the only way to any real understanding of Australian social organization.[3]

Every Australian tribe about which we have information has a classificatory system of kinship terminology. That is to say, collateral and lineal relatives are grouped together into a certain number of classes and a single term is applied to all the relatives of one class. The basic principle of the classification is that a man is always classed with his brother and a woman with her sister. If I apply a given term of relationship to a man, I apply the same term to his brother. Thus I call my father's brother by the same term that I apply to my father, and similarly, I call my mother's sister 'mother'. The consequential relationships are followed out. The children of any man I call 'father' or of any woman I call 'mother' are my 'brothers' and 'sisters'.[4] The children of any man I call 'brother', if I am a male, call me 'father', and I call them 'son' and 'daughter'. This first principle may be called the principle of the equivalence of brothers. It is the one essential principle of what are known as 'classificatory' systems of terminology.

The second principle applied in Australian systems of terminology is one which brings relatives by marriage within the classes of consanguineal relatives. Thus the wife of any man I call 'father' is my 'mother', and inversely the husband of any woman I call 'mother' is my 'father'. Similarly my father's father's brother's wife is classed with my father's mother and denoted by the same term.

The third important principle in Australian systems is what can be called the non-limitation of range. In many classificatory systems the principle of the equivalence of brothers is applied only over a certain limited range. The range may be determined, for instance, by a clan. In Australia the recognition and classification of relationships is usually extended without any limit, to embrace the whole society. In a typical Australian tribe it is found that a man can define his relation to every person with whom he has any social dealings whatever, whether of his own or of another tribe, by means of the terms of relationship. In other words, it is impossible for an Australian native to have anything whatever to do with any one who is not his relative, of one kind or another, near or distant.

Every term in an Australian system of terminology may be regarded as having a primary meaning. Thus in the Kariera tribe, although a man applies the term *mama* to a great number of men, if you ask him 'Who is your *mama*?', he will reply by naming his own father. Similarly with other terms. Within the class of persons denoted by one kinship term, the individual distinguishes degrees of nearness or distance. In Western Australia the natives express this difference in English by using the terms 'close-up' and 'far-away'. A man distinguishes between his close-up and his far-away 'fathers', 'brothers', 'mother's brothers', etc. These distinctions of degrees within a class are of the utmost importance in the classification of relatives for social purposes.

The classification of kin by means of the terminology is the basis on which the behaviour of one person to another in Australian society is regulated. The principle that applies here is that there is a certain uniformity in behaviour towards all relatives of one kind, i.e., who are denoted by one term. In some instances the uniformity is considerable. Thus in the Kariera tribe a man must carefully avoid having any direct social dealings with any woman he calls *toa*, this being the term he applies in the first instance to his own father's sister and his own mother's brother's wife. In other instances the uniformity is modified by the distinction of near and distant relatives of one kind. Thus in the Kariera tribe again there is a certain pattern of behaviour to which an individual is expected to conform in his relations with his 'father'. He would behave in this way not only to his own father, but also to his close-up 'father', i.e., his father's brother. For a distant or far-away 'father', although there would be something of the attitude towards his own father in his behaviour to him, the distance makes the relationship a much less intimate one. The behaviour to a distant 'father' is a pale reflection of that towards the actual father. However, even so, there would be a marked difference in the behaviour of a man to a distant 'father' and to a distant 'mother's brother'.

We may say, then, that in general there is a certain pattern of behaviour for each kind of relative, to which an individual is expected to conform in his dealings with any relative of that kind, subject to important modifications according as the relationship is near or distant. For some relationships this pattern is definite and well organized, for others it is vague and comparatively less important.

The kinship system, as it regulates the whole of social life, regulates marriage. In normal Australian systems since an individual is related to every person he meets it follows that he must necessarily marry a relative, and therefore the regulation of marriage takes the form of requiring an individual to marry only persons who stand to him or her in some specific relationship.

While kinship systems all over Australia are similar in many important respects, yet in other respects there are many variations. Any systematic description of these variations necessarily requires some sort of classification. The only method of classification that is at present possible is to select certain norms and then examine the relation of each particular system to these norms. This is the procedure that will be followed here. For the present it will suffice to establish two such norms, and for this purpose I shall use the system of the Kariera tribe of Western Australia and that of the Aranda tribe of Central Australia.[5]

The Kariera kinship system is based on and implies the existence of the form of marriage known as cross-cousin marriage. There are really three forms of the cross-cousin marriage which might be called respectively bilateral, matrilateral and patrilateral. In the first a man is permitted or expected to marry either his 'mother's brother's daughter' or his 'father's sister's daughter'. In the second he is permitted to marry his 'mother's brother's daughter', but not his 'father's sister's daughter'. In the third he may marry his 'father's sister's daughter' but not his 'mother's brother's daughter'. The marriage on which the Kariera system is based is the first mentioned of these three.

In the Kariera system all relatives are divided into generations, and in each generation the relatives are divided into two classes of males and two classes of females, with further distinctions in some of these classes (e.g., of brothers) between older and younger relatives. Thus in the second ascending generation the grandparents and their brothers and sisters, and all other relatives are divided into the following four kinds:

1 Father's father; with his brothers, husbands of the father's mother's sisters, and the brothers of the mother's mother.
2 Father's mother; with her sisters, wives of the father's father's brothers, and sisters of the mother's father.
3 Mother's father; with his brothers, husbands of the mother's mother's sisters, and brothers of the father's mother.
4 Mother's mother; with her sisters, wives of the mother's father's brothers, and sisters of the father's father.

Each of these groups of relatives is denoted by one term of relationship. It should be noted that the mother's mother's brother is classed with the father's father, and the father's mother's brother with the mother's father. This is a determining feature of the type.

The terms for grandparents are used reciprocally for grandchildren. That is to say, my father's father applies to me (his son's son) the same term of relationship that I apply to him, and similarly with other grandparents. In other words, I classify together and include under one term my father's father and my son's son. This is another important feature of the system.

In the first ascending (parents') generation a man distinguishes four kinds of relatives.

'Father' including own father, father's brother, mother's sister's husband, father's father's brother's son, mother's mother's brother's son, etc.

'Mother' including own mother, mother's sister, father's brother's wife, mother's mother's sister's daughter, etc.

'Mother's brother' including the brother of any woman called 'mother' and the husband of the sister of any man called 'father'.

'Father's sister' including the sister of any man called 'father' and the wife of any man called 'mother's brother'.

In his own generation a man has distinct terms for older and younger brothers and for older and younger sisters, the actual relation in age to himself being the determining factor in the use of the terms. He has names for male cross-cousins and for female cross-cousins. All persons of his own generation fall into one or other of these classes of relatives.

In the first descending (children's) generation a man again distinguishes only four kinds of relatives: 'son', 'daughter', 'sister's son' and 'sister's daughter'.

Figure 1 gives the scheme on which the relatives of a man are classified in the Kariera system.

It will be seen that in the five generations there are twenty classes of relatives, two of which (brother and sister) are further subdivided on the basis of age within the generation. There are, however, only eighteen terms for these twenty-two kinds of relatives by reason of the terms for grandparents being used reciprocally for grandchildren.

The marriage rule of the Kariera system is very simple. A man may only marry a woman to whom he applies the same term of relationship that he does to his own mother's brother's daughter. If it is possible for him to marry the daughter of an actual brother of his own mother he normally does so, but of course this only happens in a limited number of instances.

The Kariera also have the custom of sister-exchange. When a man marries a woman his sister frequently, or indeed normally, is given as wife to his wife's brother. When this happens, if one man marries his own mother's brother's daughter then the other marries his own father's sister's daughter. As a result of this custom it sometimes happens that a man's mother's brother is married to his (i.e., the man's) father's sister. The daughter, whom he may marry, is therefore at one and the same time his mother's brother's daughter and his father's sister's daughter.

The important features of the Kariera system taken as a norm are:
(1) the bilateral cross-cousin marriage with exchange of sisters.
(2) the classification of all relatives in each generation into four classes, two male and two female (leaving aside the distinction of older and younger brothers and sisters) with the consequent classification of mother's mother's brother with father's father and so on.

145

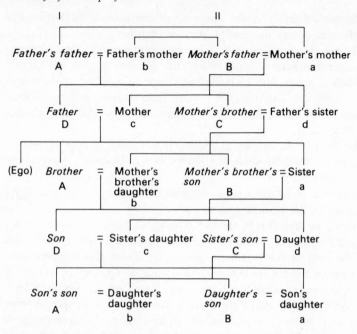

Figure 1 Kariera type of kinship terminology. Explanation of the chart: the chart shows the various classes into which a man's relatives are classified in a system of the Kariera type. The sign = connects husband and wife in each generation, and the descending line from that sign shows the children of any married pair. Thus it will be seen that a father's father's sister is classified with the mother's mother and her children are therefore classified with mother and mother's brother. Thus by means of the chart the classification of any relative, no matter how distant, can be immediately discovered. The chart also shows in vertical columns the two patrilineal lines of descent (I and II), and under each relative the section to which that relative belongs in a four-section system is shown by the letters A, B, C, D, Ego in the chart being taken as belonging to section A.

(3) the use of reciprocal terms between grandparent and grandchild.

When we turn to the Aranda we find a much more complicated system of classification of relatives. We may say roughly, as giving a clue to the relation of the two types, that where Kariera groups together a number of relatives into one class the Aranda system divides that group into two classes.

Thus in the second ascending (grandparents') generation while Kariera has two kinds of male relatives and two of female, Aranda has four of each. Kariera classes together mother's mother's brother with father's father, but Aranda distinguishes them, making two distinct classes of relatives where Kariera has one. This may be seen from the following table:

Kariera	Aranda	
1 'Father's father'	'Father's father' (1)	Father's father and his brothers, father's mother's sisters' husbands.
	'Mother's mother's brother (4)	Mother's mother's brothers, mother's father's sisters' husbands.
2 'Father's mother'	'Father's mother' (2)	Father's mother, and her sisters, father's father's brother's wives.
	'Mother's father's sister' (3)	Mother's father's sisters, mother's mother's brothers' wives.
3 'Mother's father'	'Mother's father' (3)	Mother's father and his brothers, mother's mother's sisters' husbands.
	'Father's mother's brother' (2)	Father's mother's brothers, father's father's sisters' husbands.
4 'Mother's mother'	'Mother's mother' (4)	Mother's mother and her sisters, mother's father's brothers' wives.
	'Father's father's sister' (1)	Father's father's sisters, father's mother's brothers' wives.

But while Aranda distinguishes in the second ascending generation four kinds of male relatives and four kinds of female, it has not eight terms but only four. This is because the same term that is applied to a male relative is also applied to his sister. Thus the four terms of the system apply as follows:

1 Father's father   Father's father's sister.
2 Father's mother's brother   Father's mother.
3 Mother's father   Mother's father's sister.
4 Mother's mother's brother   Mother's mother.

This, of course, gives quite a different alignment of relatives from the Kariera system. Kariera classifies father's father with mother's mother's brother under one term and father's father's sister with mother's mother under another. Aranda classifies father's father and his sister under one term and mother's mother and her brother under another.

Since, in the Kariera system only two kinds of male relatives are recognized in the second ascending generation that system brings all collateral relatives into two lines of descent. As compared with this the Aranda system has four lines of descent. Counting descent through males these are the lines of (1) father's father, to which Ego belongs, (2) father's mother's brother; (3) mother's father, and (4) mother's mother's brother.

In the first ascending generation, in addition to 'father', 'mother', 'mother's brother' and 'father's sister', four other classes of relatives are distinguished, two male and two female. Thus the son and daughter of the mother's mother's brother are distinguished from the father and father's sister with whom they are classified in the Kariera system.

So also in the other generations the Aranda system has four kinds of male relatives and four kinds of female, where the Kariera has only two of each. The accompanying chart represents the scheme of the Aranda system.

There are not, however, in the Aranda system, or in any system of the same type, forty terms of relationship used by males. The number is reduced first by the fact that the same terms are used for grandparents and for grandchildren, secondly by the use of the same term for certain male relatives and for their sisters, thirdly by the existence of certain self-reciprocal terms. In some systems which conform to this type the number of terms is further reduced by classifying together under one term a man and his son's son or a woman and her brother's son's daughter.

We have seen that the Kariera system is correlated with a particular form of marriage. The Aranda system also requires a special marriage rule, by which a man marries his mother's mother's brother's daughter's daughter or some relative who is classified with her and denoted by the same term of relationship. Amongst the women whom a man may marry there are none of his first cousins, four kinds of second cousins (mother's mother's brother's daughter's daughter, father's mother's brother's son's daughter, father's father's sister's son's daughter, and mother's father's sister's daughter's daughter), and certain of his third, fourth, etc., cousins.

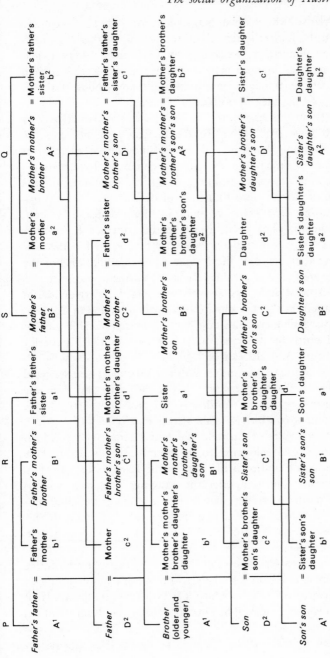

Figure 2 Aranda type of kinship terminology: Ego is male, P, A¹. Explanation of the chart: the chart is constructed on the same principles as that given for the Kariera type. It contains exactly twice as many classes of relatives as the Kariera chart. The classification of any relative however distant can be found from the chart. The chart shows the four patrilineal lines of descent of the Aranda system in vertical columns headed P, Q, R and S. These refer only to the male relatives in the column immediately beneath the letter. The line of descent of any female relative can be found by referring to her brother, since she belongs to the same line. The subsections into which a man's relatives fall in the system of eight subsections if he is A¹ are shown by the letters A¹, B¹, etc.

All the relatives whom a man may marry in the Aranda system are, of course, in the Kariera system classified with his mother's brother's daughter, and are therefore possible wives. The Aranda system divides the female relatives whom a man may marry in the Kariera system into two parts, from one of which he must now choose his wife while those of the other are forbidden to him.

The easiest way to classify the kinship system of Australia is by reference to these two norms. In the Kariera type we have the bilateral cross-cousin marriage and the classification of all relatives into two lines of descent. In the Aranda system we have marriage with the mother's mother's brother's daughter's daughter, and the classification of relatives into four lines of descent.

Systems of the Kariera type are found in a limited area in Western Australia from the Ninety-Mile Beach to the Fortescue River. It is possible that a system of the same type may have existed in the now extinct tribes at the head of the Murray River. Modifications of the Kariera type are found in Arnhem Land in Northern Australia.

Systems of the Aranda type are very widespread, but there are, of course, variations in the different regions. Such are found in Western Australia (Mardudhunera, Talaindji, etc.) in a considerable area of central and northern Australia, including part of the Kimberley district, in South Australia east of Lake Eyre, in part of New South Wales, on the Murray River and in Western Victoria. These scattered regions from the West coast nearly to the East coast and from the extreme north-west to the south-east are probably parts of one continuous area over which systems of this type obtain.

In the eastern parts of Australia are found some systems which will be referred to as belonging to the Kumbaingeri type. In these the classification of kindred is like that of the Kariera type into two lines of descent. A man marries the daughter of a man who is classified as 'mother's brother', but he may not marry the child of a near 'mother's brother' or of a near 'father's sister'. Systems of this type are found on the coast of New South Wales, and apparently in Western Queensland.

The Wikmunkan type, found in the Cape York Peninsula, agrees with the Kariera in classifying relatives into two lines of descent, but has a special marriage rule by which a man marries the daughter of his mother's younger brother, but may not marry the daughter of his mother's elder brother.

In Western Australia at the Ninety-Mile Beach, there is a system based on or implying a marriage rule whereby a man marries his mother's brother's daughter, but may not marry his father's sister's daughter. This is the Karadjeri type.

In the north-east of Arnhem Land the system is also based on this matrilateral cross-cousin marriage, but it has a much more complicated classification of relatives than the Karadjeri, involving the recognition of seven lines of descent.

In South Australia, at the mouth of the Murray River, the system of the Yaralde and other tribes is related to the Aranda type by its classification of kin into four lines of descent, but has a marriage rule which simply prohibits marriage with near relatives on the basis of clan relationship.

In the Western Kimberley District there is a system in the Ungarinyin tribe which has some similarity to the Yaralde system, and like it is also based on the recognition of four lines of descent. It permits marriage with the mother's mother's brother's son's daughter.

In the north of Dampier Land, Western Kimberley, the system of the Nyul-Nyul is an aberrant type.

Throughout a considerable part of the coastal area of north-west Australia the kinship systems are modified by the existence of a special form of marriage whereby a man marries his sister's son's daughter.

We must now return to the named divisions described earlier, and consider their relation to the kinship system. When the divisions previously described—moieties, sections, sub-sections, etc.—are examined in relation to the kinship system, it is found that they consist of certain relatives grouped together.

Let us first consider the example of the Kariera. This tribe has a system of four sections—

$$A = B$$
$$C = D$$

If we take a man of section A we find that his own section contains all the men he called 'brother', 'father's father' and 'son's son', and no others. The section D contains all the men he calls 'father' or 'son'. Section C contains all his 'mother's brothers' and 'sister's sons' and section B consists of the men he calls 'mother's father', 'mother's brother's son' and 'daughter's son'. A female relative belongs, of course, to the same section as her brother. Thus for a man of section A all his 'father's sisters' are in section D.

The relations between the sections may be shown by a table of equivalences.

$$\frac{A}{A} \quad \frac{B}{B} \quad \frac{C}{C} \quad \frac{D}{D} \qquad \text{Father's father, brother, son's son.}$$

$$\frac{A}{B} \quad \frac{B}{A} \quad \frac{C}{D} \quad \frac{D}{C} \qquad \text{Mother's father, mother's brother's son, daughter's son.}$$

$$\frac{A}{C} \quad \frac{B}{D} \quad \frac{C}{A} \quad \frac{D}{B} \qquad \text{Mother's brother, sister's son.}$$

$$\frac{A}{D} \quad \frac{B}{C} \quad \frac{C}{B} \quad \frac{D}{A} \qquad \text{Father, son.}$$

The following chart shows the distribution of relatives through the sections:

Four sections—Kariera type[6]

A		B	
Father's father	Mother's mother	*Mother's father*	Father's mother
Brother	Sister	*Mother's brother's son*	Mother's brother's daughter
Son's son	Son's daughter	*Daughter's son*	Daughter's daughter
C		**D**	
Mother's brother	Mother	*Father*	Father's sister
Sister's son	Sister's daughter	*Son*	Daughter

We have seen that a kinship system of the Kariera type groups all relatives into two lines of descent. Tracing descent through males only, the two lines are shown as follows:

I (A + D)
Father's father
Father
Brother
Son
Son's son

II (B + C)
Mother's father
Mother's brother
Mother's brother's son
Sister's son
Daughter's son

If we trace descent through females we get two different lines of descent:

X (A + C)
Father's father (=mother's mother's brother)
Mother's brother
Brother

Sister's son
Son's son (=sister's daughter's son)

Y (B + D)
Mother's father (=father's mother's brother)
Father
Mother's brother's son (=father's sister's son)
Son
Daughter's son

The patrilineal lines of descent (I and II) constitute a pair of patrilineal moieties. The matrilineal lines of descent (X and Y) constitute a pair of matrilineal moieties. The system of four sections is constituted by the crossing of patrilineal moieties and matrilineal moieties giving four divisions in all.[7]

The rules of marriage and descent of the four-section system in the Kariera tribe are now seen to be the immediate result of the more fundamental rule that a man may only marry his 'mother's brother's daughter'. If I belong to section A my 'mother's brother's daughter' is in section B. It should be noted that there are some women in that section whom I cannot marry, those I call 'father's mother' or 'daughter's daughter' being barred, even if their relationship to me is a very distant one, and they are near my own age. While my wife must be of section B, our children must belong to section D, and they in turn marry my 'sister's children,' who are all in section C.

Let us turn now to the Aranda. In the northern part of the tribe there is a system of eight subsections.

A^1	Pananka	=	Purula	B^1
A^2	Knuraia	=	Ngala	B^2
C^1	Kamara	=	Paltara	D^1
C^2	Mbitjana	=	Bangata	D^2

Each of these subsections is found, on examination, to consist of groups of relatives. If any man of subsection A^1 is taken, it is found that all his male relatives are divided up amongst the eight subsections according to the accompanying chart. (Female relatives have been omitted.)

Eight subsections—Aranda type

Ego is A^1	
A^1	**B^1**
Father's father	*Father's mother's brother*
Brother	*Mother's mother's brother's daughter's son*
Son's son	*Sister's son's son*
A^2	**B^2**
Mother's mother's brother	*Mother's father*
Mother's mother's brother's son's son	*Mother's brother's son*
Sister's daughter's son	*Daughter's son*
C^1	**D^1**
Father's mother's brother's son	*Mother's mother's brother's son*
Sister's son	*Mother's brother's daughter's son*
C^2	**D^2**
Mother's brother	*Father*
Mother's brother's son's son	*Son*

From this chart it is comparatively easy to follow out the rules of marriage and descent. If I am A^1 I may only marry my 'mother's mother's brother's daughter's daughter' who is in B^1. Our children will be D^2. My son marries my 'mother's brother's son's daughter' in C^2, and their children are in my own section A^1. My daughter marries my 'mother's brother's son's son' and their children are B^2. My sister marries my 'mother's mother's brother's daughter's son' of B^1, and their children are C^1.

In the southern part of the Aranda tribe there are not eight subsections, but only four sections.

A   Pananka   =   Purula   B
C   Kamara   =   Paltara   D

But as the kinship system is the same as in the northern part of the tribe, it follows that each of these four sections contains the relatives who are divided between two subsections in the north. Thus for a man of section A, his section contains the relatives of A^1 and A^2 in the preceding chart. Similarly section B contains B^1 and B^2 and so on.

It is clear therefore that the four sections in the southern Aranda are constituted very differently from the four sections of the Kariera. In the Kariera tribe a man of section A marries from section B a woman who is his 'mother's brother's daughter'. The relatives who are classified under this term amongst the Kariera are divided in the Aranda into two groups, 'mother's brother's daughter' and 'mother's mother's brother's daughter's daughter', and when a man of section A marries into section B, it is a relative of the second kind that he must marry, and only one of that kind.

An examination of the two charts (Kariera and Aranda) will show that in both the four-section system and the eight-subsection system the principle of classification rests on the bringing together into the same section or subsection of the father's father and his son's son. Thus I and my father's father and my son's son belong to the same section or subsection. Similarly my mother's brother's son's son belongs to the same section or subsection as my mother's brother, and so on for every relative.

We have seen (p. 152) that in the Kariera system all relatives fall into two lines of descent, tracing kinship through males. In the Aranda system there are four patrilineal lines instead of the two of the Kariera. These are (1) Ego's own line headed by the father's father; (2) the mother's line descended from the mother's father; (3) that of the father's mother's brother, and (4) that of the mother's mother's brother. A man marries into his father's mother's brother's line. It is in that line that his 'mother's mother's brother's daughter's daughter' falls, since his 'father's mother's brother's son' marries his 'mother's mother's brother's daughter'. Each patrilineal line consists of one couple of subsections.

P (A^1 + D^2)

Father's father

Father

Brother

Son

Son's son

R (B^1 + C^1)

Father's mother's brother

Father's mother's brother's son

Father's mother's brother's son's son
(= Mother's mother's brother's
    daughter's son)

Sister's son

Sister's son's son.

Q (A^2 + D^1)

Mother's mother's brother

Mother's mother's brother's son

Mother's mother's brother's son's son

Mother's brother's daughter's son

Sister's daughter's son

S (B^2 + C^2)

Mother's father

Mother's brother

Mother's brother's son

Mother's brother's son's son

Daughter's son

It is these four patrilineal lines (P, Q, R, S), existing as absolute divisions of the tribe, that constitute the four named groups in the Mara and Anyula tribes, which I have called semi-moieties.

The Aranda system of eight subsections, of course, involves the existence of a pair of matrilineal moieties though they are unnamed. One moiety includes the subsection A^1, A^2, C^1 and C^2, and the other includes B^1, B^2, D^1 and D^2. These have been referred to earlier in this paper as cycles.

The above comparison of the Kariera and Aranda systems has, I hope, been sufficient to show (1) that the sections and subsections are part of the systematic classification of relatives, and can only be understood when they are considered as such, and (2) that two tribes may both have a system of four sections, even with the same names, and yet have very different kinship systems and very different regulation of marriage. The information that a tribe has two, four or eight divisions tells us very little about the social organization or the system of regulating marriage of that tribe. Thus we can find the same type of kinship system with the same method of regulating marriage (the Aranda system) in tribes with two moieties (Dieri), in tribes with four sections (Talaindji), in tribes with eight subsections (Waramanga), and in tribes with four named semi-moieties (Mara). On the other hand, of two adjoining tribes both with a system of four sections, as the Ngaluma and the Mardudhunera, one has a kinship system of the Kariera type while the other has a system of the Aranda type.

Let us now turn to a consideration of the relation between the kinship system and the local organization. We have seen that all over Australia the important local group is what is here called the horde, and that the latter, so far as its male members are concerned, is strictly patrilineal.

In the Kariera tribe we find that all the men of any given horde belong to a single line of descent. My own horde contains only men who are 'father's father', 'father', 'brother', 'son', or 'son's son' to me. On the other hand all the men of my mother's horde belong to the other line of descent. The persons belonging to a horde by birth all belong to the same patrilineal moiety. Moreover my own horde contains all my nearest relatives in the paternal line, my father's own brothers, etc. And my mother's horde contains all my nearest relatives through my mother.

We can therefore say that in the Kariera tribe, connected with each horde there is a clan. I have defined a horde as consisting of all men born into the horde together with their wives and unmarried daughters. The clan connected with the horde consists of all persons born in the horde. The male members of the clan all remain in the horde from birth to death. The female members of the clan remain with the horde till they are married and then are transferred to other hordes.[8]

This system of local clans is not confined to the Kariera tribe. We have very little information about the composition of the horde in the great majority of tribes, but evidence is accumulating that the system of patrilineal local clans was widespread in Australia, and may even be regarded as a normal, though not quite universal, feature of Australian social organization.

In some parts of Australia there is found a system of matrilineal clans. The clan consists of a body of people who are or who regard themselves as being closely related through females. The clans are totemic i.e., they are identified by being each named after or connected with some species of animal or plant. Children belong to the clan of the mother, and consequently the members of a clan are found scattered through the tribe.

These matrilineal totemic clans can, of course, exist in the same tribe with a system of patrilineal local clans and there is evidence that in some tribes the two clan systems did co-exist.

To complete this account of the social organization of Australia it is necessary to make a brief reference to the subject of totemism. Throughout Australia we find, with many local variations, a system of customs and beliefs by which there is set up a special system of relations between the society and the animals and plants and other natural objects that are important in the social life. Some of these customs and beliefs it is usual to include under the term 'totemism'.

In the strict and narrow sense of the term the 'social structure' of a people consists of the system of formal grouping by which the social relations of individuals to one another are determined, i.e., it is a grouping of human beings in relation to one another. But there is also a larger structure in which the society and external nature are brought together and a system of organized relations established, in myth and ritual, between human beings and natural species or phenomena. It is impossible to give any succinct account of this social structure in the wider sense as it appears in Australia, as this would require a systematic treatment of the ritual and mythology. There are, however, some aspects of it that need to be mentioned.

One of the most important kinds of totemism (if it is to be called such) found in Australia is that constituted by the existence of what we may call, for lack of a better term, local totem centres. The essential basis of this is the existence of certain sacred spots each of which is associated with some natural species, and which is regarded as the 'home' or 'life-centre' of that species. Such a spot is what is meant by a 'totem centre'. The totem centre is generally a natural feature, very frequently a water-hole, sometimes a rock or a tree or clump of trees, occasionally an arrangement of stones that is obviously artificial but is not regarded as such by the natives. When the totem is a species of animal or plant, the totem centre is always a spot in the vicinity of which the species is abundant. The objects that are treated as totems in this way are the animals and plants that are used for food, and for other purposes, other natural species such as mosquitoes, also rain, fire, hot weather, cold weather, winds, the rainbow-serpent, high-tide, babies, diseases, and occasionally artificial objects such as stone-axes, nets, etc.

Normally, if not universally, there is an association between the totem centres and certain mythical beings who are believed to have existed at the beginning of the world, and who were responsible for the formation of the totem centres.

Every totem centre lies, of course, in the territory of some horde, and there is therefore a special connection between the members of the horde and the totem. Usually each horde possesses a number of different totem centres, some of them more important than others.

In its normal forms, therefore, this type of totemism is based on an association of four things.

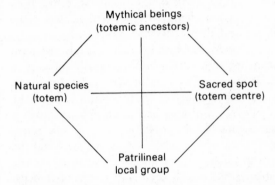

In most of the tribes that have this form of totemism there is a system of localized rites for the increase of natural species, each local totem centre having its own rite, performed usually by members of the clan or horde to which the totem centre belongs. It is convenient to denote these rites by the term *talu* by which they are known in some tribes of Western Australia (Kariera, etc.) The so-called *intichiuma*, properly *mbanbiuma*, rites of the Aranda tribe are of this type.

There is another system of rites which are not localized, i.e., not performed at a given spot, but have local references to the totem centres. These are representations of the doings of the totemic ancestors, and are really myths dramatically represented.

In some of the tribes having this totemism of local totem centres there is a special connection between each individual and some one totem. This may take the form of a conception that the individual is a reincarnation of one of the totemic ancestors or the incarnation of an emanation from the totem centre.

This form of totemism seems to be very widespread in Australia. It was first studied in detail in the Aranda tribe by Spencer and Gillen. Since then it has been found to extend over a large part of Western Australia. From the Aranda it extends to the extreme north of the continent on the one side, and to the tribes about Lake Eyre (Dieri, etc.) on the other. Miss McConnel has made a study of this type of totemism in the Wikmunkan tribe of the Cape York Peninsula. Recently it has been found in the almost extinct tribes of the east coast in northern New South Wales and southern Queensland. It seems very probably that it extended through the now extinct tribes of the south-east coastal districts as far as Victoria. Far from being confined to the centre of the continent, as has been sometimes supposed, it is found also in the extreme west, the south-east, the north-east and the north.

Another class of customs to which it is usual to apply the term totemism consists of the use of natural species (generally animals) as representatives of social divisions. In some instances the division is named after its animal representative. In the south-east of the continent each of the two sex-groups had as its representative a species of animal. For example, in the coastal regions of New South Wales the bat is the representative or sex-totem of the men, and the tree-creeper (*Climacteris* sp.) that of the women. In several regions the moieties are named after or closely associated with species of animals; for example, eaglehawk and crow, crow and white cockatoo, white cockatoo and black cockatoo, native companion and turkey, hill kangaroo and long-legged kangaroo. Similarly in the Southern Cross district of Western Australia the alternating endogamous divisions (pairs of sections) are named after two species of birds. In some of the tribes with four sections and in some of those with eight subsections, each section or subsection has a species of animal specially associated with it as its representative.

In northern and in south-eastern Australia there are tribes with matrilineal, and therefore not localized, clans, each clan being named after or represented by a natural species, generally a species of animal.

In some parts there are patrilineal local clans that have each its totem, or representative species, but, so far as we know, without the system of local totem centres described above. An example is the Yaralde tribe.

Another important element of the structural system in which man and natural objects are united in Australian tribes consists of a classification of natural species in relation to the social structure. Just as each human being has his own place in the social structure, belonging to a particular moiety, section, clan, so each of the important natural species is allotted its place as belonging to a particular moiety, section or clan. The mode of classification varies, of course, from one region to another.

We have completed our general survey of the forms of social structure in Australia. Individuals are united together into groups on the basis of sex and age, of community of language and customs (tribe), of possession and occupation of a territory (horde), and on the basis of kinship and marriage (family, clan, section, moiety). This grouping determines the relations of individuals to one another in the social and economic life.

One of the tasks of culture is to organize the relations of human beings to one another. This is done by means of the social structure and the moral, ritual and economic customs by and in which that structure functions. But another task of culture is to organize the relation of man to his environment. In Australia this involves a system of customs and beliefs by which the human society and the natural objects and phenomena that affect it are brought into a larger structure, which it is very important to recognize, but for which it is difficult to find a suitable name. The function of much of the myth and ritual is to maintain or create this structure. What is commonly called totemism is part of this structural system.

It should be noted that the most important determining factor in relation to this wider structure is the strong social bond between the horde or local clan and its territory. The strong local solidarity, which is the most important thing in the social life of the Australians, is correlated with a very strong bond between the local group and its territory. There is an equally strong and permanent association between the territory and the animals and plants that are found on it. It is this intimate association of a group of persons with a certain stretch of country, with its rocks and water-holes and other natural features, and with the natural species that are abundant in it, that provides the basis of that totemism of local totem centres that is so widespread and so important in the Australian culture.

Part II

Every human society has to provide for itself a system of social integration whereby individuals are united into groups and collective action is provided for. As no adaptation is perfect every society is constantly readjusting its integrative system, usually without any clear consciousness of what it is doing. In Australia this process of readjustment has been going on for many centuries. The details of the process itself will for ever be unknown, and it is useless to speculate about them. But the results are present in the existing different tribal systems, and these we can compare one with another. In the brief notes that follow I shall compare some of the varieties of Australian social organization with reference to differences in the mode of social integration that they provide.

Integrative systems differ in what may be called the extent of the circle of social relations, which may be defined roughly by reference to the number of persons with whom a given individual is brought into effective direct or indirect social relations. Differences of this kind may be spoken of as differences in level of integration. It is obvious that there is an enormous difference in level of integration between the Australian aborigines and the present societies of Europe or America. In two societies at approximately the same level the integration may be closer or looser.

In any society there are normally present a certain number of factors tending towards an expansion of social solidarity, and other factors tending in the opposite direction towards a contraction of social solidarity. These two sets of opposing factors may be in a state of equilibrium, or at a given time one set of factors may be stronger than the other. Some of these factors can be studied and seen at work in an Australian tribe. Thus certain religious movements tend towards a widening of solidarity and therefore to a widening of the circle of social relations. On the other hand warfare is a factor tending in the opposite direction.

It is from this strictly sociological point of view that I propose to compare a few of the varieties of Australian social organization.

One of the simplest integrative systems in Australia is that of the Kariera tribe and others of the same type. In this system a man's closest relations are with his own family, first with his parents and brothers and sisters, then after he is married with his wife and children. His intimate relations with his parents and with his brothers last as long as they are alive. Outside the family groups to which he belongs he has close, continuous and permanent relations with the other persons of his own horde. Within this narrow circle of probably not more than fifty persons all told most of his social life turns. Outside his own horde he has a fairly close relation with the horde of his own mother, being always a welcome visitor in the country of that horde. When he marries he establishes for himself a close relation with the horde from which he obtains a wife. By the Kariera system of marriage this may be his mother's horde, so that the one horde becomes for him both that of his mother and that of his wife. With all other hordes his relations are less close and definite. Everywhere within his own tribe, however, he will find persons speaking the same language as himself and practising the same customs. The linguistic group of which he is thus a member may number perhaps 500 persons. His relations, however, are not confined to members of his own tribe, but normally extend to some hordes of the neighbouring tribe or tribes.

Wherever he goes all the persons he meets are his relatives by the working of the kinship system. These are further classified for him by the section system. Outside the circle of his immediate relatives he tends to classify other persons according to the hordes to which they belong. There are certain collective terms of relationship which the individual applies to different hordes. This tendency to treat their horde as a unit is, as we shall see, a determining factor of some importance in the Australian systems. It seems to be present throughout the continent.

In the marriage system of the Kariera a man looks first for a wife to his mother's brother, i.e., to his mother's horde. If he succeeds in obtaining a wife there then his social circle remains a somewhat narrow one in which only two hordes, his own and his mother's, play important parts. If he cannot obtain a wife from his mother's horde he may seek for one in a horde into which his father's sister has married and with which, for that reason, his father is on intimate terms. The marriage system of the Kariera type therefore tends towards a contraction of the social circle. It maintains close solidarity within a narrow range.

But even in the tribes of the Kariera type there are factors tending towards the expansion of solidarity, the widening of the social circle. One or two of these may be mentioned. One of them is connected with an alternative method of obtaining a wife. When a youth is to be initiated into manhood he is sent on a journey which lasts frequently for several months. It is his grand tour. During his journey he is treated as sacred wherever he goes and may therefore visit in complete safety hordes that are at enmity with his own. He is normally taken first to a neighbouring horde of the other moiety from his own, and is passed on from one horde to another until he passes out of his own tribe and may eventually reach a tribe at some distance from his own. Here he remains for a period and acquires some knowledge of the language. He returns to his own home in due course. For the rest of his life the country through which he has travelled becomes his 'road' along which he can travel to carry messages or for other purposes. Thus in a given horde there will be men having different roads which serve to bring the horde into relation, through these individuals, with a considerable area of country. Now it seems that a man tries to obtain a wife from a distant horde on his own road, and sometimes succeeds in doing so. Normally, I think, he will be expected to give a sister in exchange. He establishes by this marriage a connection between his own children and this distant horde which is of course that of their mother. This aspect of the Kariera system is, I think, an important one intending to produce a wider integration.

Another feature may be noted. We have seen that the mother's brother is a very important relative. Now the social structure of Australian tribes is built up by the recognition of indirect relationships, and by this process a man comes into a special relation with the mother's brother of his mother's brother. In the Kariera system the mother's mother's brother is classified with the father's father. Actually a man's father's father and his mother's mother's brother may be one and the same person, by reason of cousin marriage and exchange of sisters. Even when this is not so, and the situation seems to be a rare one, a man's own mother's mother's brother may occasionally belong to his own horde. But in a considerable number of instances, probably the great majority, a man's mother's mother's brother belongs to some other horde of his own moiety. Where this is so it produces a new kind of relation between the individual and this horde. This relation seems to be recognized in the Kariera system, but is not apparently there of very much importance. It is, however, one of the factors tending towards expansion of solidarity through kinship, and becomes of very great importance in some of the other types of kinship system.

I must leave for another occasion the question of the position of totemism in the integrative system, but it may be noted here that the Kariera system, in which each local clan is a separate totemic unit, serves on the whole to emphasize the solidarity of the clan.

In the Kumbaingeri system the basis of the social organization is essentially the same as that of the Kariera although the two tribes are separated by the whole width of the continent. But in the Kumbaingeri system there are certain significant changes. A man is no longer permitted to marry his own mother's brother's daughter, nor is he, I think, permitted to marry into his mother's clan. He must marry the daughter of a man he calls 'mother's brother', but it must be a 'distant' 'mother's brother' both genealogically and geographically. The expansive tendency noticed in the Kariera is here the chief factor. It is considered desirable that every member of a horde should establish by marriage relations with some distant horde.

There is in the Kumbaingeri some differentiation between mother's brother and wife's father but it is not very marked and the two relatives are still denoted by the same term of relationship. But there is a differentiation of the wife's mother from the father's sister. The rule of avoidance which everywhere in Australia holds for the wife's mother and women classified with her, and which in the Kariera system therefore applies to the father's sister and the mother's brother's wife, does not in the Kumbaingeri system apply to the father's sister, or to any of the women of the father's generation in a man's own horde. The factor of the solidarity of the horde has here taken a different turn from the Kariera type.

The father's sister is expected to take a 'fatherly' interest in her nephew. This she may do in the Kariera tribe by giving him her daughter as a wife. In the Kumbaingeri tribe it is felt that the father's sister and all the women of his own horde are too closely bound to him by social ties to allow him to marry with their daughters. But it is still the concern of his father's sister to provide him with a wife, which she does by acting as match-maker in the distant region into which she has married. She obtains for him the daughter of a woman who is her distant 'sister'. If this means, as I think it frequently does, that the nephew obtains his wife from the horde into which his father's sister has married the arrangement is thus one of delayed exchange between hordes but not between families as in the Kariera system. The tendency apparent in the Kumbaingeri system to regard the father's sister as being so close a relative that her daughter should not be married is one that seems to be of considerable importance in a number of the Australian systems. It is to be considered, I think, as the result of an increased emphasis on family and horde solidarity.

Thus compared with the Kariera system that of the Kumbaingeri shows a somewhat wider integration while still emphasizing the solidarity of the narrow circle of the horde.

Let us now consider briefly the systems of the Aranda type. I have argued that the important principle of the Australian system as a

165

whole is the solidarity between brothers. I have further suggested that it is the solidarity between brother and sister that explains the position of the mother's brother and father's sister. As soon as we examine kinship terminologies of the Aranda type we notice that the solidarity or social equivalence of brother and sister takes a new or extended form. One feature of the kinship terminologies of the Aranda type that at first sight seems strange to a European mind is that a woman uses the same kinship term for her brother's children that he does himself and inversely the brother calls his sister's children by the same term that she does. The principle that underlies this terminology is that brother and sister are so closely connected that in spite of the difference of sex a person who stands in a certain relation to one is regarded as standing in a similar relation to the other. It is therefore merely a further application of the principle of the equivalence of brothers which we might here refer to as the equivalence of siblings.

This same tendency, to place brother and sister together in the social classification, appears in other features of the Aranda terminology. Thus in the Kariera system the father's father's sister is classified with the mother's mother, whereas in systems of Aranda type she is classified with the father's father. And so throughout the second ascending generation brother and sister are classified together under a single term. It seems that the differences between the Aranda system and the Kariera system can be traced back to this greater emphasis on solidarity of brother and sister in the former.

This is seen in the objection to marriage with the father's sister's daughter which is present not only in systems of Aranda type but also in the Kumbaingeri, Murngin and Karadjeri types. If the father's sister is to be assimilated to the father it will result in her children occupying a special place somewhat similar to that of siblings. In order to avoid marriage with the father's sister's daughter a tribe with an organization of the Kariera type must either abandon the exchange of sisters and continue the custom of marriage with the mother's brother's daughter (as in the Karadjeri and Murngin types), or it must make a compromise such as that of the Kumbaingeri type and allow marriage with a distant 'father's sister', or it must develop a more complex classification of kin as in the Aranda type.

The mechanism of the Aranda system is not very complicated when we follow it out in terms of individual relationships. We have seen that there is a close connection between a man and his mother's mother's family and therefore with his mother's mother's brother. This relative is classed in the Kariera system with the father's father, but is generally not in a man's own horde, as are the nearest of those he calls 'father's father'. If the father's sister is not to be regarded as a mother-in-law and it is necessary to find some other relative for that position one immediate possibility is the daughter of the mother's mother's brother. This involves making a definite distinction between father's father and mother's mother's brother. The possibility of the distinction already exists in the Kariera system by reason of the fact that while a man's own father's father belongs to his own horde his mother's mother's brother very frequently belongs to another horde. The making of it is aided by the tendency to classify together brother and sister, so that father's father's sister coming to be associated with the father's father must be differentiated from the mother's mother who in turn will be linked with her brother.

The mechanism of marriage in the Aranda type is the result of these differentiations. Instead of looking to the daughter of his father's father (his father's sister) for her to give him a daughter as in the Kariera system, he now has to look to the daughter of his mother's mother's brother who is now fully differentiated from his father's father. In both the Kariera and Aranda types a man looks to his mother's relatives to provide him with a wife. This is because they are specially the persons outside his own family or horde who are interested in him and are expected to be concerned for his welfare. In systems of the Kariera type it is the mother's brother who gives his daughter as a wife for his sister's son. In systems of the Aranda type it is the mother's mother's brother who gives his daughter to be a mother-in-law for his sister's daughter's child.

In terms of hordes the marriage system of the Aranda type results in a more complex integration than the Kariera system, linking an individual to four hordes in all. There is first his own, i.e., his father's horde within which his life is spent. There is secondly his mother's horde with which he has a very close connection, and from which he cannot normally obtain a wife. Through his mother and his mother's brother he is connected with their mother's brother whose horde thus becomes a third with which he is closely connected. The daughters of his mother's mother's brother are his potential wife's mothers. One of them may be specially allotted to him and when she marries she passes into a fourth horde from which he ultimately obtains his wife and with which he is consequently also closely connected. This fourth horde becomes, of course, the mother's horde of his children.

When the classification of kin is systematically carried out on the basis described above a complete system of Aranda type results. There are certain tribes, in New South Wales, for example, in which the systematization is not complete. The detailed study of those systems is of great value in enabling us to understand the principles that underlie the Aranda type generally, and will be found to confirm, I think, the analysis given above. There is no space here for any such detailed discussion.

It should be clear, I hope, from the discussion in the first part of this essay that the eight sub-sections are simply the final systematization of a kinship system of the Aranda type. An alternative systematization is provided by the four semi-moieties of the Mara and Anyula tribes, but a discussion of these would require us to consider also the totemic organization.

Amongst the vast mass of data on which this analysis of the Aranda system is based, one point may be brought forward as it is an example of those crucial instances that it is necessary to seek out in proving the validity of a sociological interpretation. I have suggested that it is the close solidarity of family and horde working in conjunction with the tendency to bring brother and sister into the same position in the social system that underlies the objection to marriage with the father's sister's daughter in the Aranda type. In systems of Aranda type the wife's father is the son of a 'father's father's sister'. Spencer and Gillen record that in the Aranda tribe where a 'father's father's sister' belongs to a man's own immediate family or locality (presumably his own horde) this woman's son may not become the wife's father. We have here, I think, a clear exemplification of a wider action of those same principles that on my view underlie the Aranda system as a whole.

When we compare the integrative systems of the Kariera type and the Aranda type we see that the latter provides apparently a wider integration bringing a single individual into social relations with a wider circle. Secondly it also provides a closer integration of the narrower groupings by giving new forms of expression to the solidarity of the family and the horde. It combines these two features, which would seem at first sight to be contrary to one another, by an increase in the complexity of the social structure.

We are thus justified, I think, in regarding the Kariera and the Aranda systems as two terms in an evolutionary process, for evolution, as the term is here used, is a process by which stable integrations at a higher level are substituted for or replace integrations at a lower level. This does not involve the assumption that the Aranda system is derived historically from one identical with the existing Kariera system.

The Aranda system of kinship involves certain difficulties of social adjustment. Chief of these is the difficulty of providing every man with a wife, owning to the very narrow restriction of marriage. And examination of different systems of this type shows what attempts have been made to overcome these difficulties by adjustments of the system.

A few remarks may be made on the Yaralde system. In this there are no moieties or sections, yet it is clearly very closely related to the Aranda type, so that we must certainly assume some historical connection between them. Some of the writers on Australia have assumed that because the moiety and section organization is absent in certain tribes such as the Yaralde, these tribes possess a social organization fundamentally different in type from the tribes with sections. That assumption, I believe, gives a quite false view of the facts.

The basis of the Yaralde system is the recognition of four patrilineal lines of descent just as in systems of the Aranda type. But instead of the four absolute divisions which are found in a systematized Aranda type of organization the four lines of descent in the Yaralde tribe exist only in relation to some given individual whose relationships are considered. We have seen that in the Aranda type the hordes or local clans are of great importance. Their importance is more obvious, if perhaps not greater, in the Yaralde system. In terms of the local clans, in the Yaralde system, a man's near relatives of his own, *i.e.*, his father's father's, line of descent, are in his own clan. He is in intimate relation with his mother's clan which contains his nearest relatives of his mother's father's line. Similarly those of his mother's mother's brother's line are to be found in one clan. Here a special feature of the Yaralde system appears, for an individual classifies under a single term or relationship all the members of this clan without regard to generation. The principle that is obviously at work here is that of the solidarity of the local clan. We have seen that in other more normal Australian

169

systems there is a tendency for the individual to group together all the members of a clan other than his own and to regard his relationship to them as being determined by his genealogically close relationship to one member of the clan. This tendency has here been given free play and has in a certain sense overcome the division into generations which elsewhere is so important. For the individual his mother's mother's clan is a single unit all the members of which are classified together under a single term and regarded as standing in the same relationship to him. In the Yaralde system therefore a man does not look to his mother's mother's local clan to provide him with a mother-in-law as in the Aranda type, and it would seem that he could not normally marry the daughter of a woman of that clan. The same situation appears with regard to the fourth line of descent. A man classifies together under a single term all persons of his father's mother's clan irrespective of generation. In the Aranda system a man obtains his wife from his father's mother's brother's line of descent. But in the Yaralde system marriage with a woman of the father's mother's clan is forbidden. Thus, while a man's relations with his own and his mother's local clan are very similar in the Yaralde system to what they are in the Aranda type, his relations to the local clans of his two grandmothers, paternal and maternal, are very different. His solidarity with these clans is emphasized, but it takes the form of making him so closely related to all members of the two clans in question that he cannot marry one of them. This destroys the possibility of the ordinary method of marriage of the Aranda type.

In the Yaralde system the tracing of relationships of an individual to different local clans is carried back to the third ascending generation. This also is an unusual feature. By this process he is brought into a relation of intimacy and close solidarity with the clans of his father's father's mother and his mother's father's mother. He regards the members of these clans as being similar to brothers and sisters, and may therefore not marry with them.

In the Yaralde system, therefore, a man is in a close relation of simple solidarity with six local clans, including his own. He enters by marriage into close relations with a seventh clan.

The essential basis of the Yaralde system is the same as that of systems of Aranda type, namely the recognition of the four lines of descent. It shows a further extension of some of the principles and tendencies present in the Aranda type, together with the absence of certain other features of the latter. Thus the importance of the local clan as a unit of structure is further emphasized in the Yaralde system. The connection of a person with the local clans of his four grandparents is also emphasized, and his relationships are traced still further back so that he is intimately connected with the clans of six out of his eight great-grandparents.[9] The recognition of this connection takes the form of prohibiting marriage into any of these six clans (one of which is of course a man's own). On the other hand the absence of moieties and sections means that the relation in which a man stands to distant clans, or to those with which he has no near genealogical connection, is indeterminate. As compared with normal Australian systems the Yaralde have adopted a different method of regulating marriage. There is no longer a simple rule that a man must marry a woman who stands to him in a particular relationship. Outside the range of his own nearer kin there are women who are sufficiently distant from him to become his wife's mother, and from any one of these he may obtain a daughter to be his wife. It seems possible that the special characteristics of the Yaralde type are connected with a greater density of population in this part of the continent, and a greater volume of the horde, which seems to have included a larger number of individuals in these tribes than is usual in Australia as a whole. It is now unfortunately too late to verify this hypothesis.

The meaning of some of the features of the Yaralde system can be made clearer by a comparison with the Ungarinyin system, the details of which, obtained by Dr Elkin, have not yet been published. The two areas, Yaralde and Ungarinyin, lie so far apart that there can be no question of the influence of one tribe on the other, and they are separated by a wide area in which systems of the Aranda type are found. The Ungarinyin have adopted the same principle as the Yaralde of applying a single kinship term to all members of the local clan of the mother's mother and the father's mother. We have thus the same sort of process occurring independently in two widely separated regions, and it seems that in both instances it is the result of an increasing emphasis on the solidarity of the local clan as a unit in the social integration.

One last subject that must be mentioned is that of tribes with matrilineal clans. Unfortunately the functioning of the social structure in these tribes has not been observed as fully as could be desired, and for most of the tribes no further observations are possible. It is, however, clear that the system of matrilineal clans marks off a man's nearest relatives in the female line from the others, just as the local clan marks off his nearest relatives in the male line. As a result of this it produces a closer integration of a man with certain of his relatives, namely those of his mother's matrilineal line, who are scattered throughout the hordes, not only of his own tribe, but of the neighbouring tribes also. The system of matrilineal clans therefore provides a powerful additional integration as compared with the tribes that lack the system.

This brief comparison of some of the variations in the Australian organization has served, I hope, to confirm the interpretation and analysis of the general type. It has shown that the terminology of kinship has a real and very close correlation with the social organization. Secondly, it has shown, I think, with sufficient clearness that throughout Australia it is the actual genealogical individual relationships resulting from the family that are the significant thing and form the basis of the whole social structure.

I hope that the whole essay has also served to show the essential homogeneity of Australia so far as social organization is concerned. In spite of the diversity of the various systems a careful comparison reveals them as being variations of a single type. Similar results are obtained by the study of other aspects of Australian culture, such as the technological system, or the mythology.

My chief purpose has been to remove certain misconceptions about the Australian social organization that are current in anthropological literature and thus to clear the way for a sociological study of the Australian culture. As a result of the researches carried out during the last four years by Lloyd Warner, Elkin, Miss McConnel, Hart, Thomson and Piddington, researches which it is to be hoped will be continued, it is now possible to undertake that study with some hope of reaching valid and important conclusions.

Notes

1 The term has been criticized, but I have failed to find a better.
2 In this and similar tables the capital letters stand for males and the lower case letters for females.
3 For the sociologist the terminology of kinship is of little or no interest in itself. Its study is only a means, though a necessary means, to the investigation of the kinship system as an element of social structure regulating the social relations (moral, economic, etc.) of individuals to

one another. Some ethnologists neglect to record the kinship terminology of the peoples they study. Many record a list of terms with their application and do nothing more. Such lists are of comparatively little value. The way in which relatives are classified for social purposes, although this is correlated with the terminology, cannot be inferred with any certainty, and in any detail, from that terminology. It needs to be observed.

4 When a term of relationship is placed within inverted commas as 'father', it is used not as denoting an individual relationship, but as the simple equivalent of a classificatory term of the native language. Thus 'father' means any man to whom a native applies the same term of relationship that he does to his own father.

5 The selection of these two tribes is not made haphazard. The discovery of the Kariera system by myself in 1911 was the result of a definite search, on a surmise, made before visiting Australia, but after a careful study of Australian data in 1909, that some such system might very well exist and that Western Australia would be a reasonable place in which to look for it. I first used these two systems as norms in a short note published in the *Journal of the Royal Anthropological Institute* in 1913, using them to define what I called kinship systems of Type I (Kariera) and Type II (Aranda). I now find it is not very satisfactory to continue this classification into numbered types, but further experience in dealing with Australian data has confirmed me in my choice of these two systems as norms with which to compare others.

6 Ego is A, and male. When Ego is female there is, of course, a different alignment of relatives in the sections.

7 The section A is constituted by all persons who are I and X, B by those who are II and Y, C by those who are II and X, and D by those who are I and Y.

8 This distinction between the horde and the associated local clan is, I think, a very important one to make and to keep in mind. A horde changes its composition by the passing of women out of it and into it by marriage. At any given moment it consists of a body of people living together as a group of families. The clan has all its male members in one horde, but all its older female members are in other hordes. It changes its composition only by the birth and death of its members.

9 There is no evidence of any special relation with the clans of the father's mother's mother and the mother's mother's mother, but this may have been overlooked.

On joking relationships

The publication of Mr F. J. Pedler's note[1] on what are called 'joking relationships', following on two other papers on the same subject by Professor Henri Labouret[2] and Mademoiselle Denise Paulme,[3] suggests that some general theoretical discussion of the nature of these relationships may be of interest to readers of *Africa*.[4]

What is meant by the term 'joking relationship' is a relation between two persons in which one is by custom permitted, and in some instances required, to tease or make fun of the other, who in turn is required to take no offence. It is important to distinguish two main varieties. In one the relation is symmetrical; each of the two persons teases or makes fun of the other. In the other variety the relation is asymmetrical; A jokes at the expense of B and B accepts the teasing good humouredly but without retaliating; or A teases B as much as he pleases and B in return teases A only a little. There are many varieties in the form of this relationship in different societies. In some instances the joking or teasing is only verbal, in others it includes horse-play; in some the joking includes elements of obscenity, in others not.

Standardised social relationships of this kind are extremely widespread, not only in Africa but also in Asia, Oceania and North America. To arrive at a scientific understanding of the phenomenon it is necessary to make a wide comparative study. Some material for this now exists in anthropological literature, though by no means all that could be desired, since it is unfortunately still only rarely that such relationships are observed and described as exactly as they might be.

The joking relationship is a peculiar combination of friendliness and antagonism. The behaviour is such that in any other social context it would express and arouse hostility; but it is not meant seriously and must not be taken seriously. There is a pretence of hostility and a real friendliness. To put it in another way, the relationship is one of permitted disrespect. Thus any complete theory of it must be part of, or consistent with, a theory of the place of respect in social relations and in social life generally. But this is a very wide and very important sociological problem; for it is evident that the whole maintenance of a social order depends upon the appropriate kind and degree of respect being shown towards certain persons, things and ideas or symbols.

Examples of joking relationships between relatives by marriage are very commonly found in Africa and in other parts of the world. Thus Mademoiselle Paulme[5] records that among the Dogon a man stands in a joking relationship to his wife's sisters and their daughters. Frequently the relationship holds between a man and both the brothers and sisters of his wife. But in some instances there is a distinction whereby a man is on joking terms with his wife's younger brothers and sisters but not with those who are older than she is. This joking with the wife's brothers and sisters is usually associated with a custom requiring extreme respect, often partial or complete avoidance, between a son-in-law and his wife's parents.[6]

The kind of structural situation in which the associated customs of joking and avoidance are found may be described as follows. A marriage involves a readjustment of the social structure whereby the woman's relations with her family are greatly modified and she enters into a new and very close relation with her husband. The latter is at the same time brought into a special relation with his wife's family, to which, however, he is an outsider. For the sake of brevity, though at the risk of over-simplification, we will consider only the husband's relation to his wife's family. The relation can be described as involving both attachment and separation, both social conjunction and social disjunction, if I may use the terms. The man has his own definite position in the social structure, determined for him by his birth into a certain family, lineage or clan. The great body of his rights and duties and the interests and activities that he shares with others are the result of his position. Before the marriage his wife's family are outsiders for him as he is an outsider for them. This constitutes a social disjunction which is not destroyed by the marriage. The social conjunction results from the continuance, though in altered form, of the wife's relation to her family, their continued interest in her and in her children. If the wife were really bought and paid for, as ignorant persons say that she is in Africa, there would be no place for any permanent close relation of a man with his wife's family. But though slaves can be bought, wives cannot.

Social disjunction implies divergence of interests and therefore the possibility of conflict and hostility, while conjunction requires the avoidance of strife. How can a relation which combines the two be given a stable, ordered form? There are two ways of doing this. One is to maintain between two persons so related an extreme mutual respect and a limitation of direct personal contact. This is exhibited in the very formal relations that are, in so many societies, characteristic of the behaviour of a son-in-law on the one side and his wife's father and mother on the other. In its most extreme form there is complete avoidance of any social contact between a man and his mother-in-law.

This avoidance must not be mistaken for a sign of hostility. One does, of course, if one is wise, avoid having too much to do with one's enemies, but that is quite a different matter. I once asked an Australian native why he had to avoid his mother-in-law, and his reply was, 'Because she is my best friend in the world; she has given me my wife'. The mutual respect between son-in-law and parents-in-law is a mode of friendship. It prevents conflict that might arise through divergence of interest.

The alternative to this relation of extreme mutual respect and restraint is the joking relationship, one, that is, of mutual disrespect and licence. Any serious hostility is prevented by the playful antagonism of teasing, and this in its regular repetition is a constant expression or reminder of that social disjunction which is one of the essential components of the relation, while the social conjunction is maintained by the friendliness that takes no offence at insult.

The discrimination within the wife's family between those who have to be treated with extreme respect and those with whom it is a duty to be disrespectful is made on the basis of generation and sometimes of seniority within the generation. The usual respected relatives are those of the first ascending generation, the wife's mother and her sisters, the wife's father and his brothers, sometimes the wife's mother's brother. The joking relatives are those of a person's own generation; but very frequently a distinction of seniority within the generation is made; a wife's older sister or brother may be respected while those younger will be teased.

In certain societies a man may be said to have relatives by marriage long before he marries and indeed as soon as he is born into the world. This is provided by the institution of the required or preferential marriage. We will, for the sake of brevity, consider only one kind of such organisations. In many societies it is regarded as preferable that a man should marry the daughter of his mother's brother; this is a form of the custom known as cross-cousin marriage. Thus his female cousins of this kind, or all those women whom by the classificatory system he classifies as such, are potential wives for him, and their brothers are his potential brothers-in-law. Among the Ojibwa Indians of North America, the Chiga of Uganda, and in Fiji and New Caledonia, as well as elsewhere, this form of marriage is found and is accompanied by a joking relationship between a man and the sons and daughters of his mother's brother. To quote one instance of these, the following is recorded for the Ojibwa. 'When cross-cousins meet they must try to embarrass one another. They "joke" one another, making the most vulgar allegations, by their standards as well as ours. But being "kind" relations, no one can take offence. Cross-cousins who do not joke in this way are considered boorish, as not playing the social game.'[7]

The joking relationship here is of fundamentally the same kind as that already discussed. It is established before marriage and is continued, after marriage, with the brothers- and sisters-in-law.

In some parts of Africa there are joking relationships that have nothing to do with marriage. Mr Pedler's note, mentioned above, refers to a joking relationship between two distinct tribes, the Sukuma and the Zaramu, and in the evidence it was stated that there was a similar relation between the Sukuma and the Zigua and between the Ngoni and the Bemba. The woman's evidence suggests that this custom of rough teasing exists in the Sukuma tribe between persons related by marriage, as it does in so many other African tribes.[8]

While a joking relationship between two tribes is apparently rare, and certainly deserves, as Mr Pedler suggests, to be carefully investigated, a similar relationship between clans has been observed in other parts of Africa. It is described by Professor Labouret and Mademoiselle Paulme in the articles previously mentioned, and amongst the Tallensi it has been studied by Dr Fortes, who will deal with it in a forthcoming publication.[9]

The two clans are not, in these instances, specially connected by intermarriage. The relation between them is an alliance involving real friendliness and mutual aid combined with an appearance of hostility.

The general structural situation in these instances seems to be as follows. The individual is a member of a certain defined group, a clan, for example, within which his relations to others are defined by a complex set of rights and duties, referring to all the major aspects of social life, and supported by definite sanctions. There may be another group outside his own which is so linked with his as to be the field of extension of jural and moral relations of the same general kind. Thus, in East Africa, as we learn from Mr Pedler's note, the Zigua and the Zaramu do not joke with one another because a yet closer bond exists between them since they are *ndugu* (brothers). But beyond the field within which social relations are thus defined there lie other groups with which, since they are outsiders to the individual's own group, the relation involves possible or actual hostility. In any fixed relations between the members of two such groups the separateness of the groups must be recognised. It is precisely this separateness which is not merely recognised but emphasised when a joking relationship is established. The show of hostility, the perpetual disrespect, is a continual expression of that social disjunction which is an essential part of the whole structural situation, but over which, without destroying or even weakening it, there is provided the social conjunction of friendliness and mutual aid.

The theory that is here put forward, therefore, is that both the joking relationship which constitutes an alliance between clans or tribes, and that between relatives by marriage, are modes of organising a definite and stable system of social behaviour in which conjunctive and disjunctive components, as I have called them, are maintained and combined.

To provide the full evidence for this theory by following out its implications and examining in detail its application to different instances would take a book rather than a short article. But some confirmation can perhaps be offered by a consideration of the way in which respect and disrespect appear in various kinship relations, even though nothing more can be attempted than a very brief indication of a few significant points.

In studying a kinship system it is possible to distinguish the different relatives by reference to the kind and degree of respect that is paid to them.[10] Although kinship systems vary very much in their details there are certain principles which are found to be very widespread. One of them is that by which a person is required to show a marked respect to relatives belonging to the generation immediately preceding his own. In a majority of societies the father is a relative to whom marked respect must be shown. This is so even in many so-called matrilineal societies, i.e. those which are organised into matrilineal clans or lineages. One can very frequently observe a tendency to extend this attitude of respect to all relatives of the first ascending generation and, further, to persons who are not relatives. Thus in those tribes of East Africa that are organised into age-sets a man is required to show special respect to all men of his father's age-set and to their wives.

The social function of this is obvious. The social tradition is handed down from one generation to the next. For the tradition to be maintained it must have authority behind it. The authority is therefore normally recognised as possessed by members of the preceding generation and it is they who exercise discipline. As a result of this the relation between persons of the two generations usually contains an element of inequality, the parents and those of their generation being in a position of superiority over the children who are subordinate to them. The unequal relation between a father and his son is maintained by requiring the latter to show respect to the former. The relation is asymmetrical.

When we turn to the relation of an individual to his grandparents and their brothers and sisters we find that in the majority of human societies relatives of the second ascending generation are treated with very much less respect than those of the first ascending generation, and instead of a marked inequality there is a tendency to approximate to a friendly equality.

Considerations of space forbid any full discussion of this feature of social structure, which is one of very great importance. There are many instances in which the grandparents and their grandchildren are grouped together in the social structure in opposition to their children and parents. An important clue to the understanding of the subject is the fact that in the flow of social life through time, in which men are born, become mature and die, the grandchildren replace their grandparents.

In many societies there is an actual joking relationship, usually of a relatively mild kind, between relatives of alternate generations. Grandchildren make fun of their grandparents and of those who are called grandfather and grandmother by the classificatory system of terminology, and these reply in kind.

Grandparents and grandchildren are united by kinship; they are separated by age and by the social difference that results from the fact

179

that as the grandchildren are in process of entering into full participation in the social life of the community the grandparents are gradually retiring from it. Important duties towards his relatives in his own and even more in his parents' generation impose upon an individual many restraints; but with those of the second ascending generation, his grandparents and collateral relatives, there can be, and usually is, established a relationship of simple friendliness relatively free from restraint. In this instance also, it is suggested, the joking relationship is a method of ordering a relation which combines social conjunction and disjunction.

This thesis could, I believe, be strongly supported if not demonstrated by considering the details of these relationships. There is space for only one illustrative point. A very common form of joke in this connection is for the grandchild to pretend that he wishes to marry the grandfather's wife, or that he intends to do so when his grandfather dies, or to treat her as already being his wife. Alternatively the grandfather may pretend that the wife of his grandchild is, or might be, his wife.[11] The point of the joke is the pretence at ignoring the difference of age between the grandparent and the grandchild.

In various parts of the world there are societies in which a sister's son teases and otherwise behaves disrespectfully towards his mother's brother. In these instances the joking relationship seems generally to be asymmetrical. For example the nephew may take his uncle's property but not vice versa; or, as amongst the Nama Hottentots, the nephew may take a fine beast from his uncle's herd and the uncle in return takes a wretched beast from that of the nephew.[12]

The kind of social structure in which this custom of privileged disrespect to the mother's brother occurs in its most marked forms, for example the Thonga of South-East Africa, Fiji and Tonga in the Pacific, and the Central Siouan tribes of North America, is characterised by emphasis on patrilineal lineage and a marked distinction between relatives through the father and relatives through the mother.

In a former publication[13] I offered an interpretation of this custom of privileged familiarity towards the mother's brother. Briefly it is as follows. For the continuance of a social system children require to be cared for and to be trained. Their care demands affectionate and unselfish devotion; their training requires that they shall be subjected to discipline. In the societies with which we are concerned there is something of a division of function between the parents and other relatives on the two sides. The control and discipline are exercised chiefly by the father and his brothers and generally also by his sisters; these are relatives who must be respected and obeyed. It is the mother who is primarily responsible for the affectionate care; the mother and her brothers and sisters are therefore relatives who can be looked to for assistance and indulgence. The mother's brother is called 'male mother' in Tonga and in some South African tribes.

I believe that this interpretation of the special position of the mother's brother in these societies has been confirmed by further field work since I wrote the article referred to. But I was quite aware at the time it was written that the discussion and interpretation needed to be supplemented so as to bring them into line with a general theory of the social functions of respect and disrespect.

The joking relationship with the mother's brother seems to fit well with the general theory of such relationships here outlined. A person's most important duties and rights attach to his paternal relatives, living and dead. It is to his patrilineal lineage or clan that he belongs. For the members of his mother's lineage he is an outsider, though one in whom they have a very special and tender interest. Thus here again there is a relation in which there is both attachment, or conjunction, and separation, or disjunction, between the two persons concerned.

But let us remember that in this instance the relation is asymmetrical.[14] The nephew is disrespectful and the uncle accepts the disrespect. There is inequality and the nephew is the superior. This is recognised by the natives themselves. Thus in Tonga it is said that the sister's son is a 'chief' (*eiki*) to his mother's brother, and Junod[15] quotes a Thonga native as saying 'The uterine nephew is a chief! He takes any liberty he likes with his maternal uncle'. Thus the joking relationship with the uncle does not merely annul the usual relation between the two generations, it reverses it. But while the superiority of the father and the father's sister is exhibited in the respect that is shown to them, the nephew's superiority to his mother's brother takes the opposite form of permitted disrespect.

It has been mentioned that there is a widespread tendency to feel that a man should show respect towards, and treat as social superiors, his relatives in the generation preceding his own, and the custom of joking with, and at the expense of, the maternal uncle clearly conflicts with this tendency. This conflict between principles of behaviour helps us to understand what seems at first sight a very extraordinary feature of the kinship terminology of the Thonga tribe and the VaNdau tribe in South-East Africa. Amongst the Thonga, although there is a term *malume* (= male mother) for the mother's brother, this relative is also, and perhaps more frequently, referred to as a grandfather (*kokwana*) and he refers to his sister's son as his grandchild (*ntukulu*). In the VaNdau tribe the mother's brother and also the mother's brother's son are called 'grandfather' (*tetekulu*, literally 'great father') and their wives are called 'grandmother' (*mbiya*), while the sister's son and the father's sister's son are called 'grandchild' (*muzukulu*).

This apparently fantastic way of classifying relatives can be interpreted as a sort of legal fiction whereby the male relatives of the mother's lineage are grouped together as all standing towards an individual in the same general relation. Since this relation is one of privileged familiarity on the one side, and solicitude and indulgence on the other, it is conceived as being basically the one appropriate for a grandchild and a grandfather. This is indeed in the majority of human societies the relationship in which this pattern of behaviour most frequently occurs. By this legal fiction the mother's brother ceases to belong to the first ascending generation, of which it is felt that the members ought to be respected.

It may be worth while to justify this interpretation by considering another of the legal fictions of the VaNdau terminology. In all these south-eastern Bantu tribes both the father's sister and the sister, particularly the elder sister, are persons who must be treated with great respect. They are also both of them members of a man's own patrilineage. Amongst the VaNdau the father's sister is called 'female father' (*tetadji*) and so also is the sister.[16] Thus by the fiction of terminological classification the sister is placed in the father's generation, the one that appropriately includes persons to whom one must exhibit marked respect.

In the south-eastern Bantu tribes there is assimilation of two kinds of joking relatives, the grandfather and the mother's brother. It may help our understanding of this to consider an example in which the grandfather and the brother-in-law are similarly grouped together. The Cherokee Indians of North America, probably numbering at one time about 20,000, were divided into seven matrilineal clans.[17] A man could not marry a woman of his own clan or of his father's clan. Common membership of the same clan connects him with his brothers and his mother's brothers. Towards his father and all his relatives in his father's clan of his own or his father's generation he is required by custom to show a marked respect. He applies the kinship term for 'father' not only to his father's brothers but also to the sons of his father's sisters. Here is another example of the same kind of fiction as described above; the relatives of his own generation whom he is required to respect and who belong to his father's matrilineal lineage are spoken of as though they belonged to the generation of his parents. The body of his immediate kindred is included in these two clans, that of his mother and his father. To the other clans of the tribe he is in a sense an outsider. But with two of them he is connected, namely with the clans of his two grand-fathers, his father's father and his mother's father. He speaks of all the members of these two clans, of whatever age, as 'grandfathers' and 'grandmothers'. He stands in a joking relationship with all of them. When a man marries he must respect his wife's parents but jokes with her brothers and sisters.

The interesting and critical feature is that it is regarded as particularly appropriate that a man should marry a woman whom he calls 'grandmother', i.e. a member of his father's father's clan or his mother's father's clan. If this happens his wife's brothers and sisters, whom he continues to tease, are amongst those whom he previously teased as his 'grandfathers' and 'grandmothers'. This is analogous to the widely spread organisation in which a man has a joking rela-tionship with the children of his mother's brother and is expected to marry one of the daughters.

It ought perhaps to be mentioned that the Cherokee also have a one-sided joking relationship in which a man teases his father's sister's husband. The same custom is found in Mota of the Bank Islands. In both instances we have a society organised on a ma-trilineal basis in which the mother's brother is respected, the father's sister's son is called 'father' (so that the father's sister's husband is the father of a 'father'), and there is a special term for the father's sister's husband. Further observation of the societies in which this custom occurs is required before we can be sure of its interpretation. I do not remember that it has been reported from any part of Africa.

What has been attempted in this paper is to define in the most general and abstract terms the kind of structural situation in which we may expect to find well-marked joking relationships. We have been dealing with societies in which the basic social structure is provided by kinship. By reason of his birth or adoption into a certain position in the social structure an individual is connected with a large number of other persons. With some of them he finds himself in a definite and specific jural relation, i.e. one which can be defined in terms of rights and duties. Who these persons will be and what will be the rights and duties depend on the form taken by the social structure. As an example of such a specific jural relation we may take that which normally exists between a father and son, or an elder brother and a younger brother. Relations of the same general type may be extended over a considerable range to all the members of a lineage or a clan or an age-set. Besides these specific jural relations which are defined not only negatively but also positively, i.e. in terms of things that must be done as well as things that must not, there are general jural relations which are expressed almost entirely in terms of prohibitions and which extend throughout the whole political society. It is forbidden to kill or wound other persons or to take or destroy their property. Besides these two classes of social relations there is another, including many very diverse varieties, which can perhaps be called relations of alliance or consociation. For example, there is a form of alliance of very great importance in many societies, in which two persons or two groups are connected by an exchange of gifts or services.[18] Another example is provided by the institution of blood-brotherhood which is so widespread in Africa.

The argument of this paper has been intended to show that the joking relationship is one special form of alliance in this sense. An alliance by exchange of goods and services may be associated with a joking relationship, as in the instance recorded by Professor Labouret.[19] Or it may be combined with the custom of avoidance. Thus in the Andaman Islands the parents of a man and the parents of his wife avoid all contact with each other and do not speak; at the same time it is the custom that they should frequently exchange presents through the medium of the younger married couple. But the exchange of gifts may also exist without either joking or avoidance, as in Samoa, in the exchange of gifts between the family of a man and the family of the woman he marries or the very similar exchange between a chief and his 'talking chief'.

So also in an alliance by blood-brotherhood there may be a joking relationship as amongst the Zande;[20] and in the somewhat similar alliance formed by exchange of names there may also be mutual teasing. But in alliances of this kind there may be a relation of extreme respect and even of avoidance. Thus in the Yaralde and neighbouring tribes of South Australia two boys belonging to communities distant from one another, and therefore more or less hostile, are brought into an alliance by the exchange of their respective umbilical cords. The relationship thus established is a sacred one; the two boys may never speak to one another. But when they grow up they enter upon a regular exchange of gifts, which provides the machinery for a sort of commerce between the two groups to which they belong.

Thus the four modes of alliance or consociation, (1) through intermarriage, (2) by exchange of goods or services, (3) by blood-brotherhood or exchanges of names or sacra, and (4) by the joking relationship, may exist separately or combined in several different ways. The comparative study of these combinations presents a number of interesting but complex problems. The facts recorded from West Africa by Professor Labouret and Mademoiselle Paulme afford us valuable material. But a good deal more intensive field research is needed before these problems of social structure can be satisfactorily dealt with.

What I have called relations by alliance need to be compared with true contractual relations. The latter are specific jural relations entered into by two persons or two groups, in which either party has definite positive obligations towards the other, and failure to carry out the obligations is subject to a legal sanction. In an alliance by blood-brotherhood there are general obligations of mutual aid, and the sanction for the carrying out of these, as shown by Dr Evans-Pritchard, is of a kind that can be called magical or ritual. In the alliance by exchange of gifts failure to fulfil the obligation to make an equivalent return for a gift received breaks the alliance and substitutes a state of hostility and may also cause a loss of prestige for the defaulting party. Professor Mauss[21] has argued that in this kind of alliance also there is a magical sanction, but it is very doubtful if such is always present, and even when it is it may often be of secondary importance.

The joking relationship is in some ways the exact opposite of a contractual relation. Instead of specific duties to be fulfilled there is privileged disrespect and freedom or even licence, and the only obligation is not to take offence at the disrespect so long as it is kept within certain bounds defined by custom, and not to go beyond those bounds. Any default in the relationship is like a breach of the

185

rules of etiquette; the person concerned is regarded as not knowing how to behave himself.

In a true contractual relationship the two parties are conjoined by a definite common interest in reference to which each of them accepts specific obligations. It makes no difference that in other matters their interests may be divergent. In the joking relationship and in some avoidance relationships, such as that between a man and his wife's mother, one basic determinant is that the social structure separates them in such a way as to make many of their interests divergent, so that conflict or hostility might result. The alliance by extreme respect, by partial or complete avoidance, prevents such conflict but keeps the parties conjoined. The alliance by joking does the same thing in a different way.

All that has been, or could be, attempted in this paper is to show the place of the joking relationship in a general comparative study of social structure. What I have called, provisionally, relations of consociation or alliance are distinguished from the relations set up by common membership of a political society which are defined in terms of general obligations, of etiquette, or morals, or of law. They are distinguished also from true contractual relations, defined by some specific obligation for each contracting party, into which the individual enters of his own volition. They are further to be distinguished from the relations set up by common membership of a domestic group, a lineage or a clan, each of which has to be defined in terms of a whole set of socially recognised rights and duties. Relations of consociation can only exist between individuals or groups which are in some way socially separated.

This paper deals only with formalised or standardised joking relations. Teasing or making fun of other persons is of course a common mode of behaviour in any human society. It tends to occur in certain kinds of social situations. Thus I have observed in certain classes in English-speaking countries the occurrence of horse-play between young men and women as a preliminary to courtship, very similar to the way in which a Cherokee Indian jokes with his 'grandmothers'. Certainly these unformalised modes of behaviour need to be studied by the sociologist. For the purpose of this paper it is sufficient to note that teasing is always a compound of friendliness and antagonism.

The scientific explanation of the institution in the particular form in which it occurs in a given society can only be reached by an intensive study which enables us to see it as a particular example of a widespread phenomenon of a definite class. This means that the whole social structure has to be thoroughly examined in order that the particular form and incidence of joking relationships can be understood as part of a consistent system. If it be asked why that society has the structure that it does have, the only possible answer would lie in its history. When the history is unrecorded, as it is for the native societies of Africa, we can only indulge in conjecture, and conjecture gives us neither scientific nor historical knowledge.[22]

Notes

1 'Joking relationships in East Africa', *Africa*, 13, 1940, p. 170.
2 'La parenté à plaisanteries en Afrique Occidentale', *Africa*, 2, 1929, p. 244.
3 'Parenté à plaisanteries et alliance par le sang en Afrique Occidentale', *Africa*, 12, 1939, p. 433.
4 Professor Marcel Mauss has published a brief theoretical discussion of the subject in the *Annuaire de l'École pratique des Hautes Études, Section des Sciences religieuses*, 1927–8. It is also dealt with by Dr F. Eggan in *Social Anthropology of North American Tribes*, University of Chicago Press, 1937 (1955), pp. 75–81.
5 op. cit., p. 438.
6 Those who are not familiar with these widespread customs will find descriptions in H. A. Junod, *Life of a South African Tribe*, Neuchâtel, 1913, vol. 1, pp. 229–37, and in *Social Anthropology of North American Tribes*, ed. F. Eggan, pp. 55–7.
7 Ruth Landes in M. Mead, ed., *Co-operation and Competition among Primitive Peoples*, McGraw-Hill, 1937, p. 103.
8 Incidentally it may be said that it was hardly satisfactory for the magistrate to establish a precedent whereby the man, who was observing what was a permitted and may even have been an obligatory custom, was declared guilty of common assault, even with extenuating circumstances. It seems quite possible that the man may have committed a breach of etiquette in teasing the woman in the presence of her mother's brother, for in many parts of the world it is regarded as improper for two persons in a joking relationship to tease one another (particularly if any obscenity is involved) in the presence of certain relatives of either of them. But the breach of etiquette would still not make it an assault. A little knowledge of anthropology would have enabled the magistrate, by putting the appropriate questions to the witnesses, to have obtained a fuller understanding of the case and all that was involved in it.

187

9 M. Fortes, *The Dynamics of Clanship among the Tallensi,* Oxford University Press, 1945.

10 See, for example, the kinship systems described in *Social Anthropology of North American Tribes* and Margaret Mead, 'Kinship in the Admiralty Islands', *Anthropological Papers of the American Museum of Natural History,* 34 (2), 1934, pp. 243–56.

11 For examples see Labouret, *Les Tribus du Rameau Lobi,* 1931, p. 248, and Sadarat Chandra Roy, *The Oraons of Chota Nagpur,* Ranchi, 1915, pp. 352–4.

12 A. Winifred Hoernlé, 'Social organisation of the Nama Hottentot'; *American Anthropologist,* n.s., 27, 1925, pp. 1–24.

13 'The mother's brother in South Africa', *South African Journal of Science,* 21, 1924, 542-55.

14 There are some societies in which the relation between a mother's brother and a sister's son is approximately symmetrical, and therefore one of equality. This seems to be so in the Western Islands of Torres Strait, but we have no information as to any teasing or joking, though it is said that each of the two relatives may take the property of the other.

15 *Life of a South African Tribe,* vol. I, p. 255.

16 For the kinship terminology of the VaNdau see Boas, 'Das Verwandtschafts-system der Vandau', in *Zeitschrift für Ethnologie,* 1922, pp. 41–51.

17 For an account of the Cherokee see Gilbert, in *Social Anthropology of North American Tribes,* pp. 285–338.

18 See Marcel Mauss, *The Gift,* Cohen & West, 1954.

19 op. cit., p. 245.

20 Evans-Pritchard, 'Zande blood-brotherhood', *Africa,* 6, 1933, pp. 369–401.

21 op. cit.

22 The general theory outlined in this paper is one that I have presented in lectures at various universities since 1909 as part of the general study of the forms of social structure. In arriving at the present formulation of it I have been helped by discussions with Dr Meyer Fortes.

11 Systems of kinship and marriage

I

A system of kinship and marriage can be looked at as an arrangement which enables persons to live together and co-operate with one another in an orderly social life. For any particular system as it exists at a certain time we can make a study of how it works. To do this we have to consider how it links persons together by convergence of interest and sentiment and how it controls and limits those conflicts that are always possible as the result of divergence of sentiment or interest. In reference to any feature of a system we can ask how it contributes to the working of the system. This is what is meant by speaking of its social function. When we succeed in discovering the function of a particular custom, i.e. the part it plays in the working of the system to which it belongs, we reach an understanding or explanation of it which is different from and independent of any historical explanation of how it came into existence. This kind of understanding of a kinship system as a working system linking human beings together in an orderly arrangement of interactions, by which particular customs are seen as functioning parts of the social machinery, is what is aimed at in a synchronic analytic study. In such an analysis we are dealing with a system as it exists at a certain time, abstracting as far as possible from any changes that it may be undergoing. To understand a process of change we must make a diachronic study. But to do this we must first learn all that we possibly can about how the system functioned before the changes that we are investigating occurred. Only then can we learn something of their possible causes and see something of their actual or probable effects. It is only when changes are seen as changes in or of a functioning system that they can be understood.

II

We have first of all to try to get a clear idea of what is a kinship system or system of kinship and marriage. Two persons are kin when one is descended from the other, as, for example, a grandchild is descended from a grandparent, or when they are both descended from a common ancestor. Persons are cognatic kin or cognates when they are descended from a common ancestor or ancestress counting descent through males and females.

The term 'consanguinity' is sometimes used as an equivalent of 'kinship' as above defined, but the word has certain dangerous implications which must be avoided. Consanguinity refers properly to a physical relationship, but in kinship we have to deal with a specifically social relationship. The difference is clear if we consider an illegitimate child in our own society. Such a child has a 'genitor' (physical father) but has no 'pater' (social father). Our own word 'father' is ambiguous because it is assumed that normally the social relationship and the physical relationship will coincide. But it is not essential that they should. Social fatherhood is usually determined by marriage. The dictum of Roman law was *pater est quem nuptiae demonstrant*. There is an Arab proverb, 'Children belong to the man to whom the bed belongs'. There was a crude early English saying, 'Whoso boleth my kyne, ewere calf is mine'. Social fatherhood as distinct from physical fatherhood is emphasized in the Corsican proverb, *Chiamu babba a chi mi da pane.*

The complete social relationship between parent and child may be established not by birth but by adoption as it was practised in ancient Rome and is practised in many parts of the world today.

In several regions of Africa there is a custom whereby a woman may go through a rite of marriage with another woman and thereby she stands in the place of a father (pater) to the offspring of the wife, whose physical father (genitor) is an assigned lover.

Kinship therefore results from the recognition of a social relationship between parents and children, which is not the same thing as the physical relation, and may or may not coincide with it. Where the term 'descent' is used in this essay it will refer not to biological but to social relations. Thus the son of an adopted person will be said to trace descent from the adopting grandparents.

The closest of all cognatic relationships is that between children of the same father and mother. Anthropologists have adopted the term 'sibling' to refer to this relationship: a male sibling is a brother, a female sibling is a sister.[1] The group consisting of a father and a mother and their children is an important one for which it is desirable to have a name. The term 'elementary family' will be used in this sense in this essay. (The term 'biological family' refers to something different, namely, to genetic relationship such as that of a mated sire and dam and their offspring, and is the concern of the biologist making a study of heredity. But it seems inappropriate to use the word 'family' in this connexion.) We may regard the elementary family as the basic unit of kinship structure. What is meant by this is that the relationships, of kinship or affinity, of any person are all connexions that are traced through his parents, his siblings, his spouse, or his children.

We must also recognize what may conveniently be called 'compound families'. Such a family results in our own society when a widower or widow with children by a first marriage enters into a second marriage into which children are born. This gives such relationships as those of half-siblings and of step-parent and stepchild. In societies in which polygynous marriages are permitted a compound family is formed when a man has two or more wives who bear him children. Families of this kind are, of course, common in Africa, and the difference between full siblings (children of the same father and mother) and half-siblings (children of one father by different mothers) is generally socially important.

Where there are truly polyandrous marriages, as among the Todas of south India, a family may consist of a woman with two or more husbands and her children.[2] But we should distinguish from this an arrangement by which the oldest of two or more brothers takes a wife, of whose children he will be the father (pater), and access to the wife for sexual congress is permitted to the man's younger brother until such time as he in turn is married. For it is not sexual intercourse that constitutes marriage either in Europe or amongst savage peoples. Marriage is a social arrangement by which a child is given a legitimate position in the society, determined by parenthood in the social sense.

The elementary family usually provides the basis for the formation of domestic groups of persons living together in intimate daily life. Of such groups there is a great variety. One common type is what may be called the 'parental' family in which the 'household' consists of the parents and their young or unmarried children. We are familiar with this type of family amongst ourselves, but it is also a characteristic feature of many primitive peoples. The group comes into existence with the birth of a first child in marriage; it continues

191

to grow by the birth of other children; it undergoes partial dis-
solution as the children leave it, and comes to an end with the death
of the parents. In a polygynous parental family there are two or more
mothers but only one father, and a mother with her children
constitute a separate unit of the group.

What is sometimes called a patrilineal extended family is formed
by a custom whereby sons remain in their father's family group,
bringing their wives to live with them, so that their children also
belong to the group. Among the Bemba of Northern Rhodesia there
is found a matrilineal extended family, a domestic group consisting
of a man and his wife with their daughters and the husbands and
children of the latter. The group breaks up, and new groups of the
same kind are formed, when a man obtains permission to leave his
parents-in-law, taking his wife and children with him.

Most men who live to maturity belong to two elementary families,
to one as son and brother, and to the other as husband and father.
It is this simple fact that gives rise to a network of relations
connecting any single person with many others. We can get a good
idea of this by considering what may be called orders of relationship
by kinship and marriage. Relationships of the first order are those
within the elementary family, viz. the relation of parent and child,
that of husband and wife, and that between siblings. Relationships
of the second order are those traced through one connecting person
such as those with father's father, mother's brother, stepmother
(father's wife), sister's husband, brother's son, wife's father, &c.
Those of the third order have two connecting links, as mother's
brother's son, father's sister's husband, and so on. So we can go on
to the fourth, fifth, or nth order. In each order the number of
relationships is greater than that in the preceding order. This
network of relationships includes both cognatic relationships and
relationships resulting from marriage, a person's own marriage, and
the marriages of his cognates.

The first determining factor of a kinship system is provided by the
range over which these relationships are effectively recognized for
social purposes of all kinds. The differences between wide-range and
narrow-range systems are so important that it would be well to take
this matter of range as the basis for any attempt at a systematic
classification of kinship systems. The English system of the present
day is a narrow-range system, though a wider range of relationship,
to second, third, or more distant cousins, is recognized in rural

districts than in towns. China, on the contrary, has a wide-range system. Some primitive societies have narrow-range systems, others have wide-range. In some of the latter a man may have several hundred recognized relatives by kinship and by marriage whom he must treat as relatives in his behaviour. In societies of a kind of which the Australian aborigines afford examples every person with whom a man has any social contact during the course of his life is a relative and is treated in the way appropriate to the relationship in which he or she stands.

Within the recognized range there is some method of ordering the relationships, and it is the method adopted for this purpose that gives the system its character. Later in this essay we shall consider some of the principles which appear in the ordering of relatives in different systems.

A part of any kinship system is some system of terms by which relatives of different kinds are spoken of or by which they are addressed as relatives. The first step in the study of a kinship system is to discover what terms are used and how they are used. But this is only a first step. The terminology has to be considered in relation to the whole system of which it is part.

There is one type of terminology that is usually referred to as 'descriptive'. In systems of this type there are a few specific terms for relatives of the first or second order and other relatives are indicated by compounds of these specific terms in such a way as to show the intermediate steps in the relation. It is necessary in any scientific discussion of kinship to use a system of this kind. Instead of ambiguous terms such as 'uncle' or 'cousin' we have to use more exact compound terms such as 'mother's brother', 'father's sister's son', and so on. When we have to deal with a relationship of the fifth order, such as 'mother's mother's brother's daughter's daughter', and still more in dealing with more distant relations, the system presents difficulties to those who are not accustomed to it. I have found it useful to invent a system of symbols to use instead of words.[3] Descriptive terminologies in this sense, i.e. those using specific terms and compounding them, are to be found in some African peoples, and illustrations are given in the section on the Yakö in [*African Systems*].[4]

In many systems of kinship terminology a single term is used for two or more kinds of relatives, who are thus included in a single terminological category. This may be illustrated by the English

193

system of the present day. The word 'uncle' is used for both the father's brother and the mother's brother and also by extension for the husband of an 'aunt' (father's sister or mother's sister). Similarly with such terms as 'nephew', 'niece', 'cousin', 'grandfather', &c.

The categories used in the terminology often, indeed usually, have some social significance. In English we do something which is unusual in kinship systems when we apply the term uncle (from Latin *avunculus,* mother's brother, literally 'little grandfather') to both the mother's brother and the father's brother. But this corresponds with the fact that in our social life we do not make any distinction between these two kinds of relatives. The legal relationship in English law, except for entailed estates and titles of nobility, is the same for a nephew and either of his uncles; for example, the nephew has the same claim to inheritance in case of intestacy over the estate of either. In what may be called the socially standardized behaviour of England it is not possible to observe any regular distinction made between the paternal and the maternal uncle. Reciprocally the behaviour of a man to his different kinds of nephews is in general the same. By extension, no significant difference is made between the son of one's mother's brother and the son of one's father's brother. In Montenegro, on the contrary, to take another European language, there is a different system. The father's brother is called *stric* and his wife is *strina,* while the mother's brother is *ujak* and his wife is *ujna,* and the social relations in which a man stands to his two kinds of uncles show marked differences.

In the eighteenth century Lafitau[5] reported the existence amongst American Indians of a system of terminology very unlike our own.

> Among the Iroquois and Hurons all the children of a cabin regard all their mother's sisters as their mothers, and all their mother's brothers as their uncles, and for the same reason they give the name of fathers to all their father's brothers, and aunts to all their father's sisters. All the children on the side of the mother and her sisters, and of the father and his brothers, regard each other mutually as brothers and sisters, but as regards the children of their uncles and aunts, that is, of their mother's brothers and father's sisters, they only treat them on the footing of cousins.

In the nineteenth century Lewis Morgan, while living with the Iroquois, was impressed by this method of referring to kin and set to work to collect kinship terminologies from all over the world. These he published in 1871 in his *Systems of Consanguinity and Affinity*. He found systems of terminology similar to that of the Iroquois in many parts of the world, and such systems he called 'classificatory'.

The distinguishing feature of a classificatory system of kinship terminology in Morgan's usage is that terms which apply to lineal relatives are also applied to certain collateral relatives. Thus a father's brother is 'father' and mother's sister is 'mother', while, as in the type described by Lafitau, there are separate terms for mother's brother and father's sister. Consequently in the next generation the children of father's brothers and mother's sisters are called 'brother' and 'sister' and there are separate terms for the children of mother's brothers and father's sisters. A distinction is thus made between two kinds of cousins, 'parallel cousins' (children of father's brothers and mother's sisters), who although 'collateral' in our sense are classified as 'brothers' and 'sisters', and 'cross-cousins' (children of mother's brothers and father's sisters). There is a similar distinction amongst nephews and nieces. A man classifies the children of his brothers with his own children, but uses a separate term for the children of his sisters. Inversely a woman classifies with her own children the children of her sisters but not those of her brothers. Classificatory terminologies of this kind are found in a great many African peoples.

There are other types of classificatory system, found less frequently, in which the term 'father' is applied to the brothers of the mother as well as to those of the father, and both mother's sister and father's sister are called 'mother'; or cousins, both parallel and cross-cousins, may all be treated as 'brothers' and 'sisters'.

In classificatory systems the principle of classification may be applied over a wide range of relationship. Thus a first cousin of the father, being his father's brother's son, whom he therefore calls 'brother', is classified with the father and the same term 'father' is applied to him. His son in turn, a second cousin, is called 'brother'. By this process of extension of the principle of classification nearer and more distant collateral relatives are arranged into a few categories and a person has many relatives to whom he applies the term 'father' or 'mother' or 'brother' or 'sister'.

The most important feature of these classificatory terminologies was pointed out long ago by Sir Henry Maine. 'The effect of the system', he wrote, 'is in general to bring within your mental grasp a much greater number of your kindred than is possible under the system to which we are accustomed.'[6] In other words, the classificatory terminology is primarily a mechanism which facilitates the establishment of wide-range systems of kinship.

There is more to it than this, however. Research in many parts of the world has shown that the classificatory terminology, like our own and other non-classificatory systems, is used as a method of dividing relatives into categories which determine or influence social relations as exhibited in conduct. The general rule is that the inclusion of two relatives in the same terminological category implies that there is some significant similarity in the customary behaviour due to both of them, or in the social relation in which one stands to each of them, while inversely the placing of two relatives in different categories implies some significant difference in customary behaviour or social relations. Some anthropologists make a great point of real or supposed exceptions to this rule, but they seem to forget that there can only be an exception when there is a general rule to which it is an exception.

There is a complication resulting from the fact that in classificatory systems there are necessarily distinctions between near and distant relatives included in the same category. Thus amongst the men referred to as 'father' the nearest relative is, of course, the actual 'own' father. After him come his brothers and after them his parallel first cousins and perhaps in some systems the husbands of the mother's sisters. So on to more and more distant relatives of the same terminological category. The attitude and behaviour of a person towards a particular relative is affected not only by the category to which he belongs but also by the degree of nearness or distance of the relationship. In classificatory systems there are many women whom a particular man calls 'sister'. In some systems he will be prohibited from marrying any of these women. In some others he may not marry any 'near' 'sister', i.e. any one of these women who is related to him within a certain degree of cognatic relationship, but may marry a more distant 'sister'.

Morgan tried to classify all terminological systems into two classes as being either classificatory or descriptive. But the ordinary English system should not be called descriptive and there are many other non-classificatory systems that are also not descriptive.[7] A people using a classificatory terminology may also make use of the descriptive principle or method in order to refer to the exact genealogical relation between two persons.[8] The study of kinship terminologies is valuable because they frequently, or indeed usually, reveal the method of ordering relationships.

The reality of a kinship system as a part of a social structure consists of the actual social relations of person to person as exhibited in their interactions and their behaviour in respect of one another. But the actual behaviour of two persons in a certain relationship (father and son, husband and wife, or mother's brother and sister's son) varies from one particular instance to another. What we have to seek in the study of a kinship system are the norms. From members of the society we can obtain statements as to how two persons in a certain relationship ought to behave towards one another. A sufficient number of such statements will enable us to define the ideal or expected conduct. Actual observations of the way persons do behave will enable us to discover the extent to which they conform to the rules and the kinds and amount of deviation. Further, we can and should observe the reactions of other persons to the conduct of a particular person or their expressions of approval or disapproval. The reaction or judgement may be that of a person who is directly or personally affected by the conduct in question or it may be the reaction or judgement of what may be called public opinion or public sentiment. The members of a community are all concerned with the observance of social usage or rules of conduct and judge with approval or disapproval the behaviour of a fellow member even when it does not affect them personally.

A kinship system thus presents to us a complex set of norms, of usages, of patterns of behaviour between kindred. Deviations from the norm have their importance. For one thing they provide a rough measure of the relative condition of equilibrium or disequilibrium in the system. Where there is a marked divergence between ideal or expected behaviour and the actual conduct of many individuals this is an indication of disequilibrium; for example, when the rule is that a son should obey his father but there are notably frequent instances of disobedience. But there may also be a lack of equilibrium when there is marked disagreement amongst members of the society in formulating the rules of conduct or in judgements passed on the behaviour of particular persons.

In attempting to define the norms of behaviour for a particular kind of relation in a given system it is necessary to distinguish different elements or aspects. As one element in a relation we may recognize the existence of a personal sentiment, what may be called the affective element. Thus we may say that in most human societies a strong mutual affection is a normal feature of the relation of mother and child, or there may be in a particular society a typical or normal emotional attitude of a son to his father. It is very important to remember that this affective element in the relation between relatives by kinship or marriage is different in different societies.

We may distinguish also an element that it is convenient to refer to by the term 'etiquette', if we may be permitted to give a wide extension of meaning to that word. It refers to conventional rules as to outward behaviour. What these rules do is to define certain symbolic actions or avoidances which express some important aspect of the relation between two persons. Differences of rank are given recognition in this way. In some tribes of South Africa it would be an extreme, and in fact unheard of, breach of the rules of propriety for a woman to utter the name of her husband's father.

An important element in the relations of kin is what will here be called the jural element, meaning by that relationships that can be defined in terms of rights and duties. Where there is a duty there is a rule that a person should behave in a certain way. A duty may be positive, prescribing actions to be performed, or negative, imposing the avoidance of certain acts. We may speak of the 'performance' of a positive duty and the 'observance' of a negative duty. The duties of *A* to *B* are frequently spoken of in terms of the 'rights' of *B*. Reference to duties or rights are simply different ways of referring to a social relation and the rules of behaviour connected therewith.

In speaking of the jural element in social relations we are referring to customary rights and duties. Some of these in some societies are subject to legal sanctions, that is, an infraction can be dealt with by a court of law. But for the most part the sanctions for these customary rules are what may be called moral sanctions sometimes supplemented by religious sanctions.

There are, first, what we may call personal rights and duties, rights *in personam* in legal terminology. *A* has a right *in personam* in relation to *B* when *A* can claim from *B* the performance of a certain duty. The right and the duty are both determinate. Thus, in the relation between an African husband and his wife each of the partners has personal rights imposing duties upon the other. Those personal rights and duties that form a most important part of relations by kinship and marriage are different from those established by contract or in a contractual relationship. In such a relationship a person accepts a certain definite obligation or certain obligations towards another. When the specific obligations on both sides have been fulfilled the contractual relation is terminated. But relations of kinship are not of this kind. They are not entered into voluntarily and they normally continue throughout life. It is true that a marital relationship is entered into; but it is not a contractual relationship between husband and wife; it is best described as a union.[9] It may be terminated by death, but in some societies not even then (witness the custom of the levirate by which a woman continues to bear children for her husband after he is dead); where divorce is recognized it may be terminated by that means. But the rights and duties of husband and wife are not like the obligations defined in a contract; they are incident to the relationship in the same sort of way as the rights and duties of parents and children.

We must distinguish from personal rights (*jus in personam*) what are designated rights *in rem*. Such a right is not a claim in relation to a certain particular person but a right 'against all the world'. The most characteristic form of such rights is in relation to things. The right which I have over something which I possess is infringed if someone steals it or destroys it or damages it. The use of the legal term *jus in rem* implies that in certain circumstances a person may be treated as a thing (*res*).[10]

> Thus when a father or master brings an action for the detention of, or for injuries inflicted upon, his child or apprentice, or when a husband sues for injuries inflicted upon his wife, the child, apprentice, and wife are in fact held to be *things*. The action is not brought in pursuance of the legal rights of the child, apprentice, or wife.

I shall refer to these rights (*in rem*) over persons as 'possessive rights', but it must be remembered that the term is used in this special sense.

In the formation of systems of kinship and marriage these possessive rights over persons are of great importance. Thus in most African systems a husband has possessive rights in relation to his wife. His rights are infringed, i.e. he suffers a wrong, if a man commits adultery with her or if someone kills her or abducts her. Later in this essay we shall have to consider the subject of possessive rights over children. It should be noted that possessive rights over persons can be shared by a number of persons or may be held collectively by a definite group of persons, just as may possessive rights over land or other property.

A kinship system is therefore a network of social relations which constitutes part of that total network of social relations which is the social structure. The rights and duties of relatives to one another are part of the system and so are the terms used in addressing or referring to relatives.

By using the word 'system' we make an assumption, for the word implies that whatever it is applied to is a complex unity, an organized whole. This hypothesis has already received a considerable measure of verification by anthropological studies. But we must distinguish between a stable system which has persisted with relatively little change for some period of time and the unstable condition of a society which is undergoing rapid change. It is in the former, not in the latter, that we may expect to find some fair degree of consistency and congruence amongst the items that make up the whole.

III

In this and following sections the more important structural principles which are found in kinship systems will be briefly indicated.

Two persons who are kin are related in one or other of two ways: either one is descended from the other, or they are both descended from a common ancestor. It is to be remembered that 'descent' here refers to the social relationship of parents and children, not to the physical relation. Kinship is thus based on descent, and what first determines the character of a kinship system is the way in which descent is recognized and reckoned.

One principle that may be adopted is the simple cognatic principle. To define the kin of a given person his descent is traced back a certain number of generations, to his four grandparents, his eight great-grandparents, or still farther, and all descendants of his recognized ancestors, through both females and males, are his cognates. At each generation that we go backwards the number of ancestors is double that of the preceding generation, so that in the eighth generation a person will have sixty-four pairs of ancestors (the great-grandparents of his great-great-grandparents). It is therefore obvious that there must be some limit to tracing kinship in this way.

The limit may simply be a practical one depending on the inability to trace the genealogical connexions, or there may be a theoretically fixed limit beyond which the genealogical connexion does not count for social purposes.

Another way of ordering the kindred may be illustrated by the system of ancient Rome. Within the body of a person's recognized cognates certain are distinguished as agnates. Cognates are agnates if they are descendants by male links from the same male ancestor.[11] In the Roman system there was the strongest possible emphasis on agnatic kinship, i.e., on unilineal descent through males.

In some other societies there is a similar emphasis on unilineal descent through females. With such a system a person distinguishes from the rest of his cognates those persons who are descended by female links only from the same female ancestress as himself. We can speak of these as his matrilineal kin.

There are few, if any, societies in which there is not some recognition of unilineal descent, either patrilineal (agnatic) or matrilineal or both. Thus in the modern English system surnames descend in the male line. In many countries, in a mixed marriage, children acquire by birth the nationality of the father, not that of the mother. But what matters in the study of any society is the degree of emphasis on the unilineal principle and how it is used.

One important way in which the unilineal principle may be used is in the formation of recognized lineage groups as part of the social structure. An agnatic lineage consists of an original male ancestor and all his descendants through males of three, four, five, or n generations. The lineage group consists of all the members of a lineage alive at a given time. A woman belongs to the lineage of her father, but her children do not. With matrilineal reckoning the lineage consists of a progenetrix and all her descendants through females. A man belongs to his mother's lineage, but his children do not. Lineage groups, agnatic or matrilineal, are of great importance in the social organization of many African peoples.

A lineage of several generations in depth, i.e. back to the founding ancestor or ancestress, will normally be divided into branches. In an agnatic lineage of which the founding ancestor has two sons each of them may become the founder of a branch consisting of his descendants in the male line. The two branches are united by the fact that their founders were brothers. As a lineage continues and increases the branching process continues, resulting in a large and complex organization. In some parts of China we find in one village a body of persons all having the same name and tracing their descent in the male line to a single ancestor who may have lived eight or nine hundred years ago. This is therefore a very large lineage which may number several hundred living persons. Genealogical records of the whole lineage are usually preserved and are sometimes printed for the use of the families of the lineage. There is a complex ramification of branches. An important feature of the Chinese system is the maintaining of the distinction of generations. A common method of giving names is one by which a man has three names; the first is the lineage or family name; the second indicates the generation to which he belongs; the third is his distinctive personal name. From the second part of the name any member of the lineage can tell to which generation any particular individual belongs.

What is here called a branch of a lineage is, of course, itself a lineage. A lineage of ten generations may include two or more branches of nine generations and one of these may contain two or more of eight, and so on. A lineage of several generations includes dead as well as living. We may conveniently use the term 'lineage group' to refer to a group formed of the members of a lineage who are alive at a particular time. Lineage groups as thus defined are important as components of the social structure in many African societies. A lineage group that is socially important may itself consist of smaller groups (branch lineages) and it may itself be part of a more extended and recognized group formed of related lineages.

It is desirable to illustrate by examples the differences in the ordering of kindred as the result of relative emphasis on the cognatic principle or on the unilineal principle. As an example of a cognatic system we may take the kinship system of the Teutonic peoples as it was at the beginning of history. This was based on a widely extended recognition of kinship traced through females as well as males. The Anglo-Saxon word for kinsfolk was *maeg* (*magas*). A man owed loyalty to his 'kith and kin'. Kith were one's friends by vicinage, one's neighbours; kin were persons descended from a common ancestor. So, for 'kith and kin' Anglo-Saxon could say 'his magas and his frŷnd', which is translated in Latin as *cognati atque amici*.

The arrangement of kin by degrees of nearness or distance was based on sib-ship (English *sib,* German *Sippe*). A man's sib were all his cognates within a certain degree. One method of arranging the sib was by reference to the human body and its 'joints' (*glied*). The father and mother stand in the head, full brothers and sisters in the neck, first cousins at the shoulders, second cousins at the elbow, third cousins at the wrists, fourth, fifth, and sixth cousins at the joints of the fingers. Finally come the nails, at which would stand the seventh cousins. On one scheme these nail kinsmen (*nagel magas*) were not included in the sib, though they were recognized as kinsmen (*magas*) if known to be such. The sib therefore included all kinsfolk up to and including sixth cousins. They were the *sibgemagas,* the sib kinsfolk.[12]

It is evident that no two persons can have the same sib, though for two unmarried full brothers, *A* and *B,* every person who was sib to *A* was sib to *B,* and *A* and *B* were sib-kinsmen of one another. A person cannot be said to 'belong' to a sib or be a member of a sib in the sense in which he can be said to belong to a lineage or a clan or a village community.

The innermost circle of the sib of an individual included his father and mother, his brother and sister, and his son and daughter—the 'six hands of the sib'. Another circle that was recognized was that of relatives 'within the knee'. This word (*cneow*) seems to have referred to the elbow, so that kinsfolk 'within the knee' would include all the descendants of the eight great-grandparents.

The sib was thus an arrangement of kindred as it were in a series of concentric circles, with the person whose sib it was at the centre. One circle included all those kin with whom marriage was forbidden. It is difficult to discover exactly where this was. In some Teutonic systems and in ancient Wales it is said that the prohibition against marriage extended to 'the fifth degree'. This would seem to include all third cousins, but the matter is not quite clear.

Another way of reckoning degrees of kinship was by 'stocks'. There were first the four 'quarters' of the sib (*klüfte,* in Frisian), the four stocks of the grandparents, each consisting of the descendants of one of the four pairs of great-grandparents. The wider sib included the eight stocks (*fechten* or *fange*) of the great-grandparents, each consisting of the descendants of one of the eight pairs of great-great-grandparents. The eight stocks (Old High German *ahta,* Old Norse *oett*) therefore included all kinsfolk as far as third cousins.

In the Middle Ages another method of reckoning was adopted, the parentelic system (Latin *parentela*). A person's sib was arranged in five parenteles: (1) his own descendants; (2) all descendants of his parents (excluding 1); (3) all descendants of his two pairs of grandparents (excluding 1 and 2); (4) all descendants of his four pairs of great-grand-parents (excluding 1, 2, and 3); (5) all descendants of his eight pairs of great-great-grandparents (excluding 1, 2, 3, and 4). This system seems to have been used principally for regulating inheritance. Within a parentele the degree of relationship was fixed by the greater or smaller distance from the common ancestor. Thus the uncle is more nearly related than his son, the cousin. But nephews (in the second parentele) are more nearly related than uncles (in the third). Both the 'stock' and the parentelic method of reckoning seem to go only as far as the wrist 'joint', i.e. as far as third cousins on both sides. They include, therefore, only part of the total sib.

In more recent times the present method of reckoning by cousinage was introduced. It has been suggested that the system of reckoning by first, second, third cousins originated in Spain and Portugal as a result of Teutonic invasions. In England this reckoning by cousins has replaced the older system of the sib.

'Sib' may be defined as meaning computable cognatic relationship for definite social purposes. We have seen that it was used for fixing the degrees within which marriage was forbidden. After the introduction of Christianity the relation between godparents and godchildren was included under sib. The godfather and godmother were 'god-sib' (modern 'gossip') to their godchildren and marriage between them was forbidden. Sib-ship also regulated the inheritance of property. Persons who were not related to a deceased person within a certain degree had no claim to inherit.

Where the functioning of the Teutonic sib can be best studied is in the customs relating to wergild, which was the indemnity that was required when one person killed another. It was paid by the person who had killed and his sib, and was received by the sib of the deceased. When the system was in full force the number of kinsmen who might be called on to contribute to the payment or who might receive a share of it was considerable. Theoretically it seems to have extended in some communities as far as sixth cousins on both sides, i.e. to all the 'joints' but not to the nail. But practically, and in some instances in theory, duties and claims seem to have been effective only as far as fourth cousins. There were laws or rules fixing the total amount of the wergild and the amounts or shares to be contributed or shared by each class of kinsfolk. The nearest kin paid and received most, the most distant paid and received least.[13]

The payment of wergild was an indemnity for homicide paid to those persons who had possessive rights (rights *in rem*) over the person who was killed. In the Teutonic system these rights were held by the cognatic relatives of the slain man by what was essentially a system similar to partnership. Each relative held as it were a share in the possession, and the consequent claim for indemnity and the share of any relative depended on the nearness of the relation so that, for example, the share claimed by the second cousins was twice that belonging to third cousins.

We have now to ask what use was made of the unilineal principle in the Teutonic systems. A man's kin were divided into those of the spear side (his paternal kin) and those of the spindle side (his maternal kin). In some of the Teutonic systems relatives on the father's side paid or received twice as much as those on the mother's side in a wergild transaction. This was so in the England of King Alfred. Similarly in ancient Welsh (British) law the *galanas* (the Celtic term for wergild) was paid two-thirds by paternal kinsmen and one-third by maternal, up to the fifth cousin, but not including the son of the fifth cousin or the sixth cousin. So far as the Teutonic peoples are concerned this may have been a late development. But in any case this did not mean the recognition of unilineal descent, but only that a father's sister's son was a nearer relative than a mother's sister's son.

Amongst some at least of the Teutonic peoples there existed large house-communities under the control of a house-father or house-lord, of the type of what it is usual to call the patriarchal family. Sons continued to live with their father under his rule and daughters usually joined their husbands elsewhere. But although the patrilineal principle was general or usual, it was not always strictly adhered to. Thus in the Icelandic *Nyal's Saga* the house-community of old Nyal included not only his wife Bergthora and his three married sons but also a daughter's husband, and, with children, men-servants, and others the household numbered some fifty persons.

The patrilineal principle also appears in the preference given to sons over daughters in the inheritance of land. But in default of sons, daughters might inherit land in some Teutonic societies. It appears that the principle of unilineal descent was only used to a limited extent in the Teutonic system.

About the Teutonic system two pseudo-historical theories have been advanced. One is that these peoples in prehistoric times had a system of matriarchy, which, whatever else it may or may not mean, implies an emphasis on unilineal descent through females. As evidence is quoted the statement of Tacitus that amongst the Germans the mother's brother was an important relative.[14]

The other theory is that in prehistoric times the Teutonic peoples had a system of patriarchy emphasizing agnatic descent. This is a deduction from the general theory that originally all the Indo-European peoples had a patriarchal system. For neither theory is there any historical evidence.

An example of an arrangement of relations of kinship on the basis of unilineal descent may be taken from the Masai of East Africa. Though the kinship system of the Masai has not been adequately studied, the arrangement of the various kin can be seen in the terminology which has been recorded by Hollis.[15]

The terminology is classificatory. The father, the father's brother, and the father's father's brother's son are called by the same term, *menye*. The sons and daughters of these men are called 'brother' and 'sister' (*ol-alashe* and *eng-anashe*). To all the children of men he calls 'brother' a man applies the same terms as to his own son and daughter (*ol-ayoni* and *en-dito*). All these persons belong to a man's own agnatic lineage (descendants of the father's father's father). We do not know how far the recognition of the lineage connexion is extended, but for our present purpose this does not matter.[16]

A feature of the Masai system is that these terms for 'father', 'brother', 'sister', 'son', 'daughter', though used as classificatory terms, are not applied except to a man's agnatic kindred. Thus while in some societies with a classificatory terminology[17] the mother's sister's husband is called 'father' and her children are 'brother' and 'sister', this is not so in Masai. Thus the Masai terminology emphasizes the distinction between agnatic and other kindred.

It is of some significance that the distinction between agnatic and other kin is not carried back into the generations of the grandparents and great-grandparents. Male relatives of the second and third ascending generations on both the father's and the mother's side are *ol-akwi* and their wives and sisters are *okoi*. Similarly, and reciprocally, the terms *ol-akwi* (grandson) and *eng-akwi* (granddaughter) are applied to daughters' children as well as sons' children and to the grandchildren, through sons or daughters, of any 'brother' of the lineage.

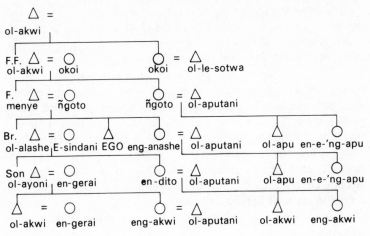

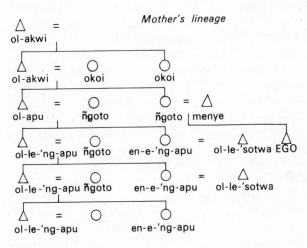

Figure 1 Masai kinship terminology

The emphasis on the agnatic lineage also appears in the fact that there are certain terms which apply only to women who have come into the lineage by marriage: *e-sindani* for the wife of any 'brother', and *en-gerai* for the wife of any 'son' or 'grandson' of the lineage.

Let us consider the women of a man's own lineage of his own and

207

the preceding generation. The sisters of the men he calls 'father' are referred to descriptively (*eng-anashe-menye*) or the term for 'mother' (*ñgoto*) is applied to them. The husband of a 'father's sister' or a 'sister' is called *ol-aputani,* which simply means 'relative by marriage', but their children are called *ol-apu* and *en-e-'ng-apu.* A man's *ol-apu* is his 'sister's son' or 'father's sister's son' and is connected with the man's own lineage through the mother. The children of his *ol-apu* are again his kin, *ol'le-'ng-apu* and *en-e-'ng-apu,* and the son of *ol-le-'ng-apu* is again *ol-le-'ng-apu.* The cognatic relationship is continued from father to son in the male line. But the offspring of an *en-e-'ng-apu* (sister's daughter, father's sister's daughter, sister's son's daughter, &c.) are *ol-le-'sotwa* and *en-e-sotwa.* It is evident from the account given by Hollis that these two terms do not refer to any definite relation of kinship but simply mean 'relative'. The husband of an *en-e-'ng-apu* is not *ol-aputani* (relative by marriage) but simply *ol-le-'sotwa.*

A man is connected through his mother with her agnatic lineage. He calls his mother's brother *ol-apu.* This is therefore a self-reciprocal term used between mother's brother and sister's son. The relationship, according to Hollis, is an important one. The mother's brother's son and daughter, the cross-cousins, are *ol-le-'ng-apu* and *en-e-'ng-apu.* Once again the relationship is continued within the lineage, i.e. through males but not through females. The son and daughter of the mother's brother's son are *ol-le-'ng-apu* and *en-e-'ng-apu,* but the children of the mother's brother's daughter are simply *sotwa* relatives. Specific kinship is also not continued through the mother's sisters, whose children are *sotwa* relatives.

A man also recognizes the mother's brother of his father as a kinsman and calls him *ol-apu,* as he does his own mother's brother. This man would call him *ol-le-'ng-apu* since he is his sister's son's son. Hollis does not inform us what a man calls his father's mother's brother's son, but it seems likely that he would be *ol-le-'ng-apu.*

The emphasis on agnatic descent is also observable in the relation of a man to his wife's lineage. All the male members of the lineage, including the wife's father's father and the wife's father's father's brother and all their male descendants in the male line, are *ol-aputani.* On the other hand, while the wife's father's sister is *eng-aputani,* the relationship does not continue and her children are only *sotwa.* In the wife's mother's lineage she is *eng-aputani* and her brothers and sisters are *ol-aputani* and *eng-aputani,* but the relationship continues no farther and the wife's mother's brother's children become *sotwa*.

The Masai kinship terminology thus presents an interesting and illuminating example of a system in which the emphasis is placed on agnatic lineage. The most important kinship relations of a man are evidently those with the members of his own agnatic lineage. But the children of his sister and father's sister (female members of his lineage) are persons with whom his kinship is important. The kinship connexion is maintained in the male line but not in the female line. The other side of this relationship is that of a man with his mother's lineage. Here again he is related to the members of the lineage, his mother's sister and his mother's brother, but the relationship only continues in the male line to the children and the son's children of his mother's brother, and not to the children of his mother's sister or to the children of his mother's brother's daughter. By marriage he is related to his wife's agnatic lineage, to female members as well as male, and again the relationship is only continued in the male line. His relationship to his wife's mother is continued to her brothers and sisters but not to the rest of her lineage.

The emphasis on the agnatic line is shown clearly in the fact that the husband of the father's sister is *ol-aputani,* a relative by marriage, and her children are kinsfolk, while the husband of a mother's sister, far from being a 'father', as he is in some systems, is merely a relative (*sotwa*), as also are her children. The general principle is that relationships, including those established through females or by marriage, continue in the male line only.

An interesting and distinctive feature of the Masai system is the use of the terms *ol-le-'sotwa* and *en-e-sotwa.* Hollis tells us that *sotwa* means 'peace' or 'relative'. It does not connote any definite kind or degree of relationship either by kinship or by marriage. Thus *sotwa* relatives may marry. Hollis states that the restrictions on marriage are two: (1) a man may not marry a woman of his own sub-clan, which is a patrilineal group; (2) 'No man may marry a nearer relation than a third cousin, and then only if the terms of address used are *ol-le-sotwa* and *en-e-sotwa.'* This statement as it stands implies that there are certain *sotwa* relatives who may not be married, for example, the mother's sister's daughter and the mother's mother's sister's daughter's daughter. On such a point as this it would be better if we had more precise information. The fact is clear, however, that the *sotwa* relationship is not itself a bar to marriage while other kinship relations are.

The Masai system arranges a man's kin into a few large categories.(1) His agnatic relatives belonging to his own lineage (or sub-clan); (2) his *apu* kin, if we may call them so, the descendants of those women of his lineage who are his father's sisters or his sisters, and on the other hand, the members of the mother's lineage: the relationship is established through a female and is then continued in the male line only; (3) his *aputani* relatives, i.e. relatives by marriage, either the kin of his wife or persons who have married one of his kinswomen; (4) those relatives to whom he applies the classificatory terms 'grandfather', 'grandmother', 'grandson', 'grand-daughter', some of whom belong to his lineage while others do not; (5) his *sotwa* relatives, a sort of fringe of persons not belonging to the first four classes, with each of whom some indirect connexion can be traced: they are vaguely his 'relatives', persons with whom he should be at peace.

The structural difference between organization by sib and by lineage can be readily seen by comparing a 'stock' with a 'lineage'. A 'stock' includes all the descendants of a man and his wife counting descent through females as well as males. In the sib system a man belongs to each of the eight stocks of his eight pairs of great-great-grandparents and all descendants of these ancestors are his kin. With a patrilineal lineage system he belongs to a lineage which includes the descendants of a male ancestor counting through males only. The persons of his mother's lineage are his kin, but he does not belong to the lineage.

We are here concerned with the ways in which different societies provide an ordering of the kin of an individual within a certain range, wide or narrow. One way is by tracing kinship equally and similarly through males and through females. There is a close approximation to this in modern European societies and in some primitive societies. In various societies we find some greater or less emphasis placed on unilineal descent, but there are many different ways in which this principle can be applied. In the Masai system there is marked emphasis on the male line, so that the most important of a man's social connexions are with the members of his own agnatic lineage and with those of his mother's agnatic lineage and those of the agnatic lineage of his wife. In other societies there may be a similar emphasis on the female line, so that a man's chief relations through his father are with the latter's matrilineal lineage. There are also systems in Africa and elsewhere in which unilineal descent through males is given recognition and also unilineal descent through females.

There are a great variety of ways in which the unilineal principle may be used. It is therefore only misleading to talk about matrilineal and patrilineal societies as was formerly the custom of anthropologists. Some more complex and systematic classification is needed to represent the facts as they are.

IV

Reference has already been made to the classificatory systems of kinship terminology which are found in very many African peoples. The theory of pseudo-history is that this method of referring to kin is a 'survival' from a time in the past when the family as it now exists had not made its appearance. In those remote days it is imagined that there existed a system of 'group-marriage' in which a group of men cohabited with a group of women and when a child was born all the men were equally its fathers and all the women equally its mothers. This fantastic example of pseudo-history was put forward by Lewis Morgan in his *Ancient Society* (1878).

The theory here proposed is not in any way concerned with the origins of classificatory terminologies, which are found widely distributed in Asia, Africa, America, and Australasia, but with their social functions. It starts from the simple and obvious postulate that in order to have a system of kinship it is necessary to have some way of distinguishing and classifying a person's kin, and that one very obvious and natural means of doing this is through the kinship nomenclature. We give the same name to a number of things when we think that in some important respect they are similar. We use in English the same name—uncle—for the mother's brother and the father's brother because we think of them as similar, as relatives of the same kind. In a classificatory system a man uses the same term for his father and his father's brother because he thinks of them as relatives of one general kind.

The principle on which the classificatory terminology is based may be called the principle of the unity of the sibling group. This refers not to the internal unity of the group as shown in the relations of its members to one another but to the fact that the group may constitute a unity for a person outside it and connected with it by a specific relation to one of its members. Thus a son may, in a

211

particular system, be taught to regard his father's sibling group as a united body with whom he is related as their 'son'.

The sibling group, i.e. the body of brothers and sisters of common parentage, has its own internal structure. In the first place there are the very important social distinctions between the sexes, which divide the brothers from the sisters. These distinctions are differently exhibited in usages in different societies, and the relation between brother and sister is therefore an important feature of any particular kinship system. Secondly there is the order of birth, which is translated into social terms in the distinction of senior and junior. The importance of this distinction in African tribes is shown by the existence of separate terms for 'senior brother' and 'junior brother'. In a polygynous family there is the further difference between full siblings and half-siblings, and in African peoples this is usually, if not always, important.

Within an elementary family, i.e. amongst full brothers, the discrimination between older and younger siblings is made on the basis of order of birth. But in a polygynous compound family the wives may be unequal in rank, the great wife, or the first wife, having a higher rank than others. In the Kaffir tribes of the Transkei a son of a wife of inferior rank will apply to all the sons of the great wife (his half-brothers) the term used for 'elder brother' even when they are younger than himself. The two words are therefore better translated as 'senior brother' and 'junior brother'.

In these same tribes (which have a classificatory terminology) the sons of an older brother of the father must be called 'senior brother' irrespective of actual age, and those of the father's younger brother will be called 'junior brother'. Amongst the Yao, who have matri-lineal descent, not only the sons of the older brother of the father, but also those of the older sister of the mother, must be called 'senior brother' (Sanderson).

The main principle of the classificatory terminology is a simple one. If A and B are two brothers and X stands in a certain relation to A, then he is regarded as standing in a somewhat similar relation to B. Similarly if A and B are two sisters. In any particular system the principle is applied over a certain range. The similarity of the relation is indicated by applying a single term of relationship to A and B. The father's brother is called 'father' and the mother's sister is called 'mother'. The father's father's brother is regarded as similar to the father's father and therefore his son is also called 'father'. Once the principle is adopted it can be applied and extended in different ways. However the principle is used, it makes possible the recognition of a large number of relatives and their classification into a relatively few categories. Within a single category relatives are distinguished as nearer or more distant.

As a general rule, to which, of course, there may be exceptions, towards all persons to whom a given term of relationship is applied there is some element of attitude or behaviour by which the relationship is given recognition, even if it is only some feature of etiquette or an obligation to exhibit friendliness or respect. Rules of behaviour are more definite and more important for near relatives than for more distant ones.

It is a general characteristic of classificatory terminologies that the father's brother is called 'father' and the mother's sister 'mother'. When we come to the mother's brother and the father's sister, for these relatives there is a possible choice between two different structural principles. One may be called the 'generation' principle. There are a few examples in Africa of peoples with classificatory systems who call the father's sister and the mother's brother's wife 'mother'. The Masai provide one example, and there are others. This means that female cognates of the first ascending generation are placed in a single category. It is only rarely, and not, so far as I am aware, anywhere in Africa, that the mother's brother is called 'father'. Where this principle is used the emphasis is on generation and sex.

The other principle is that of the unity of the sibling group. The father's sister belongs to the father's sibling group and therefore she is a relative of the same general kind as the father and the father's brother, and similarly the mother's brother is a relative of the same kind as the mother and her sister. This way of thinking about uncles and aunts is shown in the kinship terminology of many African societies. Writing about the Kongo, Father van Wing says: 'All the sisters and brothers of the mother are considered as the mothers (*ngudi*) of the Mukongo (*ngudi nsakela* or *ngudi nkasi*) while all the brothers and sisters of the father (*se*) are considered by the Mukongo as fathers (*mase*).'[18] The term for 'mother's brother' in many Bantu tribes is *umalume*, which is literally 'male mother', *uma* being the term for 'mother' and *lume* meaning 'male'. Similarly, in a number of African peoples the father's sister is referred to by the term for 'father' or is called 'female father'. Examples are the Kitara, the Ndau, the Yao, the Huana, and there are others.

213

To some Europeans this use of the terms 'female father', 'male mother' may seem the height of absurdity. The reason for this is simply a confusion of thought resulting from the ambiguity of our own words for father and mother. There is the purely physical relation between a child and a woman who gives birth to it or the man who begets it. The same relation exists between a colt and its dam and sire. But the colt does not have a father and a mother. For there is the social (and legal) relation between parents and children which is something other than the physical relation. In this sense an illegitimate child in England is a child without a father. In the African tribes with which we are dealing it is the social and legal relationship that is connoted by the words which we have to translate 'father' and 'mother'. To call the father's sister 'female father' indicates that a woman stands in a social relation to her brother's son that is similar in some significant way to that of a father with his son. It is more exact, however, to say that a father's sister is regarded as a relative of the same kind as a father's brother, with such necessary qualifications as result from the difference of sex.

The principle of social structure with which we are here concerned is therefore one by which the solidarity and unity of the family (elementary or compound) is utilized to order and define a more extended system of relationships. A relationship to a particular person becomes a relation to that person's sibling group as a social unit. This shows itself in two ways. First, in some similarity in behaviour, as when the kind of behaviour that is required towards a father's brother is in some respects similar to that towards a father. Second, in the provision that in certain circumstances one relative may take the place of another, the two being siblings. Thus in some African societies the place of a father, a husband, or a grandfather may be taken by his brother. In the custom known as the sororate the place of a deceased wife is taken by her sister. In one form of the levirate the brother of a deceased man becomes the husband of the widow and the father of her children. Amongst the Hehe the grandmother plays an important part in the life of a child. This should be the child's own grandmother, but if she is dead her sister can take her place.[19]

Miss Earthy[20] says that amongst the Lenge the father's sister (*hahane,* female father) 'ranks as a feminine counterpart of the father, and sometimes acts as such, in conjunction with or in the absence of the father's brothers'. She may offer a sacrifice on behalf of her brother's child, in case of illness, in order that the child may recover. Such sacrifice would, of course, normally be made by the father or his elder brother.

The purpose of this section has only been to indicate the existence of a structural principle which is of great importance in a very large number of kinship systems not only in Africa but also in many other parts of the world. Where the principle influences the terminology of kinship it may appear in the form of a classificatory terminology. But the absence of such a terminology does not mean that the principle of the unity of the sibling group is not effectively present in the social structure and in the organization of norms of behaviour. The classificatory terminology in its most characteristic form is the utilization of the principle of the unity of the sibling group to provide a means for ordering relatives in a system of wide-range recognition of relationships.

V

Within the elementary family there is a division of generations; the parents form one generation, the children another. As a result, all the kin of a given person fall into generations in relation to him, and there are certain general principles that can be discovered in his different behaviour towards persons of different generations.

The normal relation between parents and children can be described as one of superordination and subordination. This results from the fact that children, at least during the early part of life, are dependent on their parents, who provide and care for them and exercise control and authority over them. Any relationship of subordination, if it is to work, requires that the person in the subordinate position should maintain an attitude of respect towards the other. The rule that children should not only love but should honour and obey their parents is, if not universal at least very general in human societies.

There is therefore a relation of social inequality between proximate generations, and this is commonly generalized so that a person is subordinate and owes respect to his relatives of the first ascending generation—that of his parents. To this rule there may be specific exceptions, for the mother's brother in some African societies, for example, or for the father's sister's husband in some societies in other parts of the world, whereby these relatives may be treated disrespectfully or with privileged familiarity. Such exceptions call for explanation.

The relation between the two generations is usually generalized to extend beyond the range of kinship. Some measure of respect for persons of the generation or age of one's parents is required in most if not all societies. In some East African societies this relation is part of the organization of the society into age-sets. Thus among the Masai sexual intercourse with the wife of a man belonging to one's father's age-set is regarded as a very serious offence amounting to something resembling incest. Inversely, so is sexual connexion with the daughter of a man of one's own age-set.

The social function of this relation between persons of two proximate generations is easily seen. An essential of an orderly social life is some considerable measure of conformity to established usage, and conformity can only be maintained if the rules have some sort and measure of authority behind them. The continuity of the social order depends upon the passing on of tradition, of knowledge and skill, of manners and morals, religion and taste, from one generation to the next. In simple societies the largest share in the control and education of the young falls to the parents and other relatives of the parents' generation. It is their authority that is or ought to be effective. All this is obvious, and it is unnecessary to dwell upon it.

But the further effects of this in the organization of the relations of generations are not always so immediately obvious. We shall be concerned in what follows with the relations between persons and their relatives of the second ascending generation, that of their grandparents.

If the exercise of authority on the one side and respect and obedience on the other were simply, or even primarily, a matter of relative age, we should expect to find these features markedly characteristic of the relations between grandparents and grandchildren. Actually we find most commonly something almost the opposite of this, a relation of friendly familiarity and almost of social equality.

In Africa generally there is a marked condition of restraint on the behaviour of children in the presence of their parents. They must not indulge in levity or speak of matters connected with sex. There is very much less restraint on the behaviour of grandchildren in the presence of their grandparents. In general also, in Africa as elsewhere, grandparents are much more indulgent towards their grandchildren than are parents to their children. A child who feels that he is being treated with severity by his father may appeal to his father's father.

The grandparents are the persons above all others who can interfere in the relations between parents and children. The possibility of this interference has important social functions. Elizabeth Brown remarks that 'in Hehe society the presence of the grandmother minimizes possible friction between mother and daughter'.[21] In any relation of subordination and superordination conflict is always possible. This is true of the relation of fathers and sons and of mothers and daughters in a great many societies. The son is subordinate to his father, but the latter is subordinate to his father in turn, and similarly with a mother and mother's mother. Control of the behaviour of parents towards their children therefore falls in the first place to their parents. In South Africa a man who is appealing to his ancestors for help, as when he is offering them a sacrifice, frequently, perhaps usually, makes his first appeal to his deceased father's father, and asks him to pass on the request to the spirit of his father and to the other ancestors.

In the passage of persons through the social structure which they enter by birth and leave by death, and in which they occupy successive positions, it is not, properly speaking, children who replace their parents, but those of the grandparents' generation are replaced by those of the grandchildren's generation. As those of the younger generation are moving into their positions of social maturity those of the older generation are passing out of the most active social life. This relation of the two generations is recognized in some African peoples. In East Africa, where age-sets are arranged in cycles, the cycles are such that a son's son may frequently belong to the same one as his father's father. This explains also some of the African customs as to the relation of a child to its great-grandparent. Rattray reports for the Ashanti that a great-grandchild is called 'grandchild don't touch my ear', and the touch on the ear of such a relative is said to cause speedy death. Remembering the way in which small infants frequently reach for the ear of anyone close to them, this is a way of indicating the existence of a social distance between men and the children of their grandchildren. In the normal organization of generations there is no place for any close definite relation between these two relatives. For any man the birth of children to his grandchildren is the sign that he is approaching the end of his life.

The relation between grandparents and grandchildren that has here been briefly indicated is institutionalized in various ways in African and other societies. There is a widespread custom of privileged familiarity between grandchildren and grandparents. The grandchild may tease his relative and joke at his expense. This custom of permitted disrespect to grandparents is found in tribes of Australia and North America as well as in many African peoples. A good example is one from the Oraons of India reported by· Sarat Chandra Roy.[22]

The replacement of grandparents by their grandchildren is in a way recognized in the widespread custom of giving a child the name of a grandparent. Amongst the Henga, when a child is born the husband is greeted with the words 'A father has been born to you today', having reference to the fact that the child will be given the name of its grandfather. A further step is taken in some peoples by the formation of a belief that in some sense the grandparent is 'reincarnated' in a grandchild.

One aspect of the structural principle with which we are here concerned is that one generation is replaced in course of time by the generation of their grandchildren. Another aspect of the same principle is that the two generations are regarded as being in a relation, not of superordination and subordination, but of simple friendliness and solidarity and something approaching social equality. This may sometimes result in what may be called the merging of alternate generations, a structural principle of fundamental importance in the native tribes of Australia and in some Melanesian peoples. A man with his 'father's fathers', his 'son's sons', and his 'brothers' in the classificatory sense form a social division over against his 'fathers' and 'sons', who constitute another division.

Where the principle makes itself apparent in some African peoples is in a peculiar feature of the kinship terminology, whereby the term that primarily means 'wife' is applied by a man to his granddaughters or his grandmothers, and a woman applies to her grandson the term meaning 'husband'. The custom has been reported for the Ganda, the Pende, the Ila, the Yao, the Ngonde, and the Henga. Thus amongst the Ngonde the term *nkasi* which is applied to the wife and to the brother's wife is also applied to all a man's 'granddaughters' in the classificatory sense (but not to the 'granddaughters' of his wife) and to the wives of his 'grandsons', own and classificatory. Inversely it is applied to the wives of the men who are called 'grandfather'. The real significance of this is that these women are thus merged with those of his own generation. That this is the real meaning of the custom may be seen by reference to the term *mwinangu* which Sanderson translates 'compeer' and which is applied primarily to persons of one's own generation and implies equality. 'For a grandson *mwisukulu-mwinangu* is always used in preference to *mwisukulu* by itself, and indicates that a grandson is treated as a "brother", a younger "brother" but an equal.' Similarly the term *wamyitu*, meaning 'kinsman', is used for relatives of one's own generation, and may also be used for any relative or connexion except the generation immediately above or below that of the speaker (e.g. father or son) as it implies a degree of intimacy not permitted with those degrees.[23]

The use of a term meaning 'wife' for a granddaughter must not be assumed to imply the existence of a custom of marriage with a granddaughter either in the present or in the past. Amongst the Ngonde and Henga such marriages are not permitted. But once the granddaughters and grandmothers have been included in one's own generation by this merging of alternate generations, the possibility of marriage suggests itself. There are therefore African tribes in which such marriages are regarded as permissible. It is said to be legal, though rare, amongst the Yao for a man to marry the daughter of his own child (Sanderson). Amongst the Kaonde a man may marry the daughter of his brother's son or of his brother's daughter, but may not marry the daughter of his sister's daughter (Melland). In the reverse direction, in the Ngonde tribe a man may be required to marry a 'grandmother' on the death of his 'grandfather', apparently in order to provide for her if she would otherwise be destitute.

There is therefore discoverable in African societies, as in many other societies in various parts of the world, a social structure based on relations of generation. Between two proximate generations the relation is normally one of essential inequality, authority, and protective care on the one side, respect and dependence on the other. But between the two generations of grandparents and grandchildren the relation is a contrasting one of friendly familiarity and near equality. The contrast between the two kinds of relation is itself an important part of the structural system and is emphasized in some of the accompanying institutions; for example, the contrast between restraint in the presence of a father or his brother and the freedom of joking with a grandfather. The way in which this structural principle provides for a condition of equilibrium in social relations is one deserving of careful investigation. There is not room to deal with it here.

In most African kinship terminologies no distinction is made

219

between grandparents on the father's side and those on the mother's side. We have seen that even in a system such as that of the Masai, where there is great emphasis on the distinction between agnatic and other cognatic relatives, this distinction is not made in the second ascending generation. This seems to be associated with a single general pattern of behaviour towards all those one calls 'grandfather' or 'grandmother', which does not, of course, exclude the existence of certain special relations, such as that of a man with his own father's father.

VI

In what might perhaps be called the normal use of the generation principle in kinship structure, the generations provide basic categories. Any category of relatives can be placed in one particular generation: uncles in the first ascending, nephews in the first descending, and so on. But in some terminologies a single term may be used for relatives of two or more generations. A study of instances of this serves to throw light on the principles involved in the various methods of ordering relationships.

In order to deal with this subject we have to consider the question of interpersonal rank or status in relationships. In a social relation two persons may meet as equal or approximately equal in rank, or one may be of superior rank to the other. Differences in rank may show themselves in many different forms. They are perhaps most easily seen in the rules of etiquette, or in an attitude of deference that the inferior is expected to show to his superior.

There may be inequality of rank within one generation. There are systems in Oceania and Africa in which a father's sister's son is superior in rank to his mother's brother's son. In a great number of systems an older brother, or a classificatory 'senior brother', is superior in rank to his junior. The difference in rank may be more emphasized in some systems than in others.

There seems to be universally some more or less marked inequality of rank between certain relatives belonging to two proximal generations, as between father and son, and there is some evidence of the existence of a tendency to extend this to all relationships between two such generations, the person who is senior by generation being superior to the one who is junior. But, as we shall see, this general tendency is sometimes overborne. We have already seen

that between the alternate generations (of grandparents and grandchildren) there is a widespread tendency to make the relationship one
of approximate equality.

A relationship of unequal rank is necessarily asymmetrical. A
symmetrical relationship is one in which each of the two persons
observes the same, or approximately the same, pattern of behaviour
towards the other. In an asymmetrical relationship there is one way
of behaviour for one of the persons and a different, complementary
behaviour for the other; as when a father exercises authority over a
son, and the son is deferential and obedient. Terminology can also
be symmetrical or asymmetrical. In the former case each applies the
same term of relationship to the other; in the latter there are two
different, reciprocal terms, as uncle—nephew. Where terminology in
a relationship is symmetrical it is frequently an indication that the
relationship is thought of as being approximately symmetrical in
respect of behaviour.

We sometimes find terms of relationship that have no generation
reference. An example is provided by the Masai term *sotwa,* which
may be applied to relatives of any generation. It refers to persons
who are 'relatives' in a general sense but do not belong to any one
of the specific categories into which nearer relatives are divided. It
corresponds to some extent to the Old English term 'sib', and it is
interesting that both these terms have reference to 'peace'; sib or
sotwa are those with whom one should live at peace.

The English 'cousin' can be used for kin of different generations,
and generation position has to be indicated by terms such as 'once
removed'. The word is derived from the Latin *consobrinus* (mother's
sister's son), and therefore originally had a generation reference to
one's own generation, but in the Middle Ages it seems to have been
regarded as equivalent to the Latin *consanguineus.*

The frequently observed absence of marked inequality between
grandparents and grandchildren may be occasionally reflected in the
terminology, either by the use of a single self-reciprocal term between
these relatives or by applying to grandparents and to grandchildren
a term that is normally used for relatives of one's own generation.
This has been noted in the last section.

An interesting example of a system in which terms having a
primary reference to one generation are applied to relatives of other
generations is provided by the Nandi of East Africa. The term *kamet*
refers in the first instance to the mother and her sisters (first

221

ascending generation). But the mother's brother's daughter is also called *kamet* and is addressed by the same term of address as the mother. Correspondingly the term *imamet* refers primarily to the mother's brother, but is also applied to the mother's brother's son. Further, the children of the mother's brother's son, who belong to the first descending generation, are also called 'mother's brother' and 'mother'.

The same feature appears amongst the Bari and the Kitara. In the former a single term *(mananye)* is used for the mother's brother, his children, and his son's children, and we may note that the wife of any male *mananye* is called 'grandmother' *(yakanye)*. Amongst the Kitara the mother's brother and his son are both called 'male mother' *(nyina rumi)* and the mother's brother's daughter is called 'little mother' *(nyina ento)* like the mother's sister. Reciprocally a man calls both his sister's son and his father's sister's son by the same term *mwhiwha*. There is a partial application of the same principle amongst the Masai, where the mother's brother is *ol-apu* and his children and his son's children are *ol-le-'ng-apu* and *en-e-'ng-apu*.

This peculiar type of terminology has been found in a number of societies in different parts of the world, and is called by anthropologists the Omaha type. Its widespread occurrence shows that it cannot be regarded as the product of some accident of history; we should seek some theoretical explanation. It can be regarded as a method of expressing and emphasizing the unity and solidarity of the patrilineal lineage group. A man belongs to a patrilineal lineage. He is closely connected with his mother's lineage, which plays an important part in his life, second only to that of his own. His connexion with that lineage, being through his own mother, is with the first ascending generation. By the terminology he treats all the members of that group, through three (or more) generations, beginning with that of his mother, as belonging to a single category; the females are 'mothers' to him and the males are 'mother's brothers'. For all these persons, and for the group as a whole, he is a 'sister's son'. Thus in its relation to this person the lineage of three generations is a unity; we can therefore speak of the structural principle that is applied in these systems as the principle of the unity of the lineage.

In systems of the Omaha type the principle is applied not only to the mother's lineage but also to other lineages with which a person is closely connected by some individual relationship. Amongst the

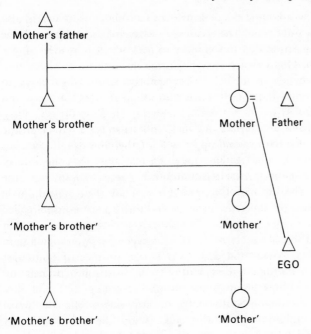

Masai, for example, all the members of the lineage of a man's wife, beginning with his wife's father's father, are his *aputani*.

In a previous section the classificatory terminology in general was interpreted as a way of recognizing the principle of the unity of the sibling group. The special Omaha form of the classificatory system is here interpreted as a way of recognizing the unity of the lineage group. Thus a single method of interpretation is applied throughout, and this gives a simplification or economy of theory. If the whole question were merely one of the use of terms of relationship the subject would not be of any importance; but it is here held that the terminology is used as a means of ordering relationships for social purposes, and of this there is already abundant evidence.[24]

For the purpose of the analysis that is to follow we must note here that in some of the tribes of this region of Africa there is a single self-reciprocal term for mother's brother and sister's son. In Masai this term is *ol-apu*. In Nandi the two relatives may each address the other as *mama*. This symmetrical terminology suggests that the social relation may also by symmetrical, i.e. that there is a single pattern of behaviour towards an *ol-apu* or a male *mama* whether he is a mother's brother or a sister's son. The accounts we have of these tribes do not permit the assertion that this is really so, though there is some slight indication in Hollis that it may be so for the Nandi.

The use of a symmetrical (self-reciprocal) terminology between mother's brother and sister's son is also found in some of the tribes of the Nuba Hills in Kordofan, namely, Heiban, Otoro, Tira, Mesakin, Koalib, and Nyima. All these tribes also use a self-reciprocal terminology for the relationship of wife's father and daughter's son, as do the Masai. Also, the first four of the Nuba tribes mentioned above use a self-reciprocal terminology between grandparent and grandchild. The use of self-reciprocal terms for these relationships puts relatives of different generations into one terminological category.

There is a special variety of the Omaha type of terminology found in the Shona, Ndau, and Shangana-Tonga peoples of Southern Rhodesia and Portuguese East Africa.[25] The most southerly tribe of the Shangana-Tonga group is the Ronga; according to Junod this tribe uses the common Southern Bantu term *malume* (literally 'male mother') for the mother's brother and his son, the reciprocal being *mupsyana,* which thus applies to the sister's child and the father's sister's child; the mother's brother's daughter is called *mamana* ('mother'). Thus the Ronga terminology is similar to that of the Kitara.

The other tribes of this cluster have a different system involving an extended use of the term for grandfather. The mother's brother is called 'grandfather'—*sekuru* in Shona, *tetekulu* in Ndau, *kokwana* in Lenge and other tribes of the Shangana-Tonga group; both the Shona and the Ndau terms are derived from a stem meaning 'father' and *kulu* or *kuru* meaning 'great'. The sons and son's sons of the mother's brother are also called 'grandfather'. The reciprocal of 'grandfather' is, of course, 'grandchild'—*muzukuru* in Shona, *muzukulu* in Ndau, *ntukulu* in Shangana-Tonga. This term, which is used by a man for the children of his son or daughter, is thus also applied to his father's sister's child and his sister's child, both of whom call him 'grandfather'. A man thus may have 'grandchildren' who are older than himself and 'grandfathers' who are younger.

In these tribes, as in the Ronga, the daughter and the son's daughter of the mother's brother are called 'mother'—*mayi* or *mayi nini* (little mother) in Shona, *mai* in Ndau, *manana* in Shangana-

Tonga. The children of these women are therefore called 'siblings' (*makwabu* or *makweru* in Shangana-Tonga).

This terminology expresses the unity of the mother's lineage. All the female members of a man's mother's lineage in her own and succeeding generations are his 'mothers'. All the men of the lineage through several generations fall into a single category, but instead of being called 'mother's brother' they are called 'grandfather'. The male members of the lineage are placed in a category that refers primarily to the second ascending generation, while the females are placed in one that refers primarily to the first ascending generation.

The principle of lineage unity is recognized in these tribes in other features of the terminology. Thus in the Shona tribes a man calls all the men and women of all generations of the lineages of his father's mother and his mother's mother 'grandfather' and 'grandmother', and they all call him 'grandchild'. In each of these lineages his individual genealogical relation is with a grandmother, so the whole lineage as a unity becomes a collection of 'grandfathers' and 'grandmothers'. When a man marries, all the women of his wife's lineage are his 'wife's sisters'; the term in the Hera tribe is *muramu*, and Holleman translates this as 'potential or even preferential wife or husband', the term being a self-reciprocal one. The term for wife's father is *mukarabghwa* or *mukarahwe*, reciprocal *mukwasha*; all the male members of the wife's lineage through all generations are called 'father-in-law'. There is inequality of rank between father-in-law and son-in-law, the former having the position of superiority, and this applies apparently to all relationships in which these terms are used. These systems of terminology are clearly based on the principle of the unity of the lineage. But that does not explain why the mother's brother is called 'grandfather'. To understand that we must refer to certain features of the social relationship between mother's brother and sister's son in these tribes.

In the type of kinship system with which we are now dealing a person is under the authority and control of his agnatic kin, his father and father's brothers and the male, and sometimes the female, members of his own agnatic lineage. It is with this group and its members that a person has his most important jural relationships, i.e. relationships defined by duties and rights. The mother does not belong to this group, though she is attached to it by marriage and is to some extent herself under its control, particularly under the control of her husband. A father, however affectionate he may be to

225

his son, is a person to be respected and obeyed, and so are his brothers and, in most of the systems of this type, his sisters. The mother, though she must, of course, exercise some discipline over her young children, is primarily the person who gives affectionate care. Just as the relation to the father is extended to his sibling group, so the relation to the mother is extended to hers. The mother's sisters are also 'mothers' and the mother's brothers are 'male mothers'. The mother's brother is not a person to exercise authority over his sister's son; that right is reserved to his 'fathers'. It is the mother's brother's part to show affectionate interest in his nephew and give him aid when he needs it. In the family of his mother's brother a man is a specially privileged person.

To establish and maintain a fixed pattern of behaviour for a particular type of relationship it is useful, and in some instances necessary, to adopt some conventionalized symbolic mode of behaviour which expresses in some way the character of the relationship. In the type of kinship system we are here considering the kind of relationship that is appropriate for a sister's son is symbolically expressed in certain definite customs of privileged familiarity exercised by the nephew. He may, for example, be permitted, or indeed expected, to joke at his uncle's expense, as in the Winnebago and other tribes of North America. He may be permitted to take his uncle's property, as in the *vasu* custom of Fiji and Tonga and as described for South Africa by Junod.[26]

This relation of privileged behaviour may be extended from the mother's brothers to the whole of her lineage, though it will be primarily exercised towards the own mother's brother. The extension sometimes takes in the dead members of the lineage, the ancestral spirits. In Southeast Africa a man's own ancestors of his own lineage are believed to watch his conduct and punish him for any breach of duty. His mother's ancestors have no business to exercise authority over him in this way; on the contrary he may go to them for help, not approaching them directly, but through his mother's brother or mother's brother's son, who can sacrifice to his own ancestors to obtain their help for his nephew or cousin. Junod gives an account of how the sister's sons and daughter's sons of a dead man symbolically express their relation at the final funeral ceremony, interrupting the prayers and grabbing and running away with the sacrificial offering, which they then eat.

There is an East African custom which has, I think, been misinterpreted. This is the custom of the mother's brother's curse. It is said that a man fears the curse of his mother's brother more than that of any other relative. This is sometimes interpreted as though it means that the mother's brother regularly exercises authority over his nephew and that his authority is greater than that even of a father. I suggest that the proper interpretation is that the mother's brother will be the last person to use his power of cursing and will only do so in exceptional and serious situations, and that it is for this reason that it is feared more than the curse of the father. A matter that ought to be inquired into is whether, where the relationship appears to be symmetrical, as in the Nandi, the uncle may also be cursed by his sister's son.

In these systems the behaviour towards a mother's brother is in marked contrast to that towards a father. A man's relation to his mother's relatives is as important as that to his father's kin, but of a different and contrasting kind. In the matter of interpersonal rank the father is very definitely superior to his son. But the mother's brother is not, or not markedly, superior to his nephew. The relationship may be treated as one of approximate equality, or the nephew may even be treated as superior. Thus in Tonga and Fiji the sister's son is quite definitely superior in rank to his mother's brother and to his mother's brother's son. In Tonga the term *eiki* (chief) is used to indicate a person of superior rank, and a sister's son is said to be *eiki* to his mother's brother. Similarly, Junod reports from the Ronga that a nephew is described as being a 'chief' to his mother's brother.

If there is, indeed, as there seems to be, a general tendency to attribute superior rank in interpersonal relations to relatives of the parents' generation, the special relation to the mother's brother that exists in these societies is directly contrary to it. The 'normal' rank relation of proximal generations, if we may venture to call it so, is destroyed in the relation to a mother's brother. There are two ways in which this may be reflected in the terminology. One is the use of a self-reciprocal term between mother's brother and sister's son, as in the Masai and Nandi and some Nuba tribes, whereby the relationship is treated as one that is symmetrical and therefore of approximate equality. Another is to place the mother's brother in the second ascending generation (by a sort of fiction) and call him 'grandfather'. We have already seen that there is a widespread tendency to make the relation between the grandparent generation and the grandchild generation one in which there is an absence of marked inequality of rank and one in which the junior generation is privileged in its behaviour towards the senior. This does not prevent the recognition of some measure of superiority for some relatives of the second ascending generation, for example, the father's father and his sister in some patrilineal systems. The inclusion of the mother's brother in the category of 'grandfathers' removes him from that generation-category to which there is a tendency to attach superiority of interpersonal rank and places him, by a fiction, in one towards which the relation is one of easy familiarity, approximate equality, or privilege.

In the system of the Shona–Ndau–Tonga cluster of tribes, therefore, we have first of all the application of the principle of unity of the lineage. For any person his mother's lineage is a single united group. The women of the lineage, who are mostly dispersed amongst the families into which they have married, are all relatives of one kind, his 'mothers'. Amongst the men of the group his closest connexion is with his mother's father and brother and his mother's brother's son. With them he stands in a specially privileged position; they are expected to show him affectionate indulgence. They and all the other males of the lineage constitute a single unity of which the representative individual is the mother's father; they are all 'grand-fathers' and he is for them a 'grandchild'. For the lineage as a unity the women born into it are its children, but their children are not. In Africa the term 'child of our child' is sometimes used for the child of a woman of the family, a sister's or daughter's child. So for the lineage treated as a unity the children borne by its female members into other lineages are 'children of our children'—grandchildren.

It may be noted, for the purpose of comparison, that our English word 'uncle' is derived from the Latin *avunculus,* which was the term for mother's brother but not for father's brother, and which is literally 'little grandfather', from *avus.* Moreover, the philologists believe that the Old English term for mother's brother, *eme* or *eam,* was originally a modification of the word for grandfather.

One purpose of this section has been to show how the division of kin into generations can be used as a means of formalizing relations of interpersonal rank. One further example may be added by referring to the arrangement of nominal generations in the Nkundo of the Belgian Congo. Although Father Hulstaert's statements are not very clear, it would seem that the important social group, which he speaks of as a clan or exogamous group, is a patrilineal lineage of seven generations or so. The brothers and sisters of the father and members of the lineage of that generation are all 'fathers' (*baise*). The children of a female 'father' (father's sister) are also 'fathers' male and female, and therefore the children of a mother's brother (male mother— *nyangompane*) are 'children' (*bana*). There is thus established a difference of rank between cross-cousins, the father's sister's children ranking above their mother's brother's children in a way similar to that in which a father ranks above his child. That this is a matter not merely of terminology but also of behaviour is evident from Father Hulstaert's account. Consistently with this a man treats the children of his father's sister's son (who is 'father' to him) as 'brothers' and 'sisters'. A diagram may help to make the matter clear.

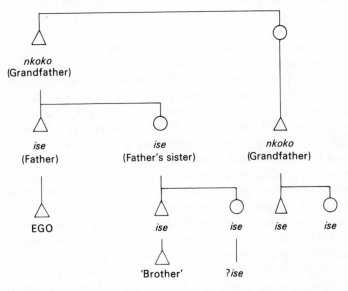

Since my father calls his father's sister's children 'fathers' I call them 'grandparents', and I call the children of my father's father's sister's son 'fathers' male and female. Father Hulstaert does not tell us the relation of a man to the children of his father's sister's daughter (who is his female 'father'). It seems very probable that they also are male and female 'fathers'. If this be so, then for any person there is a series of female lines each stemming from his own lineage; the descendants through females of a father's sister or a father's father's sister are 'fathers' to him and rank above him, he being 'child' to them. For our present purpose the Nkundo system affords another example of the use of terms having a generation reference to establish relations of rank, together with the use of such terms to establish categories containing relatives of different real generations. Relatives of one's own generation are given superior rank by being called 'father'.

VII

Every kinship system provides each person in a society with a set of dyadic (person to person) relationships, so that he stands, as it were, at the centre of a narrower or wider circle of relatives. During his life the body of his relatives is constantly changing by deaths and births and by marriages—his own marriage and the marriages of his relatives.

In many societies the kinship system also includes a different kind of structure by which the whole society is divided into a number of separate groups, each consisting of a body of persons who are or who regard themselves as being a unilineal body of kindred. Such kinship groups are moieties, clans, and lineages. Moieties, by which the society is bisected, do not exist in Africa except amongst the Galla, though they are important in some parts of the world. The distinction between clan and lineage is that in a lineage group each member can actually, or at least theoretically, trace his genealogical connexion with any other member by descent from a known common ancestor, whereas in a clan, which is usually a larger body, this is not possible. A moiety may be divided into clans and usually is so. Clans may be divided into sub-clans, and clans or sub-clans may be divided into lineages. A lineage of any considerable size is usually divided into branches, which are themselves smaller lineages, and these again may be subdivided. For structures having successive segmentations the term 'polysegmentary' has been suggested. Such systems have been excellently described by Evans-Pritchard for the Nuer, and by Fortes for the Tallensi.

It is usual to apply the term 'clan' to both patrilineal and matrilineal groups, but some American ethnographers use the term 'clan' only for matrilineal groups and 'gens' for patrilineal and Dr Nadel has adopted this usage in describing in [*African Systems* . . .] the two sets of groups of the Nyaro. Some writers in the volume have made use of compounds—patri-clan, matri-clan, patri-lineage, and matri-lineage. If these seem to some readers somewhat barbarous it must be remembered that some technical terms are needed for concise description, and have to be invented.

The term 'clan' has often been used without any clear definition. There are, of course, many different kinds of clan systems, but the term should be used only for a group having unilineal descent in which all the members regard one another as in some specific sense kinsfolk. One way of giving recognition to the kinship is by the extensive use of the classificatory terminology, so that in a system of patrilineal clans a man regards all the men of his clan as being his classificatory 'fathers', 'brothers', 'sons', 'grandfathers', or 'grandsons'. Frequently, but not universally, the recognition of the kinship bond uniting the members of the clan takes the form of a rule of exogamy which forbids marriage between two members of the same clan. Where clans are divided into sub-clans it may be only to the smaller group that the rule of exogamy applies.

Membership of a clan is normally determined by birth: where clans are matrilineal the children of a woman belong to her clan; where they are patrilineal the children belong to the father's clan. But in some tribes there is a custom of adoption. Where a man is adopted into a patrilineal clan, thereby abandoning his membership of the clan into which he was born, his children belong to the clan of his adoption, not that of his birth. In some African tribes the position of a child in the social structure depends on the source of the marriage payment for his mother. Thus, among the Lango children belong to the clan that has provided the cattle for the marriage payment for their mother. The father might not be a clansman, but might be a war captive or the sister's son of a clansman who was provided with a wife through cattle belonging to the clan, or the children might have been born outside marriage and the mother later married into the clan.[27]

If we look at a structure of clans or lineages from the point of view of an individual it appears as a grouping of his relatives. In a patrilineal system the members of his own clan are his agnatic kinsfolk, and the nearest of these to him are the members of his own lineage. The members of his mother's clan or lineage are also his kin, through his mother. He may apply to them the appropriate classificatory terms, and in some systems he may be forbidden to marry any woman of his mother's patrilineal clan. The members of

231

his father's mother's clan and his mother's mother's clan may also be recognized as relatives, and those of his wife's clan or lineage may all have to be treated as relatives by marriage.

A clan system, however, also provides a division of the tribe into a number of distinct separate groups, each having its own identity. The clans may then, as groups, play an important part in the social, political, or religious life of the tribe. The extent to which they do this depends on the degree to which they are corporate groups. A group may be spoken of as 'corporate' when it possesses any one of a certain number of characters: if its members, or its adult male members, or a considerable proportion of them, come together occasionally to carry out some collective action—for example, the performance of rites; if it has a chief or council who are regarded as acting as the representatives of the group as a whole; if it possesses or controls property which is collective, as when a clan or lineage is a land-owning group. In parts of Africa it is very common to find that land is held or owned by lineage groups, which are thus corporate groups.

An example of a society in which there are both patrilineal and matrilineal corporate kin groups is provided by the Yakö, described in [*African Systems*] by Professor Daryll Forde. There are corporate patrilineal lineages (*yeponema*) each having a leader and collectively owning landed property. There are also corporate patrilineal clans (*yepun*), each containing several lineages, and the ideal arrangement is one by which the clan has a ritual head, a shrine for clan rites, and a meeting-house for the men. The Yakö have, in addition, a system of matrilineal clans (*yejima*) divided into lineages, and these also are corporate groups uniting for clan rituals. The patrilineal clans are 'compact', i.e. the male members with their families live together in one delimited area; whereas the matrilineal clans are 'dispersed', the various members being scattered through the village settlement and living in the different areas of the patrilineal clans.

It should be noted that as a rule it is the adult men who really constitute the corporate kin group, and this is so for those systems that have descent through females. A good example is provided by the tribes of the lower Congo, described by Dr Richards in [*African Systems*]. Villages or hamlets are formed of matrilineal lineages; all the men of a single lineage live together with their wives and young children, boys when they reach a certain age leaving their parents to join their mother's brother and his village. It is therefore the men of the lineage who form the corporate group, holding rights over land and acting collectively in various ways.

Professor Gluckman regards the absence of corporate kin groups (clans or lineages) as an important distinguishing characteristic of a number of tribes of Central Africa. The typical corporate group in that region is a village constituted by the persons who attach themselves to a headman. This group is an open, not a closed group; that is, individuals or families may join or leave it, moving from one village to another. It is usual that a number of the inhabitants of a village at any time should be related, either by cognatic ties or through marriage with the headman or with one another, but they do not form a unilineal kin group, which is by its constitution a 'closed' group.

Some of these tribes have clans, patrilineal in some instances, matrilineal in others, but the clans are dispersed and not corporate. Thus the Ila and Bemba and other tribes have dispersed matrilineal clans. The members of one clan are scattered through the tribe; they do not ever come together to take any kind of collective action, and have no single authority (headman or clan council). They have no positive clan rites; the identity of the clan, and its unity as a separate group of kindred, is maintained by negative ritual observances common to all the members, such as refraining from killing or eating a certain animal (the 'totem' of the clan). A member of the clan does not know all the other members, but if two persons meet who know or discover that they belong to the same clan they are expected to behave towards one another as kinsfolk, and since all members are kin they may not intermarry. It does not seem that in these tribes matrilineal lineages are given social recognition except in royal families.

One of these Central African tribes, the Lozi, described in [*African Systems*] does not recognize either clans or lineages. The system, though it shows a slight preference in some respects for kinship in the male line, is characteristically one of cognatic kinship, tracing relationship through males and females. Theoretically the range of recognized kinship extends to the descendants of a common great-great-grandparent, i.e. to third cousins.

The unilineal principle of reckoning relationship in one line (male or female) is utilized in a great variety of ways in different kinship systems. Where it is used to create a system of clans it facilitates that wide-range recognition of relations of kinship to which there is a tendency in many societies. A person will thereby find himself connected by specific social ties, subject to established institutional modes of behaviour, with a large number of other persons. In the absence or weak development of political structure this gives an effective system of social integration. It is not possible to provide such very wide range in a system based on cognation, since that implies the tracing of genealogical relationships through all lines. But even more important is that unilineal reckoning makes it possible to create corporate kin groups having continuity in time extending beyond the life of an individual or a family. There are innumerable social activities that can only be efficiently carried out by means of corporate groups, so that where, as in so many non-literate societies, the chief source of social cohesion is the recognition of kinship, corporate kin groups tend to become the most important feature of social structure.

Thus it is the corporate kin group, whether clan, sub-clan, or lineage, that controls the use of land, whether for hunting, for pastoral life, or for cultivation; that exacts vengeance for the killing of a member, or demands and receives an indemnity. In the sphere of religion the kin group usually has its own cult, whether of its ancestors or connected with some sacred shrine. A continuing social structure requires the aggregation of individuals into distinct separated groups, each with its own solidarity, every person belonging to one group of any set. The obvious instance is the present division of the world into nations. In kinship systems cognatic kinship cannot provide this; it is only made possible by the use of the principle of unilineal descent. This is, indeed, obvious, but there have been writers who have used much misplaced ingenuity in trying to conjecture the origin of clans.

VIII

In order to understand the African customs relating to marriage we have to bear in mind that a marriage is essentially a rearrangement of social structure. What is meant by social structure is any arrangement of persons in institutionalized relationships. By a marriage certain existing relationships, particularly, in most societies, those of the bride to her family, are changed. New social relations are created, not only between the husband and the wife, and between the husband and the wife's relatives on the one side and between the wife and the husband's relatives on the other, but also, in a great many societies, between the relatives of the husband and those of the wife, who, on the two sides, are interested in the marriage and in the children that are expected to result from it. Marriages, like births, deaths, or initiations at puberty, are rearrangements of structure that are constantly recurring in any society; they are moments of the continuing social process regulated by custom; there are institutionalized ways of dealing with such events.

We tend, unless we are anthropologists, to judge other people's customs by reference to our own. To understand African marriage we must remember that the modern English idea of marriage is recent and decidedly unusual, the product of a particular social development. We think of a marriage as an event that concerns primarily the man and woman who are forming a union and the State, which gives that union its legality and alone can dissolve it by divorce. The consent of parents is, strictly, only required for minors. Religion still plays some part, but a religious ceremony is not essential.

We may compare English marriage with the following account of a 'wedding' in early England.[28]

If people want to wed a maid or a wife and this is agreeable to her and to her kinsmen, then it is right that the bridegroom should first swear according to God's right and secular law and should wage (pledge himself) to those who are her forspeakers, that he wishes to have her in such a way as he should hold her by God's right as his wife—and his kinsmen will stand pledge for him.

Then it is to be settled to whom the price for upfostering her belongs, and for this the kinsmen should pledge themselves.

Then let the bridegroom declare what present he will make her for granting his desire, and what he will give if she lives longer than he does.

If it is settled in this way, then it is right that she should enjoy half the property, and all if they have a child, unless she marries another man.

All this the bridegroom must corroborate by giving a gage and his kinsmen stand to pledge for him.

If they are agreed in all this, then let the kinsmen of the bride accept and wed their kinswoman to wife and to right life to him who desires her, and let him take the pledge who rules over the wedding.

If she is taken out of the land into another lord's land, then it is advisable that her kinsmen get a promise that no violence will be done to her and that if she has to pay a fine they ought to be next to help her to pay, if she has not enough to pay herself.

The marriage here is not any concern of the State or political authorities; it is a compact between two bodies of persons, the kin of the woman who agree to wed their daughter to the man, and his kinsmen who pledge themselves that the terms of the agreement will be carried out. The bridegroom and his kinsmen must promise to make a payment (the 'marriage payment') to her father or other legal guardian. He must also state what present he will give to his bride for permitting the physical consummation of the marriage; this was the so-called 'morning-gift' to be paid after the bridal night. There was further an agreement as to the amount of the dowry, the portion of the husband's wealth of which the wife should have the use during her lifetime if her husband died before her. The agreement is concluded by the giving of the *wed,* the symbolic payment made by the bridegroom and his kin to the woman's kinsmen.

In modern England the pledge or gage, in the form of a 'wedding' ring, is given, not to the bride's kinsmen when the marriage arrangement is made, but to the bride herself at the wedding ceremony. The change in custom is highly significant. The 'giving away' of the bride is a survival of something which at one time was the most important feature of the ceremonial of marriage.

Thus in Anglo-Saxon England a marriage, the legal union of man and wife, was a compact entered into by two bodies of kin. As the Church steadily increased in power and in control of social life, marriage became the concern of the Church and was regulated by canon law. There was a new conception that in marriage the man and woman entered into a compact with God (or with His Church) that they would remain united till parted by death. The marriage was under the control of the Church; matrimonial cases were dealt with in the ecclesiastical courts.

At the end of the Middle Ages there came the struggle for power between Church and State in which the State was, in Protestant countries, victorious. Marriage then came under State control. At the present day to legalize a union of man and wife the marriage, whether there is or is not a religious ceremony, must be registered by someone licensed by the State and fee must be paid. It is the State that decides on what conditions the marriage may be brought to an end by a divorce granted by a court which is an organ of the State.

A most important factor in the development of the modern English (and American) conception of marriage was the idea of romantic love, a theme that was elaborated in the nineteenth century in novel and drama and has now become the mainstay of the cinema industry. In its early development romantic love was conceived as not within but outside marriage, witness the troubadours and their courts of love and Dante and Petrarch. In the eighteenth century Adam Smith could write: 'Love, which was formerly a ridiculous passion, became more grave and respectable. As a proof of this it is worth our observation that no ancient tragedy turned on love, whereas it is now more respectable and influences all the public entertainments.' The idea that marriage should be a union based on romantic love leads logically to the view that if the husband and wife find they do not love one another they should be permitted to dissolve the marriage. This is the Hollywood practice, but conflicts with the control of marriage by the Church or by the State.

Another very important factor has been the change in the social and economic position of women during the nineteenth and twentieth centuries. A married woman may now hold property in her own right; she may take employment that has no connexion with her family life but takes her away from it. In the marriage ceremony many women now refuse to promise that they will obey their husbands.

Not only are marriage and ideas about marriage in England and America the product of a recent, special, and complex development, but there is good evidence that they are still changing. The demand for greater freedom of divorce is one indication of this. Yet it is clear that despite all this some people take twentieth-century English marriage as a standard of 'civilized' marriage with which to compare African marriage.

The African does not think of marriage as a union based on romantic love although beauty as well as character and health are sought in the choice of a wife. The strong affection that normally exists after some years of successful marriage is the product of the marriage itself conceived as a process, resulting from living together and co-operating in many activities and particularly in the rearing of children.

An African marriage is in certain respects similar to the early English marriage described above. The dowry or dower does not exist in Africa, though writers who do not know, or do not care about, the meanings of words use the term 'dowry' quite inappropriately to refer to the 'marriage payment'.[29] There is also in Africa nothing exactly corresponding to the English 'morning-gift' regarded as a payment for accepting sexual embraces, though it is usual for the bridegroom to give gifts to his bride. The two other features of the early English marriage are normally found in African marriages. Firstly, the marriage is not the concern of the political authorities but is established by a compact between two bodies of persons, the kin of the man and the kin of the woman. The marriage is an alliance between the two bodies of kin based on their common interest in the marriage itself and its continuance, and in the offspring of the union, who will be, of course, kin of both the two kin-groups. The understanding of the nature of this alliance is essential to any understanding of African kinship systems. Secondly, in Africa generally, as in early England, and in a great number of societies in ancient and modern times in all parts of the world, a marriage involves the making of a payment by the bridegroom or his kin to the father or guardian of the bride. Africans distinguish, as we do, between a 'legal' marriage and an irregular union. In modern England a marriage is legal if it is registered by a person licensed by the State. Only children born of such a union are legitimate. But in Africa the State or political authority is not concerned with a marriage. How, then, are we to distinguish a legal marriage? The answer is that a legal marriage, by which the children who will be born are given definite 'legitimate' status in the society, requires a series of transactions and formalities in which the two bodies of kin, those of the husband and those of the wife, are involved. In most African marriages, as in the early English marriage, the making of a payment of goods or services by the bridegroom to the bride's kin is an essential part of the establishment of 'legality'.

Some people regard payments of this kind as being a 'purchase' of a wife in the sense in which in England to-day a man may purchase a horse or a motor-car. In South Africa it was at one time held officially that a marriage by native custom with the payment of cattle (*lobola*) was 'an immoral transaction' and not a valid marriage. The Supreme Court of Kenya in 1917 decided that 'a so-called marriage by the native custom of wife-purchase is not a marriage'. The idea that an African buys a wife in the way that an English farmer buys cattle is the result of ignorance, which may once have been excusable but is so no longer, or of blind prejudice, which is never excusable in those responsible for governing an African people.

A marriage in many, perhaps most, African societies involves a whole series of prestations[30] (payments, gifts, or services), and while the most important of these are from the husband and his kin to the wife's kin, there are frequently, one might say usually, some in the other direction. One of the best accounts of the whole procedure is that given by Father Hulstaert for the Nkundo of the Belgian Congo.[31] The procedure begins with the presentation, on the part of the future husband, of the *ikula,* at one time an arrow, now two copper rings. The acceptance of this by the woman and her kin constitutes a formal betrothal. The marriage, i.e. the 'tradition' of the bride, may take place before any further payment. At the marriage, gifts are made to the bride by the parents of the bridegroom, by other of his relatives, and by the bridegroom himself. The next step is the formal prestation of the *ndanga,* formerly a knife, to the bride's father. It signifies that the husband thereafter becomes responsible for accidents that might befall his wife. In return there is a prestation from the bride's family to the husband and his family. This is part of the *nkomi,* the payment that is made to the bridegroom by the wife's family. The marriage is not fully established until the husband pays his father-in-law the *walo,* a substantial payment consisting chiefly of objects of metal. After this the woman becomes fully the man's wife. When the *walo* is handed over the woman's family make a return payment (*nkomi*) and give a present of food to the husband's family. The husband must also make a special payment to his wife's mother and must give a considerable number of presents to the father, mother, brothers, and other relatives of the bride. The relatives of the husband then demand and receive presents from the wife's family. The final payment to be made by the husband is the *bosongo,* formerly a slave, now a quantity of copper rings.

There is, of course, an immense diversity in the particulars of prestations connected with betrothal and marriage in different societies and in each case they have to be studied, with regard to their meanings and functions, in relation to the society in which they are found. For general theory, however, we have to look for general similarities. In the first place it is necessary to recognize that whatever economic importance some of these transactions may have, it is their symbolic aspect that we chiefly have to consider. This may be made clear by the English customs of the engagement ring, the wedding ring, and the wedding presents. Though an engagement ring may have considerable value (more than many Africans 'pay' for their wives), the giving of it is not regarded as an economic or at

239

least not as a business transaction. It is symbolic.

In what follows the term 'marriage payment' will be used for the major payment or payments made by the bridegroom to the wife's kin. Where there is a payment from the wife's kin to the husband (as in the Nkundo) this will be called the 'counter-payment'. The rule in many African societies is that if there is a divorce the marriage payment and the counter-payment must be returned. There are qualifications of this; for example, in some tribes where on divorce there are children and they belong to the father the marriage payment may be not returnable, or returnable only in part. Also, there are tribes in Africa in which, instead of a payment in goods, the bridegroom must serve for his wife by working for her kin, just as Jacob served his mother's brother Laban seven years for each of the two sisters, Leah and Rachel, his cousins, whom he married (Genesis xxix). This service, the equivalent of the marriage payment or of part thereof, is of course not returnable if there is divorce.

Let us return to the early English marriage. In the formulary quoted above the marriage payment was called 'the price of up-fostering' and was thus interpreted as a return to the father or guardian of the expense of rearing a daughter. But in somewhat earlier times the payment was differently interpreted. It was a payment for the transfer of the woman's *mund* from the father or guardian to the husband, whereby the latter gained and the former lost certain rights. The term for a legitimately married wife in Old Norse law was *mundi kjöbt,* meaning one whose *mund* has been purchased. In Sweden the transfer of *mund* was not by purchase but by gift, and the expression for marriage was *giftarmal.* In Roman law the marriage by *coemptio,* sometimes called 'marriage by purchase', was not the sale of a woman but the legal transfer of *manus* to her husband, and *mund* and *manus* are roughly equivalent terms. In these Roman and Teutonic marriages the important point is that to legalize the union of a man and a woman, so that it is really a marriage, legal power over his daughter must be surrendered by the father and acquired by the husband, whether the transfer be by gift or by payment. The Early English marriage was of this type.

In Africa an unmarried woman is in a position of dependence. She lives under the control and authority of her kin, and it is they who afford her protection. Commonly, if she is killed or injured her guardian or her kinsfolk can claim an indemnity. At marriage she passes to a greater or less extent, which is often very considerable, under the control of her husband (and his kin), and it is he (and they) who undertake to afford her protection. (Note the *ndanga* payment amongst the Nkundo, by which the bridegroom accepts responsibility for accidents that may befall the bride.) The woman's kin, however, retain the right to protect her against ill treatment by her husband. If she is killed or injured by third parties it is now the husband and his kin who can claim an indemnity. It is this transfer of *mund,* to use the Old English term, that is the central feature of the marriage transaction.

To understand African marriage we must think of it not as an event or a condition but as a developing process. The first step is usually a formal betrothal, though this may have been preceded by a period of courtship or, in some instances in some regions, by an elopement. The betrothal is the contract or agreement between the two families. The marriage may proceed by stages, as in the instance of the Nkundo mentioned above. A most important stage in the development of the marriage is the birth of the first child. It is through the children that the husband and wife are united and the two families are also united by having descendants in common.

We may consider African marriage in three of its most important aspects. First, the marriage involves some modification or partial rupture of the relations between the bride and her immediate kin. This is least marked when the future husband comes to live with and work for his future parents-in-law while his betrothed is still a girl not old enough for marriage. It is most marked when, as in most African societies, the woman when she marries leaves her family and goes to live with her husband and his family. Her own family suffers a loss. It would be a gross error to think of this as an economic loss.[32] It is the loss of a person who has been a member of a group, a breach of the family solidarity. This aspect of marriage is very frequently given symbolic expression in the simulated hostility between the two bodies of kin at the marriage ceremony, or by the pretence of taking the bride by force (the so-called 'capture' of the bride). Either the bride herself or her kin, or both, are expected to make a show of resistance at her removal.

Customs of this kind are extremely widespread not only in Africa but all over the world, and the only explanation that fits the various instances is that they are the ritual or symbolic expression of the recognition that marriage entails the breaking of the solidarity that unites a woman to the family in which she has been born and grown up. Ethnographical literature affords innumerable instances. One example may be given here. In Basutoland, or at least in some parts of it, on the day fixed for the marriage the young men of the bridegroom's group drive the cattle that are to constitute the marriage payment to the home of the bride. When they draw near, the women of the bride's party gather in front of the entrance to the cattle kraal. As the bridegroom's party try to drive the cattle into the kraal the women, with sticks and shouts, drive them away so that they scatter over the veld and have to be collected together again and a new attempt made to drive them into the kraal. This goes on for some time until at last the cattle are successfully driven into the kraal. The women of the group make a show of resistance at the delivery of the cattle which will have as its consequence the loss of the bride. The proper interpretation of these customs is that they are symbolic expressions of the recognition of the structural change that is brought about by the marriage.

When this aspect of marriage is considered the marriage payment can be regarded as an indemnity or compensation given by the bridegroom to the bride's kin for the loss of their daughter. This is, however, only one side of a many sided institution and in some kinship systems is of minor importance. In societies in which the marriage payment is of considerable value it is commonly used to replace the daughter by obtaining a wife for some other member of the family, usually a brother of the woman who has been lost. A daughter is replaced by a daughter-in-law, a sister by a wife or sister-in-law. The family is compensated for its loss.

A second important aspect of legal marriage is that it gives the husband and his kin certain rights in relation to his wife and the children she bears. The rights so acquired are different in different systems. Some of these are rights of the husband to the performance of duties by the wife (rights *in personam*) and he accepts corresponding duties towards her. He has, for example, rights to the services of his wife in his household. But the husband usually also acquires rights *in rem* over his wife. If anyone kills or injures her, or commits adultery with her, he may claim to be indemnified for the injury to his rights.

The husband acquires his rights through an action by the wife's kin in which they surrender certain of the rights they have previously had. The marriage payment may be regarded in this aspect as a kind of 'consideration' by means of which the transfer is formally and 'legally' made. It is the objective instrument of the 'legal' transaction of the transfer of rights. Once the payment, or some specific portion of it, has been made the bride's family have no right to fetch their daughter back, and in most tribes, if the union is broken by divorce at the instance of the husband, the payment has to be returned and the woman's family recover the rights they surrendered.

The rights obtained by a husband and his kin are different in some respects in different systems. The most important difference is in the matter of rights over the children the wife bears. An African marries because he wants children—*liberorum quaerendorum gratia.* The most important part of the 'value' of a woman is her child-bearing capacity. Therefore, if the woman proves to be barren, in many tribes her kin either return the marriage payment or provide another woman to bear children.

In a system of father-right, such as the Roman *patria potestas,* the rights of the father and his kin over the children of a marriage are so preponderant as to be nearly absolute and exclude any rights on the part of the mother's kin. On the other hand, in a system of mother-right such as that formerly existing amongst the Nayars of southern India, the father has no legal rights at all: the children belong to the mother and her kin. This does not, of course, exclude a relationship of affection between father and child. Both father-right and mother-right are exceptional conditions; most societies have systems which come between these extremes and might be called systems of joint right or divided right. The system of division varies and there may be an approximation either to father-right or to mother-right.

Some societies in Sumatra and other parts of the Malay Archipelago have two kinds of marriage. If a full marriage payment is made the children belong to the father; we may call this a father-right marriage. But if no payment is made the children belong to the mother and her kin, the marriage being one of mother-right.

The same sort of thing is reported from some parts of Africa, for example from Brass in Southern Nigeria.[33] The father-right marriage, with a substantial marriage payment, is the usual form, but if only a small payment is made the children belong to the mother's kin. The most definite example is from the Nyamwezi. In the *kukwa* form of marriage there is a payment (*nsabo*) made by the bridegroom to the father or guardian of the bride; children of such a marriage fall into the possession of the husband and his agnatic kin. In the

243

butende form of marriage there is no payment and the children belong to the mother and her kin.

There is another aspect of marriage that must be taken into account. In Africa a marriage is not simply a union of a man and a woman; it is an alliance between two families or bodies of kin. We must consider the marriage payments in this connexion also.

In so-called primitive societies the exchange of valuables is a common method of establishing or maintaining a friendly relation between separate groups or between individuals belonging to separate groups. Where material goods are exchanged it is common to speak of gift-exchange. But the exchange may be of services, particularly those of a ritual character. There are societies in which there is an exchange of women, each group (family, lineage, or clan) providing a wife for a man of the other. The rule governing transactions of this kind is that for whatever is received a return must be made. By such exchanges, even by a single act of exchange, two persons or two groups are linked together in a more or less lasting relation of alliance.[34]

There are societies in some parts of the world in which the marriage payment and the counter-payment are equal or approximately equal in value. We may regard this as an exchange of gifts to establish friendship between two families, of which the son of one is to marry a daughter of the other. The kind, and to some extent the amount of the gifts is fixed by custom. But where the marriage payment is considerable in amount and there is a much smaller counter-payment, or none at all, we must interpret this as meaning that the bride's family is conferring a specific benefit on the bridegroom by giving him their daughter in marriage, a benefit that is shared by his kin, and that the marriage payment is a return for this. The transaction can still be regarded as a form of 'gift-exchange' and as such establishes a relation (of alliance) between the parties.

It is characteristic of a transaction of purchase and sale that once it has been completed it leaves behind no obligations on either the buyer or the seller. (This does not, of course, exclude claims based on warranty.) In an African marriage the position is very different. For one thing the marriage payment may in certain circumstances have to be repaid. In some tribes where the payment consists of cattle it is the same cattle with all their increase that should be returned. Further, in some African societies the family that has made the marriage payment continues to have an interest in the cattle or other goods of which it consists. The payment received for a woman's marriage may be used to obtain a wife for a member of her family, usually her brother. This sets up a number of important relations between the persons involved.

```
     ┌────────────┐   ┌────────────┐
 A = b        B = c        C = d
```

B and *b* are brother and sister, and so are *C* and *c*. *A* marries *b* and makes a marriage payment which is used to obtain a wife (*c*) for *B*. In various tribes the marriage payment establishes a series of special personal relations between *b* and *B*, between *A* and *B*, between *b* and *c*, and between *A* and *c*. These are defined differently in different tribes. We may briefly consider three varieties.

It is usual to speak of *B* and *b* as 'linked' brother and sister, and *B* is the 'linked' mother's brother of the children of *A* and *b*, while *b* is the 'linked' father's sister of *B*'s children. In the Shangana-Tonga tribes there is a very special relation between *A* and his 'great *mukonwana*' *c*, the wife that *B* married with the payment provided by *A*. *A* can claim in marriage a daughter of *c*, particularly if his wife *b* dies and there is no younger sister to take her place.[35]

In the Lovedu the relations between the families of *A*, *B*, and *C* ought to be continued in the next and succeeding generations. A son of *A* should marry a daughter of *B* and a son of *B* should marry a daughter of *C*. There is thus established a chain of connected families. The *B* family (or lineage) gives brides to and receives cattle from the *A* family and gives cattle to and receives brides from *C*. The linked sister *b* is said to have 'built the house for her brother' *B*, and she 'has a gate' by which she may enter the house. She has the right to demand a daughter of the house to come as her daughter-in-law, to marry her son and be her helper. Thus in this tribe cross-cousin marriage is systematized in terms of marriage payments, and a complex set of relations between persons and between families is created.[36] In the Shangana-Tonga tribes *b* can demand a daughter of *c* as her co-wife or 'helper', the wife of her husband, not as her daughter-in-law.[37]

Amongst the Nkundo the relationships are given a different form. There is a special relation of *b* to *c*, the wife of her linked brother whose marriage was provided for by her marriage payment. The sister *b* is the *nkolo* of *c,* who is her *nkita.* The *nkolo* (*b*) stands in a position of superiority to the *nkita* (*c*). This relation is continued in the succeeding generations; the children of *b* (the *nkolo*) are in a position of superiority to the children of *c.* This is connected with a peculiar ordering of relations amongst the Nkundo by which the relation between cross-cousins is an asymmetrical one in which they are treated as if they belonged to different generations. The children of the father's sister are 'fathers', male and female (*baise*), to their cousins, the children of the mother's brother who are their 'children' (*bana*). The 'children' must show respect to their 'fathers' and help them. As a consequence a man regards the son of his father's sister's son as his 'brother' and uses that term for him.[38]

It should now be evident that the marriage payment is a complex institution having many varieties in form and function. In any given society it has to be interpreted by reference to the whole system of which it is a part. Nevertheless, there are certain general statements that seem to be well grounded. In Africa the marriage payment, whether it be small or large, is the objective instrument by which a 'legal' marriage is established. In some instances it is a compensation or indemnity to the woman's family for the loss of a member. This is particularly so where the marriage payment is considerable and is used to obtain a wife for the woman's brother. The payment may in some instances be regarded as part of an exchange of a kind that is used in many parts of the world to establish a friendly alliance between two groups. In some societies of South Africa and the Nilotic region it is the derivation of the cattle used in the marriage payment that fixes the social position of the children born of the union. Where the same cattle or other goods are used in two or more successive marriages this is in some tribes held to establish a special relation between the families thus formed. Where cattle are sacred in the sense that the cattle of a lineage are the material link between the living and their ancestors (having been received from those ancestors and being used for sacrifices to them), the use of cattle in marriage payments has a significance which a transfer of other goods would not have. This is not intended as a complete survey, which would be impossible within the limits of this essay. It is only an indication of how this institution, which is the procedure by which a husband acquires those rights which characterize a legal marriage (rights that vary in different societies), may be elaborated in different ways.

IX

It has been said above that an African marriage has to be regarded as a developing process. One aspect of this is the development of the relation between the two allied families as children are born and grow up. We think of kinship only as a relation between two persons who have a common ancestor. But there is a kind of reverse kinship between persons who have a common descendant, and it is relationships of this kind that are created by the marriage conceived as a process. When a child is born the father-in-law of the child's father becomes the grandfather (mother's father) of the child, and the man's brother-in-law becomes his child's uncle. It is usual to speak of the relation of a man to his brother-in-law as an affinal relation and to trace it through the wife. But the real relation that is established as the marriage proceeds is between the father and the mother's brother of a child or children. This is an elementary observation to make, but the failure to recognize clearly this simple fact is an obstacle to the understanding of a number of features of kinship systems.

African systems differ as to the rules concerning marriage between kin. In many the general rule is that a man and woman who are kin, or at any rate closely related, may not marry, and thus no bonds of kinship unite the two families before the marriage. On the other hand, there are many African societies in which it is thought very appropriate that a man should marry his cross-cousin, most usually the daughter of his mother's brother, more rarely the daughter of his father's sister. In such marriages the two families are already related before the marriage occurs. In marriage with the mother's brother's daughter a connexion between the families or lineages that has been formed in one generation is repeated in the next. There is also the very exceptional case of the Tswana, where a man may marry not only a mother's brother's daughter but such a near relative as the father's brother's daughter. We may expect that the social relations that result from a marriage alliance will differ in these different kinds of marriage, and a comparative study of the difference is desirable. It cannot be undertaken here. This section will deal only with certain features that characterize the relations of a man to his wife's relatives in a great number of African peoples and are also found among many other peoples in many parts of the world.

For seventy years anthropologists have paid a good deal of attention to a custom found in many parts of the world and commonly referred to as 'mother-in-law avoidance'. This is a custom by which social contact between a husband and his wife's mother is limited in significant ways or in extreme cases entirely prohibited.

A theory favoured by a number of anthropologists is that the purpose of this custom is to prevent incestuous intercourse with the wife's mother. It is not explained why such special and in some instances drastic measures are necessary, when incest with the mother or sister and other relatives is avoided without them. It would seem to be assumed that in some societies every man has a strong desire to have connexion with his wife's mother. It is an example of the kind of speculative theory that has been all too frequent in anthropology, made, in defiance of scientific method, without consideration of the relevant facts.

What is really the same custom varies from complete or nearly complete avoidance to the maintenance of social distance by a reciprocal attitude of reserve and respect. Amongst the Ganda 'no man might see his mother-in-law or speak face to face with her'.[39] Amongst the Galla a man must not mention the name of his mother-in-law (actual or prospective), but he does not appear to be prohibited from speaking to her. But he may not drink milk from a cup she has used nor eat food of her cooking.[40] Thus the custom has many varied forms.

It is not confined to a man's own mother-in-law. In some societies a man must practise the same sort of avoidance towards the mother-in-law of his brother. In many there is a similar avoidance of the sisters of the mother-in-law, and occasionally of the wife's grandmother. But a man must also avoid, or maintain a respectful distance from, some of his wife's male relatives, particularly her father, sometimes her father's brothers, and in some societies her mother's brothers. It is said that amongst the Toro of Albert Nyanza the avoidance between son- and father-in-law is even more rigid than that between son- and mother-in-law; and amongst the Lendu, another tribe in Uganda, the father-in-law can never visit his son-in-law except in the event of the serious illness of his daughter, whereas the mother-in-law may visit her son-in-law and his wife when two months have passed since the marriage.[41]

With this custom of maintaining a respectful distance between a man and his wife's parents and other relatives of the same generation there is frequently associated a directly contrary relation between a man and his wife's brothers and sisters. This is the kind of relationship that is usually called the 'joking relationship'. It is fundamentally a relation expressed in disrespectful behaviour. Persons between whom such a relationship exists are not merely permitted but are expected to speak and behave to one another in ways that would be insulting and offensive between persons not so related.[42]

These customs of 'avoidance' and 'joking' are too frequently found together for us to treat the association as accidental, particularly as in them we find two directly contrary modes of behaviour used in a single social context, that created by a marriage. We cannot regard as worthy of serious consideration any theory or explanation that does not deal with both of them.

As a first step towards the formation of a theory we must bear in mind that in these relationships (both of 'avoidance' and of 'joking') behaviour is highly conventionalized. In any society the kinds of abusive speech or behaviour that joking relatives may use are defined by custom. The rules that must be observed towards the wife's parents are similarly defined in detail, such as the Galla rule that a man must not drink milk from a cup that his wife's mother has used, while this does not apply to *dadi,* the intoxicating drink made from honey or from the fruit of the Borassus palm, because this drink is 'a thing of great kindness'. A very widespread rule is that forbidding the uttering of the personal name of an avoidance relative. Thus much of the behaviour imposed in these relationships must be described as symbolic behaviour and the rules are essentially similar to rules of etiquette. The acts and abstentions imposed by such rules are the conventionalized symbolic expression of the relative position of persons in a particular social relation or situation.

The view taken here is that the customs of 'avoidance' and 'joking' have the same general social function. The differentiating principle between them is that by which, as a general rule (to which, as we have seen, there are exceptions which require special explanation), behaviour towards relatives of the parents' generation should be respectful while towards relatives of one's own generation there is a nearer approach to equality and familiarity. But within one's own generation there is often a differentiation of senior and juinor with a rule that the junior person must show respect to the senior. So in some societies the rules of avoidance are applied to the wife's elder sister as well as to the wife's mother, even where there is a joking relationship with the wife's younger sister.

In the building of social structures means must be provided for avoiding, limiting, controlling, or settling conflicts. In the new structural situation resulting from marriage there are possibilities of conflict. While there is a union of the husband and wife the two families (in the sense of bodies of kin) remain separated, only linked together by their separate connexion with the new family that is coming into existence. It is the separateness of the two groups, with the need of maintaining friendly relations between them, that has to provide the basis for their personal relations.

The 'joking' relationship in its reciprocal form can be regarded as a kind of friendliness expressed by a show of hostility. The mutual abusive behaviour would be simple hostility in other connexions, but the joking relatives are required not to take offence but to respond in the same way. The social separation of the man and his wife's relatives is symbolically represented in the sham hostility, ruled by convention, and the friendliness is exhibited in the readiness not to take offence. This interpretation applies to other instances of the reciprocal joking relationship that have nothing to do with marriage.[43]

The joking relationship is clearly only appropriate between persons who in the general social structure can treat each other as equals, and this generally means persons of the same generation or those related as 'grandparent' and 'grandchild'. For the wife's parents and other relatives of that generation, and sometimes for the wife's elder sister, an attitude of respect is required. But it must be a different kind of respect from that which a man shows in some African tribes to his father and in others to his mother's brother as the person who is entitled to exercise authority over him. This respect is totally incompatible with any open show of hostility. In a man's relations with his wife's parents the social separation is symbolically expressed in conventional rules such as the avoidance of the utterance of their personal names or the Galla prohibition against eating food cooked by the wife's mother. In the most extreme form of the custom there is complete avoidance of social contact with the wife's mother, to whom a man may never speak and whom he may never meet face to face, and there is sometimes a similar complete avoidance of the wife's father.

There might be a temptation to regard this avoidance as a form of hostility, since we tend to avoid persons with whom we do not get on well. This would be a mistake. Amongst the Australian aborigines there is complete avoidance of the wife's mother. When

I asked a blackfellow why he had to avoid his mother-in-law his reply was: 'She is my best friend in the world: she has given me my wife.' Though this may seem strange to our way of thinking, I think his answer was logical and adequate. What disturbs or breaks a friendship is a quarrel. You cannot quarrel with a person with whom you have no social contact, or with whom your contacts are strictly limited and regulated by convention.

A marriage produces a temporary disequilibrium situation. In the small and close-knit groups with which we are here concerned any removal of a member results in disequilibrium. The event that most markedly produces this result is a death. But on a smaller scale the removal of a daughter by marriage is also a disturbance of equilibrium in her family. Moreover, the intrusion of a stranger into a group of kin is similarly a disturbance. Among the Nguni of South Africa the bride during the early period of her marriage has to give presents to and perform services for the women of her husband's group and only after a lapse of time is she accepted as one of themselves. Any reconstruction of a disturbed equilibrium inevitably takes time—longer or shorter as the case may be.

The establishment of a new equilibrium after a marriage requires that in certain types of kinship or family structure there is a need felt for emphasizing the separateness of the two connected families. There are many customs in which this is shown, but a single example must suffice. In the Nguni tribes the personal name that a woman has in her own family, as a daughter, may not be used by her husband's family, who have to provide her with a new name, which again will not be used by her own relatives. She is a different person in the two groups.

The principal points of tension in the situation created by a marriage are between the wife and the husband's parents and between the husband and his wife's parents. In order to condense and simplify the argument we are considering only the latter, but we must remember that the former is equally important. The point of maximum tension seems to be between the wife's mother, who is the person most closely and intimately connected with the wife before the marriage, and the son-in-law to whom have been transferred control and sexual rights over her daughter. This is, of course, what lies behind the vulgar English jokes about the mother-in-law.[44] The conventionally maintained 'distance' between son-in-law and wife's mother does have the effect of avoiding conflict between them.

In Bantu languages the customs of avoidance are referred to by a word of which some of the various forms are *ntloni, nthoni, hloni.* Some writers translate this as 'shame'. Thus Torday and Joyce report that amongst the Huana a man may never enter the house of his parents-in-law, and if he meets them on a road he must turn aside into the bush to avoid them. 'Repeated inquiries as to the reason of this avoidance on the part of a man of his parents-in-law elicited the invariable reply "that he was ashamed"; to a further inquiry of what he was ashamed, the answer would be "of marrying their daughter". No other reason could be obtained.'[45]

This 'shame' has been interpreted by Westermarck and other writers as being specifically sexual shame, but it is something much more fundamental and general than that, and indeed the English word 'shame' is not adequate as a description. What is really referred to is a felt constraint of one person in the presence of another, which limits his behaviour and keeps him at a distance from that other. Shyness is a similar phenomenon, and both shyness and shame are commonly associated with blushing. But it is to be noted that this constraint on a person in his relations with his wife's parents is not the spontaneous product of his own feelings, but is imposed upon him by social custom and the rules of etiquette that give expression to it, just as is the relative absence of constraint that is exhibited in the joking relationship with a wife's brothers or sisters.

Westermarck makes much of the fact that in Morocco all indecent talk is particularly prohibited in the presence of a man and his parent-in-law. But in a great many African tribes it is not only the father-in-law but also the father in whose presence one may not utter or listen to such talk. Obscene expressions are used in many societies as expressions of hostility, as in swearing. Their use is therefore often considered appropriate in joking relationships, and since these are the polar contrary of the relationship to parents-in-law, it is easy to see the meaning of avoiding obscenity in the presence of these relatives. Freedom to refer to sexual topics is in general characteristic of a certain kind of social intimacy, and is directly contrary to the distant reserve that has to be observed towards the wife's parents.

The argument could be supported by the examination of other features of the etiquette relating to parents-in-law, but only one can be mentioned here. It has been noted above that amongst the Galla a man may not eat food cooked by his wife's mother nor drink from a cup that she has used. In many other African tribes a man may not eat food from his wife's family, and where there is not complete avoidance of all contact a man may not eat food in the presence of his parent-in-law. Dr Nadel, in his book on the tribes of the Nuba Hills, suggests that such customs also express, symbolically, sexual shame; though he has himself indicated their true significance by referring to rules that forbid members of different clans to eat meat or drink milk together, stating that these eating avoidances are the medium 'through which these tribes express social proximity and distance'. The sharing of food, and still more, eating and drinking together (commensality), are all over the world expressions of social solidarity. The symbolism of customs of etiquette in the matter of eating is obvious in the customs themselves, and there is no need to search for obscure Freudian symbols by which eating is a sexual activity. Amongst the Nguni of South Africa a bride may not drink the milk of her husband's kraal until after a lapse of time, usually not till after she has borne a child, and after a ceremony has been performed. This is the symbolic expression of the fact that she is no longer a stranger or outsider but a member of the group.

Customs about the avoidance of names can be interpreted in the same way as customs about eating, and it has not yet been suggested that they have sexual significance. All these various rules, it is here held, are conventional rules by which a man is obliged to maintain social distance between himself and his wife's parents. By maintaining this kind of relationship any tensions that exist or may arise are prevented from breaking, by open conflict, what should be a friendly relation.

In some societies in Africa and elsewhere, the rules of avoidance are somewhat relaxed in the course of time, i.e. as the marriage develops through the birth of children. This is, for example, reported of the Kamba.[46] It is probably true of many other societies from which it has not been reported. This is easy to understand if we think of the marriage as a developing process. Whatever tensions or dangers of conflict there may be between the son-in-law and his wife's parents are at a maximum in the early period of the marriage. The imposed 'shyness' between them is functionally most significant immediately after the marriage.

X

A part of every kinship system is a set of regulations concerning marriage between persons related by kinship or through marriage. There are, in the first place, rules which prohibit marriage between persons who stand in certain relationships. An example is afforded by the list of prohibited degrees in the English Book of Common Prayer. The rules vary greatly from one system to another, and in a given society may vary from one period of its history to another. In many societies there is what is called a rule of exogamy, by which a man is forbidden to take a wife from amongst the women of his own group (lineage, sub-clan, clan, or moiety). On the other hand, in some systems there are certain relatives between whom marriage is not merely permitted but is regarded as desirable. The term 'preferential marriage' is commonly applied to customs of this kind. The commonest examples are cross-cousin marriage (marriage with the daughter of the mother's brother or of the father's sister) and marriage with the wife's sister or the wife's brother's daughter.

There are also rules relating to sexual intercourse outside marriage. Incest is the sin or crime of sexual intercourse between persons related either by kinship or through marriage within degrees defined by law or religion. Marriage and sexual intercourse outside marriage are not the same thing, and the rules relating to them must be separately considered. Most of the discussions about these rules have been vitiated by the failure to distinguish two distinct, though obviously related, problems. Here we are concerned primarily with the problem of the rules relating to marriage.

There is, in most societies, a tendency to condemn sexual intercourse between persons who are forbidden to marry. But there are many instances in which a man and woman who may not marry may carry on a temporary affair without this being considered the grave offence to which we give the name of incest, and without being subjected to any legal or religious sanction. Amongst the Tallensi of West Africa there are women whom a man is prohibited from marrying but with whom intercourse is not regarded as incestuous; the Tallensi themselves say 'copulation and marriage are not the same thing'. Similarly, amongst the Nkundo of the Belgian Congo there is a special term (*lonkana*) for sexual intercourse with women whom a man may not marry but with whom such connexion does not constitute incest; they are women of a clan (or lineage?) which is related to his own and into which he may not marry for this reason.[47]

Confining our attention to the regulation of marriage, we can see that there are certain requirements that must be met by a theory if it is to be worthy of any consideration. It must offer a general theory of the variations in these rules in different societies, and it must therefore deal not only with prohibited but also with preferred marriages. It must give some significant clue towards an understanding of why any given society has the rules it does. The test of a scientific theory is in its application to the explanation of particular instances. By this criterion many of the speculative hypotheses that have been put forward are entirely useless and it would be waste of time to discuss them. To anyone propounding a theory we might put the following question: How does the theory give us a clue to the understanding of why, amongst the Nkundo, a woman is forbidden to marry (in a second marriage) the husband's father's brother's son of her first husband's mother's brother's daughter; or why, amongst the Hera of Mashonaland, a man may not marry a woman of the lineage of his wife's brother's wife, although he may marry his wife's sister or a woman of the lineage of his mother's brother's wife?

The theory here proposed is simply a special application of the general theory that the *raison d'être* of an institution or custom is to be found in its social function. The theory is, therefore, that the rules or customs relating to prohibited or preferred marriages have for their social function to preserve, maintain, or continue an existing kinship structure as a system of institutional relations. Where a marriage between relatives would threaten to disrupt or throw into disorder the established system it tends to be disapproved or forbidden, and the greater and more widespread the disturbance that would be caused by a marriage, the stronger tends to be the disapproval which it meets with. Inversely, preferential marriages are those which have for their effect to renew or reinforce the existing system.

What is here called a tendency is something that can be discovered by observation. In some instances the objection to a certain type of marriage takes a quite definite form, as in a system of law. But in other instances there may be, in a given society at a particular time, a disagreement between individuals as to the desirability of encouraging, permitting, or prohibiting a certain type of marriage. This can be illustrated from English history. Until the Reformation marriage with a deceased wife's sister was forbidden by the canon law of the Roman Church. But persons of influence who could pay for

255

the privilege could obtain a special dispensation permitting the marriage to take place. By an Act of King Henry VIII dispensations were abolished and marriage with a deceased wife's sister or with a deceased husband's brother was made illegal. An Act of Queen Mary legalized marriage with a deceased husband's brother but not with a deceased wife's sister. In 1835 Lord Lynhurst brought forward in the House of Lords a Bill to legalize marriage with the deceased wife's sister; from that date till 1907, when an Act was finally passed permitting such marriages, there was a continued and passionate controversy. This can be studied in the debates on the subject that occurred at intervals in the Lords and Commons and were reported in Hansard. An association called the Marriage Law Defence Union was formed to prevent the passing into law of the proposal. Articles and pamphlets were printed on both sides of the controversy and of these a bibliography by Huth has 257 entries between the years 1840 and 1887. After the law permitting such marriages was passed some clergymen refused to solemnize them in church; though permitted by the law of the State they were judged by some to be contrary to religion.

This episode from the history of the English kinship system has been mentioned for several reasons. It illustrates the fact that while in a particular society there may sometimes be unanimity of opinion as to the desirability or otherwise of a particular kind of marriage, there may sometimes exist a marked divergence of opinion. In England there was, and still perhaps is among some people, a very strong sentiment against marriage with the sister of a deceased wife, while others feel that such marriage is permissible or even desirable. Similar divergence of opinion can sometimes be noted in primitive societies and its existence calls for theoretical explanation and affords a good means of testing any general theory.

An examination of the documents of the controversy that lasted in England for seventy years shows that the objection to this kind of marriage is based on sentiment rather than on any sort of reason. It is just felt to be wrong.

Nevertheless, it is possible, by analysis of the English kinship system, to see how this divergence of opinion and sentiment was possible. The decline in the social importance of kinship which has been taking place in England for several centuries, and is still continuing, resulted in a situation in which there was no clearly defined and generally accepted pattern of behaviour as between a man

256

and the brothers and sisters of his wife. In the absence of any institutional norm this kind of relationship could be, and inevitably was, differently treated by different persons. Since thought and sentiment may be very strongly influenced by words, the English term 'sister-in-law', understood as 'sister' by marriage, served to provide some persons with a pattern for the relationship; the sister-in-law is a sort of sister. Marriage with any sort of 'sister', implying sexual intimacy, was emotionally felt to be a sort of symbolic incest. Other persons felt that sister-in-law and brother-in-law are not really relatives at all. If any man, on the death of his wife, wishes to enter another marriage, the wife's sister should be just as eligible as any unrelated person. There was a third view: the relation between two sisters is, or should be, one of affection and intimacy; for a widower with young children there is no one who could so suitably replace his wife as her unmarried sister; on this view marriage with the wife's sister was viewed as a marriage to be preferred.

From this well-documented historical instance, and from the parallel instance of the discussions in South Africa over the proposal to legalize marriage with a deceased husband's brother, which had previously been forbidden by Roman–Dutch law, we can draw a generalization. Where the kinship system is one that has a structure with a set of clearly defined institutional relationships there is likely to be complete agreement as to whether a particular kind of marriage should be prohibited, permitted, or preferred. Divergence of opinion or sentiment indicates an absence of rigidity, and that, of course, is not a bad thing in itself. A political system, such as that of England, may depend essentially on the differences of opinion and sentiment of political parties. But in a system of law some rigidity is necessary, even though from time to time the law may be modified. A law works best when it is backed by a nearly unanimous public opinion.

There are significant differences in human societies in this matter of prohibiting, permitting, or preferring marriage of a woman with her husband's brother, or of a man with his wife's sister. Polyandry, the marriage of a woman to two or more husbands, is an institution that is only rarely found, but its most usual form is adelphic polyandry, in which the woman marries two or more brothers. Corresponding to this there is the much more widespread institution of sororal polygyny, in which a man marries two or more sisters. Amongst the Australian aborigines this is regarded as the ideal form

257

of marriage, and still more ideal is the arrangement by which an elder brother marries the two eldest sisters of a family and his younger brother marries one or two of the younger sisters.

There are very widespread marriage customs that are commonly referred to by the terms 'levirate' and 'sororate', but we have to distinguish different institutions to which these terms are applied. In the true levirate, exemplified by the customs of the Hebrews, and in Africa by the Nuer and Zulu and many other peoples, when a man dies and his wife has not passed the age of child-bearing it is the duty of the man's brother to cohabit with the widow in order to raise children, which will be counted, not as his, but as children of the deceased. The widow remains the wife of the dead man, for whom the brother is a surrogate and thus not strictly speaking her husband. A different institution is widow inheritance, in which a brother takes over the position of husband and father to the widow and her children.

There is a similar distinction with regard to the sororate. In some tribes of South Africa, such as the Zulu, if a woman proves to be barren her kin will provide a sister to bear children who will be counted as children of the barren wife. This is parallel to the true levirate. A different custom is that by which when a wife dies her kin may supply a sister to replace her. In sororal polygyny a man, having married an older sister, also marries her younger sister.

All these customs of preferential marriage can be seen to be continuations or renewals of the existing structure of social relations. All of them are also examples of the principle of the unity of the sibling group, since brother replaces brother and sister replaces or supplements sister.

Professor Gluckman's paper in [*African Systems* . . .] gives an illuminating comparison between the Lozi and the Zulu in this matter of the sororate and sororal polygyny. The Zulu have both; they approve of marriage with the wife's younger sister which reinforces the relationships established by the first marriage, and which, if sisters behave in a 'sisterly' way, increases the solidarity of the family group. The Lozi object to marriage with even a classificatory 'sister' of the wife, and say that the competition and rivalry between co-wives is likely to destroy the relationship that ought to exist between sisters. But there is really more in the matter than this and it may be held that the basis of this difference between the Zulu and the Lozi lies in certain very important differences of social structure. The unity of the sibling group, with its implication of substitution of brother for brother and sister for sister, is a major principle of the Zulu system and a relatively minor feature in that of the Lozi. Following this the Zulu system emphasizes the solidarity of the lineage group, and this can hardly be said to exist in Lozi. In sororal polygyny one woman of a sibling group as part of a lineage supplements another; in the sororate she replaces her. Her duties are imposed on her by her lineage affiliation. To quarrel with her sister or neglect her sister's children is not simply a neglect of her marital duties; it is contrary to her obligations to her own closest kin. In the Zulu system a marriage establishes a relation between a man and his brothers and the family of his wife, which should be permanent. Divorce is objected to because it is destructive of this permanence. If the man dies his wife passes to a brother. If the woman dies the relation can only be fully continued if she is replaced by a sister, unless she has borne children or is beyond the child-bearing age. In the very different Lozi system the levirate and sororate could not possibly have the functions they have in the Zulu system.

Marriage with the wife's sister is, on the whole, more frequently found in association with the patrilineal lineage and what may be called father-right marriage, and it is precisely in such circumstances that it functions most effectively to maintain or strengthen the relationships set up by a marriage. In societies with matrilineal institutions there are variations. Thus the Ashanti do not permit marriages of this kind, and the paper by Dr Fortes enables us to see why. On the contrary, amongst the Bemba such marriages are approved, and the reason again lies in the social structure. By his first marriage a man becomes attached to the family of his wife, with whom, for at least some time, he must take up residence. Marriage with the wife's sister would strengthen this bond and introduce no new factor; whereas if, in a second marriage he unites himself with a different family this must complicate and is likely to disturb the existing system of relations. Theoretically one would expect that the Bemba should have given, at any rate in former times, a definite preference to marriage with the wife's sister.

In a number of African tribes there is a custom by which a man is given his wife's brother's daughter as a wife. This is in a sense a variant of marriage with the younger sister of the wife. It exists in tribes in which the patrilineal lineage is a predominant feature of the social structure, and in such tribes a marriage of this sort renews by repetition the relationship set up by a first marriage between a man

259

and the patrilineal lineage of his wife; he takes a second wife from the same lineage group, just as in the sororate he receives a second wife from the sibling group of the first wife. The second wife supplements or replaces, not her elder sister, but her father's sister. The structural principle involved is that of the unity of the lineage group.

In some African societies a man is not permitted to marry the daughter of his mother's brother, and this rule is extended to the whole lineage to which she belongs, and sometimes to the clan. Other societies permit such marriages of cross-cousins, and in some they are given preference. (It must be noted that in a system of lineages or clans, whether patrilineal or matrilineal, cross-cousins belong to different groups.) There is no space available here for a general discussion of the reasons for this variation, as the subject is complex. Where the institutionalized relations of a man to his mother's brother (and his wife) are in important respects incompatible with his relations to his wife's father and mother, marriage with the mother's brother's daughter tends to be forbidden. Where there is no reason of this kind, then marriage of this sort renews in one generation a relation between families that was established in the preceding generation, and thus tends to be approved or preferred. A man takes a wife from a certain family or lineage and establishes a relation with her kinsfolk. His wife's brother becomes the mother's brother of his children; if his son marries the daughter of this man there is a repetition of the previous connexion.

The Hehe of East Africa do not forbid marriages of this kind. Gordon Brown has reported the existence of a difference of opinion in this tribe. Some people think that marriage with the mother's brother's daughter is desirable because it renews the already established relation between the families, but others think that the tensions that are likely to arise between the kin of a man and those of his wife may disrupt the existing friendly relations that have resulted from a former successful marriage, and therefore think it better to avoid a marriage of this kind. By way of contrast it is apparently the unanimous opinion of the Lobedu of the Transvaal that a relationship established in one generation by a marriage should if possible be renewed or repeated in the next generation through marriage with the mother's brother's daughter.

The paper on the Ashanti by Professor Fortes gives us further insight. The Ashanti formerly gave definite preference to marriage with the mother's brother's daughter, and had their own particular rationalizations for the custom. This kind of marriage is becoming less frequent as a result of social changes, and there is now a divergence of opinion as to the desirability of what was apparently formerly accepted as an established custom. Recognizing the existence of a number of factors in the minds of the people themselves, Professor Fortes sees the change as one involved in the gradual transformation that is taking place in the social structure of the Ashanti people.

There is a very important general difference in the regulation of marriage between societies that build their kinship system on cognatic relations traced equally through males and through females and those that adopt the unilineal principle. In a purely cognatic system, such as that of Anglo-Saxon England or ancient Wales, the prohibition against marriage applies to all cognates within a certain degree of kinship; marriage is forbidden between persons who have a common ancestor or ancestress within a certain number of generations. For example, two persons who have a common great-great-grandparent may be forbidden to marry. In a unilineal system the primary rule is that two persons may not marry if they both belong to a socially recognized unilineal descent group. This may be a lineage, or it may be a clan. A rule of this kind is called 'exogamy'. Perhaps the most extreme example is the Chinese rule, not always, I believe, observed in these days, that two persons having the same surname may not marry, since such names are patrilineally inherited and therefore the two persons of one name may be supposed to have had an ancestor in common, though it may be three thousand years ago. There is no special problem about exogamy. The exogamy of a clan is the same thing as the exogamy of a lineage, with a wider recognition of kinship. The essence of the system of clans is that a man is required to recognize all the members of his own clan as his kin and to behave to them accordingly. The rule of exogamy, where it exists, is a way of giving institutional recognition to this bond of kinship. Like the classificatory system of terminology, which is frequently found associated with clans, exogamy is part of the machinery for establishing and maintaining a wide-range kinship system.

In unilineal systems cognatic kinship outside the unilineal group may also be recognized. Thus in ancient Indian law a man might not marry a *sapinda,* a person descended patrilineally from one of his patrilineal ancestors within seven generations. He might also not marry certain cognatic kin, but the connexion had to be a nearer one, within five, or in another system of law within three generations. There is also such a thing as lineal-cognatic kinship. In a system of patrilineal lineages or clans the rule of exogamy forbids marriage within the group; but there may also be a prohibition against marriage with a person of the mother's group. Inversely, in a system of matrilineal groups a man may be forbidden to marry a woman of his father's group; the relationship is what is here called lineal-cognatic.

It is evident from these remarks that in societies that make use of the unilineal principle there is an immense variety in the rules relating to marriage. The contrast between a cognatic system and a unilineal system is brought out in the comparison of the Lozi with the Zulu. Amongst the Lozi, with a cognatic kinship system, the regulation of marriage takes the form that marriage is forbidden between any two persons who are cognatically related within a certain degree; for this purpose genealogical relationships are not traced farther back than the fourth generation, and in fact marriages do take place within theses limits. The rule, therefore, even if it is not always observed, is that third cousins, descendants of one great-great-grandparent, should not marry. This seems to have been the rule at one time in England and Wales.

The Zulu have a system of agnatic lineages, as did the ancient Romans, and marriage between agnates recognized as such within a certain range is forbidden. The Zulu also recognize lineal-cognatic kinship and forbid the marriage of a man with a woman of his mother's lineage. The regulation of marriage is very different in the Lozi and the Zulu, and the difference corresponds to a fundamental difference in social structure.

In the construction of a kinship system it is necessary to fix in some way the range over which relationships are to be institutionally recognized. In this the rules relating to marriage may have great importance. The system of the Australian aborigines is one in which every person in the society is related to every other person with whom he has any social contact whatever. The regulation of marriage therefore takes the form of a rule that a man may only take a wife from some one category, or some categories, of kin. Endogamy is a rule one of the functions of which, at any rate in some parts of India, is to circumscribe the range of relationships, since a member of an endogamous group cannot possibly be related, by kinship or through marriage, with any person outside the group. In a cognatic system the range of relationships depends on how far any person traces his genealogical connexions. In the Teutonic system of the sib, theoretically, any descendant of any of the sixty-four pairs of the grandparents of one's great-great-grandparents was a sib-kinsman, thus including all cousins up to sixth cousins. It would seem quite impossible that anyone would recognize as kinsmen all of these; it was a theoretical construction of the lawyers, not something used in daily practice. It illustrates the fact that a wide-range cognatic system is not very practicable. In setting up rules for marriage, therefore, a cognatic system, such as the Lozi, rarely, if ever, goes beyond third cousins, descendants of a common great-great-grandparent.

Unilineal systems have to work in quite a different way. Unilineal kin groups normally tend to increase in size in successive generations. A clan may grow into a group numbering many hundreds; but membership of the same clan in the case of dispersed clans may only be of significance amongst persons in regular and frequent social contact. Lineages also tend to expand in volume, and in lineage systems we find some procedure by which a lineage that has grown to a size in which the institutions that maintain its unity do not function well can be divided into two or more separate but still connected lineages. A method by which this is sometimes brought about in the Nguni tribes of South Africa is interesting as illustrating the thesis of this section. It may happen that when a lineage group has grown to a considerable size a young man may decide that he wants to marry a girl of the lineage who is not closely related to him. The natives themselves say that a marriage within the lineage is disruptive of its unity, since it would create within the group relationships by marriage which are entirely incompatible with the established lineage relations. There will therefore be resistance to the proposed marriage. But if there is sufficient opinion in favour of it the lineage can be divided into two separate connected lineages between which marriage becomes possible. Even when a lineage has become too large to be functionally fully effective the Nguni are inclined to try to maintain its unity, and therefore tend to wait for such an occasion as the one here described. Marriage within the lineage group would be thoroughly disruptive of its structure, and therefore cannot be permitted; but if the structure is changed by fission of the group the marriage is permissible between the two newly created groups. This illustrates the relation between rules as to marriage and the kinship structure.

A brief reference must be made to the Tswana, whose system is described in [*African Systems . . .*] by Professor Schapera. The Tswana are decidedly exceptional in Africa, and might almost be regarded as an anomaly; but in the comparative study of social systems exceptions and apparent anomalies are of great theoretical importance. There is a strong contrast between the Tswana and the Nguni tribes. The Tswana recognize patrilineal lineage; they seem to have had a preference for marriage with mother's brother's daughter, which is characteristic of a number of tribes with whom they are ethnically related. But they also permit marriage within the lineage to the daughter of a father's brother. This would be impossible amongst the Nguni, who indeed refer to the Sotho, related to the Tswana, with expressions of disgust as 'those people who wear breeches and marry their sisters.' How the Tswana arrived at their present system is an historical question about which we can unfortunately only speculate. But the way the system works can be studied. Amongst the Nguni the way a man is required to behave towards the relatives of his wife is entirely incompatible with the way in which he behaves to persons of his own patrilineal lineage, his father's brother, with the wife and children of the latter. The absence of such incompatibility amongst the Tswana, while it makes possible the marriage with father's brother's daughter, also marks their system as being of an unusual type amongst indigenous African peoples. The Arabic peoples also practise marriage with the father's brother's daughter, but their kinship system is in many respects very different from that of the Tswana or those of African peoples in general.

It is only possible here to deal very briefly with the subject of incest in its relation to the regulation of the marriage of kin. Incest is properly speaking the sin or crime of sexual intimacy between immediate relatives within the family, father and daughter, mother and son, brother and sister. In human societies generally such conduct is regarded as unthinkable, something that could not possibly occur, and the idea of it arouses a strong emotional reaction of repugnance, disgust, or horror. It is characteristically conceived as an 'unnatural' action, contrary not so much to law and morals as to human nature itself. It is this emotional reaction that we have to explain if we are to have a theory of incest. Another example of a kind of action frequently regarded as 'unnatural' is parricide, the killing of a father or mother. The parallel between incest and parricide is illustrated in Greek drama.

Almost everywhere in human societies as we know them the first experience that any person has of society is in the parental family, the intimate domestic group of father, mother, and children. Certain emotional attitudes are developed in such a group with sufficient force to come to be thought of as 'natural' in the sense of being part of human nature itself. The kind of emotional attitude existing in sexual intimacy, and the kinds of emotional attitude developed in the family towards the nearest kin, are felt to be violently contrary, incapable of being combined or reconciled. This is a matter of the logic of sentiments, not the logic of reason, and this is what is really meant when writers say that the repugnance to incest is instinctive, for there is a certain logic of the emotions which is the same in all human beings and is therefore inborn, not acquired. Individuals who behave contrary to this logic of sentiment, as by the murder of a mother, are behaving 'unnaturally'.

The study of what are regarded as 'unnatural' offences, incest, bestiality, in some societies homosexuality, patricide, and matricide, is a special branch of the comparative study of morals. One offence that is frequently thought of as 'unnatural' is witchcraft in the sense of working evil on members of one's own social group. (Black magic used against one's enemies in other groups, as amongst the Australian aborigines, is an altogether different matter.) In Africa incest and witchcraft are often thought of as connected. A South African native with whom I was discussing the subject remarked about sexual intimacy with a sister, with horror in his voice, 'That would be witchcraft.' There is a widespread belief in Africa that a man can obtain the greatest possible power as a sorcerer by incestuous intercourse with his mother or sister. Intercourse with a more distant relative would be quite ineffective.

In Europe in Christian times incest, bestiality, homosexuality, witchcraft, as 'unnatural' offences were quite logically regarded as offences against the Creator, and therefore the concern of the Church. In England it is only recently that incest has been treated as a crime to be dealt with by the secular courts. In many primitive societies it is thought that incest will be punished by supernatural sanctions. These points are all significant for an understanding of the attitude towards incest. The family is normally regarded as something sacred; incest, like patricide or matricide, is sacrilege.

The attitude towards incest, in the narrow sense, may be extended to sexual intimacy between other relatives, but in different ways in different societies. In some primitive societies sexual intimacy with the wife's mother is felt to be not less evil than with one's own mother. But there are other societies in which a man may be married at one time to a woman and to her daughter by another husband. Sexual intercourse between husband and wife is an element in the institutional complex of marriage. Every society therefore makes a distinction between this and sexual intimacy outside marriage. There is a tendency to make a distinction between persons between whom marriage is prohibited and other persons, a tendency that is much more powerful in some societies or in some instances than in others. There is very great variation in such matters.

The categories of relationship recognized in classificatory terminologies undoubtedly have considerable effect. If a woman is to be called 'mother' or 'sister' or 'daughter' the relationship with her is thought of as being similar to that with one's own mother or sister or daughter, and it is obvious that this will very frequently be felt to forbid any sexual intimacy. It would be a sort of 'symbolic' incest and as such objectionable; to have a sexual relation with a classificatory 'mother' is a symbolic offence against one's own mother. Such symbolic incest, except ritually on specific occasions, is strongly reprobated amongst the Australian aborigines.

Some writers assume, or seem to assume, that prohibitions against marriage are the result of feelings that sexual intercourse between the persons concerned would be wrong. The truth, in the majority of instances, is the reverse of this; sexual intercourse is felt to be wrong between two persons if by the rules of society they may not marry. It is extremely rarely, however, that the reaction to such conduct, or to the idea of it, is of the same kind and intensity as reaction to the idea of real incest with immediate relatives. This is exemplified in the laws of modern states where sexual intimacy between relatives who are by law forbidden to marry is not in all cases punishable as a crime.

Theoretical discussions on the subject of incest and the regulation of marriage are often, one might even say usually, full of confusions. The theory outlined here attempts to get rid of these. (1) Incest is the sin or crime of sexual intercourse between members of a parental family. It is not a question of prohibition of marriage. There are societies in which intercourse between brother and sister is incestuous, but kings or chiefs may marry, or may even be expected to marry, their own sisters. The condemnation of incest is based on the emotionally or 'instinctively' felt violent incompatibility between sexual intimacy and family relations of affection and respect. This may be rationalized in different ways. (2) The rules relating to marriages between related persons in any society are an intrinsic part of the complex of institutions that make up a kinship system. In each instance the rules can only be understood by reference to the system to which they belong and the social structures that constitute the basis of the system. The general law which each instance exemplifies is that the rules have for their function to maintain the continuity of the general system of institutional relationships, either by preventing marriages which would be disruptive or by encouraging marriages which reinforce the existing arrangement of persons. (3) The strong feelings about incest, by a readily recognizable psychological process, tend to spread, so that sexual intimacy between persons who may not marry tends to be regarded as being somewhat of the same kind as incest, though differing in the degree with which it meets with condemnation or reprobation.

The whole theory is therefore one of social structure and of the necessary conditions of its stability and continuity. Incest, as here defined, is not merely disruptive of the social life of a single family, it is disruptive of the whole system of moral and religious sentiments on which the social order rests. Prohibited marriages are for the most part simply those which would prevent the continuance of normal relations between the few persons who would be immediately affected. There are, however, instances in which a marriage between kin, not necessarily closely related, is felt to be an attack on the whole social order; this is so in the kinship systems of Australian aborigines. Such a marriage, if attempted, is a sort of crime against society and is likely to be treated as such.

XI

One of the most famous pseudo-historical speculations of the anthropology of the last century was the idea that the earliest form of society was one based on 'matriarchy' or 'mother-right'. One definition of this, given in the *Encyclopaedia Britannica* of 1910, is 'a term used to express a supposed earliest and lowest form of family life, typical of primitive societies, in which the promiscuous relations of the sexes result in the child's father being unknown'. An alternative definition, frequently used, was a social condition in which kinship is reckoned through females only, and in which there would be no recognition of any social relationship of fatherhood. We have no knowledge of any societies of this kind in the present or in the past; it is, as Robertson remarked in his *History of America* in the eighteenth century, a pure product of imagination.

But early anthropologists also applied the term 'mother-right' to certain existing societies, McLennan to the Nayars of southern India, and Tylor to the Menangkabau Malays. We may take these two societies as providing us with a special type of system to which we may continue to apply the term 'mother-right', and we may add to them the Khasi of Assam. It is to be noted that the Nayars and the Malays, so far from being 'primitive', are advanced, literate, and cultivated peoples. The Nayars are a military, ruling, and land-owning aristocracy in a civilized community; they esteem learning and the arts and have produced an extensive, and according to accounts, admirable, literature in their own language, Malayalam. The Malays similarly have an extensive literature which is admired by those who know it. Though the Khasi are less advanced they are very far from being savages. Thus the typical instances of mother-right are found, not amongst the more primitive peoples, but in advanced or relatively advanced societies.

The Nayars are sometimes referred to as a caste, but they are a numerous people divided into a number of subdivisions, 130 such being enumerated in the census of 1901. There are undoubtedly differences of custom in different sections of this large community. Their system of marriage and kinship has been undergoing change during the past seventy years, and with regard to some of its features there is a lack of agreement in different accounts. I believe that what follows is a substantially accurate generalized account of the system as it formerly existed. It is put in the past tense because it is not an accurate description of the conditions of the present day.[48]

The important unit of structure in the Nayar kinship system was a matrilineal lineage group called *taravad*. It consisted of all the descendants through females of a single known ancestress, and might number more than a hundred persons. It is spoken of in Indian law as a 'joint family', since the property is jointly owned by the group as a corporate unity; but this is not a family in the ordinary sense, since it includes women and their daughters and sons and brothers, but not their husbands. All sons of the *taravad* inherited from their mothers the right to share during their lives in the produce of the land or other property, but could transmit no rights to their children. The control of the property was in the hands of the *karanavan* (known in legal terminology as the 'manager'), who was normally the oldest male member. If a *taravad* became too large, or for other reasons, it might be divided. If the first ancestress had three daughters, all of whom had left descendants, three new lineage groups would be formed, the property being divided into three equal portions. The partition of property did not destroy the relationship, and kinship therefore extended beyond the *taravad*. A number of related *taravad* formed a group for which the name in north Malabar is *kulam;* we may call this a clan, though it may have been a very large lineage. The clan was exogamous, and the various lineages of one clan shared pollution, a birth or death in one lineage group causing pollution in the other groups of the clan. A number of clans constituted a sub-caste, and in south India the sub-caste is normally the endogamous group. Within the sub-caste it would seem that a *taravad* had a special relationship with one or more other lineages, not belonging to the same clan, whose members were their *enangar* (allies). This was an important feature of the kinship system. The Nayars had a cult of the ancestors or deceased members of the lineage; once a year an offering of food and drink was made to the ancestral spirits, including the mother's brothers and mother's mother's brothers of the living members.[49]

Before a Nayar girl reached puberty she had to undergo a ceremony of which the essential feature was the tying on of an ornament, usually of gold, called a *tali*. A number of girls of one *taravad* might pass through the ceremony together provided that they were all of the same generation. The *tali* was tied by a man invited for the purpose, called the *manavalan,* selected from the *enangar* of the *taravad*. There is some evidence that, at least in former times, the ceremony included the ritual defloration of the girl. There are two interpretations of the ceremony. One is that it is a sort of religious marriage which was dissolved at the end of the ceremony. The rite of tying the *tali* is a marriage or betrothal rite amongst some of the peoples of south India. At the end of the Nayar ceremony, which lasted four days, a cloth was severed in two parts and one part given to the *manavalan* and the other to the girl; this is a rite commonly used in south India as a rite of divorce. When the *mana-*

valan died the girl or woman on whom he had tied the *tali* had to observe formalities of mourning. Dr Aiyappan, on the other hand, holds that amongst the Nayars the tying of the *tali* is nothing more than a rite of initiation into womanhood.[50] For present purposes it does not matter which view we accept, and indeed it is largely a matter of the choice of words. The *manavalan* does not become the real effective husband of the girl on whom he ties the *tali*.

When a Nayar young woman reached a suitable age she formed a union which will here be called a marriage. The most usual union was with a man of her own sub-caste, who must be of the same generation as the woman and must be older. It seems that marriage with an *enangan* was regarded as specially suitable. While the evidence is imperfect, what there is points to the members of the allied *taravad* of the girl's own generation being all her cross-cousins; so that the Nayar system, like so many others in Dravidian India, would be based on cross-cousin marriage; the woman would take a husband preferably from the *taravad* of her father's sister. These marriages were referred to by the Sanskrit term *sambandham,* and the Nayars did not apply to them the usual Malayalam term for marriage. The Sanskrit *bandhu* refers to friendship, and may sometimes be used for the relation between a woman and her lover. The rite of marriage was of a simple kind, the essential feature being a gift of clothing (*pudaka*) from the man to the woman, which is a rite of marriage observed in some other castes of south India.

An important feature of the Nayar system was that a woman might form a *sambandham* union with a man of the caste of Nambutiri Brahmans. That caste had a patrilineal system in which only the oldest son of a family might marry a woman of his own caste and bring her home with him to raise up children. The children born of a union of a Nambutiri man and a Nayar woman would have no legal position in the family of the father.

The *sambandham* husband did not take his wife to live with him, but visited her in her own home. He did not have any legal rights over her or her property or over any children that resulted from the union. It seems that the wife could divorce her husband by asking him to discontinue his visits. It would appear that he was expected to offer her gifts from time to time. The Nayars have been often quoted as a people practising polyandry, but on this subject there is a difference of opinion amongst recent writers.[51] It seems clear from the historical evidence that in former times, at any rate amongst some of the Nayars, a woman might form a union with two or more men who might be simultaneously her *sambandham;* the Nayar marriage did not give a man exclusive right to sexual relations with the woman.

There has been discussion whether the Nayar *sambandham* union is or is not marriage; this obviously depends on how the word is defined. The Malabar Marriage Commission of 1894 decided that it did not constitute a legal marriage according to systems of law accepted in India. We may say that it was a marriage in the sense of a socially recognized union which always had some permanence and might continue through a life-time. It was, however, a union based not on legal bonds but on ties of personal affection.

We can use the Nayars to define a certain type of kinship organization to which the term 'mother-right' may be suitably applied. The system of the Menangkabau Malays was similar in essentials, and so was that of one section of the Khasis. The domestic group (the joint family of Indian legal terminology) is a matrilineal lineage of fewer or more generations. The parental family, the domestic group of man and wife with their young children living together as a household, does not exist. Jural relationships are practically confined to persons connected in the female line; so also are those religious relationships that are constituted by ancestor worship. All important property passes down in the matrilineal lineage, and only members of the lineage have claims over it; inversely the most important duties of a person are towards his or her lineage group and its members.

In the purest form of the system a man does not acquire by marriage any rights of possession over his wife and her children. His relationship with them contains no jural element, but is one of mutual affection. He gives his wife gifts, but cannot transfer to her or to his children property which belongs to his lineage or over which the lineage members have a claim. There are some variations. Amongst the Khasi a man did have certain rights over his wife since adultery was severely punished, and in this system there was an elaborate religious ceremony for marriage. The Khasi father occupies a position of respect and is revered by his children after his death. A widow may keep her deceased husband's bones for a time (thus keeping his spirit with her), but sooner or later the bones must go back to the man's lineage and clan. But yet divorce is common and may occur for a variety of reasons.

271

Mother-right is contrasted with 'father-right' and the people chosen by anthropologists as affording a typical example of the latter were the ancient Romans, or rather one form of family that existed in Rome, characterized by *manus mariti* and *patria potestas*. There was a structure of patrilineal clans (*gentes*) and lineages. The father-right type of marriage must be distinguished from what is sometimes called 'free marriage' or marriage *sine manu,* which also existed in Rome, and in which a woman retained her connexion with her own family. In the father-right marriage possessive rights over a woman were ceremonially transferred from her father or guardian to her husband, and in the *coemptio* marriage a payment was made to the woman's family in consideration of this transfer of rights. The wife thus passed under the power and authority of her husband; she transferred her allegiance from her own household deities and ancestral spirits to those of her husband. The father, the *paterfamilias,* had exclusive possessive rights over his children; they were under his power, the *patria potestas*. Over his sons he had the power of life and death, and might sell a son—the *jus vitae et necis et vendendi*. With this right the law or the mother's relatives could not interfere, but in his exercise of his power the father had to observe the duties of religion, and for an abuse of power might receive censure from the members of his gens, or at one period perhaps from the Censors.

While in one sense mother-right and father-right are opposite types of system, there is another sense in which they are only contrasting varieties of a single type. What they have in common is the extreme emphasis on the lineage, matrilineal or patrilineal, and they both contrast strongly with systems based mainly on cognatic kinship; in both, the jural relations in kinship are rigidly confined to one lineage and clan. Possessive rights over the children belong entirely to the lineage, and inversely it is within the lineage that the individual has his most important duties and also his most significant rights, such as the right of support and rights of inheritance over property. In religion also (remembering that the Romans had patrilineal ancestor worship) it is the lineage or clan ancestors to whom one owes religious duties, and from whom one may ask for succour. The institutional complex of which mother-right and father-right are contrasting forms is thus one that can hardly make its appearance except at a relatively high stage of social development, where property and its transmission have become important, and where social continuity has come to be based on lineage.

272

We have to ask, therefore, what is the differentiating principle between the two contrasting forms of the complex. It has sometimes been supposed that mother-right is the result of emphasis on the social bond between mother and child, but an examination of evidence gives no support whatever to this view. In primitive societies, whether they have matrilineal or patrilineal institutions, it is normally recognized that the closest of all kinship bonds is that between mother and child. Even in societies that incline to father-right it is felt that a child is of the same flesh and blood as its mother. So children born from one womb have the same flesh and blood, and in the patrilineal tribes of Africa children of the same mother are much more closely connected than children of the same father by different mothers. As Gluckman, following Evans-Pritchard, points out, in strongly patrilineal societies such as the Nuer and Zulu it is through the mother that the social position of a child is determined. We have only to consider the position of the *mater-familias* in the Roman family to realize that under father-right the most intimate personal bond is with the mother.

The contrast between father-right and mother-right is one of two types of marriage. A woman is by birth a member of a sibling group; strong social bonds unite her to her brothers and sisters. By marriage she enters into some sort of relation with her husband. To provide a stable structure there has to be some sort of institutional accommodation of the possibly conflicting claims and loyalties, as between a woman's husband and her brothers and sisters. There are possible two extreme and opposite solutions, those of father-right and mother-right, and an indefinite number of compromises.

In the solution provided by mother-right the sibling group is taken as the most important and permanent unit in social structure. Brothers and sisters remain united, sharing their property, and living together in one domestic group. In marriage the group retains complete possession of a woman; her husband acquires no legal rights at all or a bare minimum but at the same time he has few duties towards her or her group. Rights of possession over children therefore rest with the mother and her brothers and sisters. It is these persons to whom the child must go for every kind of aid and comfort, and it is they who are entitled to exercise control or discipline over the child.

It must be emphasized that this is a matter of jural (including legal) relations only, and these do not constitute the whole of social

273

life. We may revert to the theory of Aristotle that the two chief factors on which social harmony depends are justice and *philotes*. Justice corresponds to what are here being called jural elements in social relationships. We may take the other term as applying to all personal relationships of attachment and affection. A system of mother-right, in which a father has no, or almost no, legal rights over or legal duties towards his children, does not debar, but possibly encourages, mutual affection; for affectionate attachment can perhaps flourish best where there is a minimum of the kind of constraint that may result from the obligations of a jural relationship. Certainly there is evidence of frequent instances of strong and lasting affection between a man and his wife and children under a system of mother-right. The system simply separates out the jural relations, which are confined within the lineage, and the personal relations of affection, esteem, and attachment.

The solution offered by father-right is opposite. Possession of a woman, and therefore of the children of her body, are surrendered by marriage to her husband and his kin. The Roman husband acquires *manus* over his wife and her children fall under his *potestas*. The mother's kin, her brothers and sisters, in this kind of marriage, have no rights over the children, who, in turn, have no rights over them. The jural bonds between a woman and her siblings are severed by her marriage. But this leaves open the possibility of relations of personal affection. It is characteristic of systems that approximate to father-right that the mother's brothers and sisters are expected to extend to her children affectionate care and friendly indulgence, and that the sister's child is expected to exhibit affection towards the maternal uncles and aunts. Once again there is a separation made between jural relations and relations of personal attachment.

Mother-right as represented by the Nayars, and father-right as represented by one form of marriage in Rome, give us useful points of reference for an attempt to establish a systematic typology of kinship systems. In both these types the structure is one in which legal and jural relationships are as nearly as may be possible limited to the lineage and its connexions. The contrary of this is to be found in what are here called cognatic systems, in which jural relations are based on cognatic kinship traced equally through males and females. Such systems, or close approximations, are found in some primitive societies such as the Andaman Islands, and in advanced societies such as Anglo-Saxon and modern England.

In Africa a system that approximates fairly closely to the ideal type of a cognatic system is that of the Lozi, in which there is a minimal emphasis on unilineal kinship, so that lineages can hardly be said to exist as features of social structure. Professor Gluckman has brought out the marked contrast there is between the Lozi system and that of the Zulus which is a very close approximation to father-right. The Lozi system also contrasts with one of mother-right.

Relations of kinship involving rights and duties may also be traced through both male and female lines in a double lineage system in which the structure includes both patrilineal and matrilineal lineages or clans. An example of this type of system is provided in [*African Systems*] by the paper on the Yakö by Professor Daryll Forde. Every individual has a well-defined set of relationships within his patrilineal lineage and clan, and another within his matrilineal lineage and clan.

Thus we have four types of systems (ideal types based on empirical examples) to give us a framework within which to construct a typology: father-right, mother-right, purely cognatic systems, and double lineage systems.

In Africa the nearest approach to pure mother-right is the system of Ashanti, of which an analytical description is given in [*African Systems*] by Professor Fortes. The system is undergoing modification under European influences of various kinds, but still retains some of its former features. What has in this discussion been held to be the basic structural feature of mother-right, the close and continued solidarity of the sibling group of brothers and sisters of one flesh and blood, is illustrated in Professor Fortes's paper. It is true that the parental family exists, but it is not the standardized form of the domestic group. The importance of lineage transmission of property is well illustrated, and also the religious bonds that unite persons of common descent in the female line.

What can be called 'qualified' systems approximating not very closely to mother-right are characteristic of some parts of central Africa and have been compared [in the paper] by Dr Audrey Richards. In the system of the lower Congo, the type A of Dr Richards, there is an interesting compromise in the form of a division of rights. The male members of a matrilineal lineage continue to live together in a corporate group owning property and having their own religious cult. But the group surrenders certain rights over its female members to her husband when she marries. She retains a significant connexion with the group of her brothers, but

275

does not live with them. The domestic unit is the parental family, man, wife, and young children. Boys, when they reach a certain age, leave the parental family to join the group which consists of the male members of the lineage. The system is one of a division of rights; the father has rights over his wife and his young children within the parental family, and of course corresponding duties. But his sons ultimately fall under the power and authority of the brothers of their mother.

The system of certain tribes of Rhodesia and Nyasaland is a compromise formation in which the division of rights does not seem to be clearly defined, so that there are variations in practice not only from one tribe to another, but also within a tribe. This is connected with the local structure of this region, with its marked mobility by which persons move from one village to another, or establish new villages, so that the personnel of a particular village varies from time to time. The structural principle of mother-right appears in a contrary form to that of the Congo tribes, in the tendency for the group of sisters to continue living together, at any rate for some time. This is illustrated by the enlarged domestic group of the Bemba, consisting of a man and his wife and their married daughters with their husbands and children; the group breaks up when a man with his daughters forms a new domestic group of the same kind.

Both Professor Fortes and Dr Richards draw attention to the existence of tensions and strains in the kinship systems of the Ashanti and the Bemba. But tensions and strains and possibilities of conflict exist in any system of rights and duties. The constraint of social obligations may often be felt as irksome. There is an unfortunate tendency for human beings in some circumstances to insist on their rights rather than to be punctilious in performance of duty. But it is obvious that a system based on compromise or on successive compromises is more likely to reveal tensions or conflicts than one in which jural relations are clearly defined and socially accepted. There is no reason why a system of mother-right should present more difficulties for individual adjustment than a system of father-right. But a system like the Bemba, with its division of rights and its occasions of rearrangement of structure, must obviously depend on the way in which individuals make personal adjustments with each other.

The Ila appear to have a mixed system which is farther removed from mother-right clans and some other matrilineal features.

The Nguni peoples of South Africa, represented in [*African Systems . . .*] by the Swazi and the Zulu, may be described as having father-right. Possession of children is determined by the marriage payment. 'Cattle beget children' and 'The children are where the cattle are not' is the way the people themselves express this. But during their infancy the children belong to their mother. This is symbolically expressed in the custom by which she may protect them from sickness by making for them necklaces of hairs from the tail of her *ubulunga* cow, which belongs to the ancestral herd of her own lineage, and which she takes with her on marriage, so that during the first period of her marriage she can drink the milk of her own lineage cattle. The *ubulunga* beast, cow for a woman and bull for a man, is a link between the individual and the *sacra* of his or her lineage, the cattle, the kraal, and the ancestral spirits. A woman after her marriage is entitled to the protection of the gods of her own family, and so also are her infant children who are attached to her more than to their father. It is at adolescence that a boy or girl becomes fully incorporated in the father's lineage. There is something similar in the Ashanti system, and still more definitely in the Congo systems, in the way in which a boy's relation with his mother's brothers becomes the preponderant fact in his life after adolescence.

This section illustrates the method of typological analysis applied to institutions of kinship. The procedure is to select certain types which can be used as standards with which to compare others. For the type of mother-right it was necessary to go outside Africa, since even the Ashanti have only a qualified system of mother-right and, moreover, the Nayar and Menangkabau systems had been selected by anthropologists of the last century as best representing actual mother-right or matriarchy. It has also long been customary to take the ancient Romans as an example of father-right or patriarchy, though if we want an African example it might be possible to take the Zulu. It has been argued that the major structural principle of both father-right and mother-right is the maximum emphasis on the lineage as the source of jural and legal relations. The opposite type is therefore that of cognatic systems in which lineage has very little or no recognition. This gives three fixed points on what can be pictured as a chart on which systems could be given position by reference to these points.

To understand certain features of kinship we have to recognize that in many systems the structural unit consists of a woman and her children. This is very clearly seen in the patrilineal tribes of South Africa in which a polygynous family consists of two or more such units, each with its separate dwelling and food-supply, united by the relation to the man who is husband and father. It is by the position of this structural unit in the total kinship structure that we can define the contrast between mother-right and father-right. In true mother-right the unit group of mother and children is completely incorporated, jurally or legally, in the group of the woman's brothers and sisters. In true father-right the unit group is incorporated for jural purposes in a group consisting of brothers with their wives and children.

In trying to classify kinship systems a most important feature to consider is the way in which the relationship of a person to his mother's siblings and to his father's siblings is institutionally defined. In any system that approximates to the cognatic type there is a tendency to treat the father's brother and the mother's brother as relatives of the same kind, and similarly with father's sister and mother's sister; but the assimilation may be less complete where there is some recognition, even though it be slight, of unilineal relationships. The degree of assimilation may sometimes be indicated in the terminology, as in the English use of 'uncle' and 'aunt'. In classificatory terminologies it may appear in the inclusion of the mother's brother under the term for 'father' and of father's sister under the term for 'mother'. In the Lozi system a man calls all the cognatic relatives of his mother in her generation (the children of her father's and mother's brothers and sisters) 'mothers', male and female, and classifies as 'fathers' all the cognatic relatives of his father. It is therefore not patrilineal or matrilineal lineage that is recognized in this terminology, but the Old English distinction amongst the cognates of a person between those on the 'spear' side (through the father) and those on the 'spindle' side (through the mother). It contrasts with the common Bantu custom of using 'father' for the father's brothers and sisters and other persons of the father's lineage and generation, which is an application of the unilineal principle.

Cognatic systems are rare, not only in Africa but in the world at large. The reasons have already been indicated: it is difficult to establish and maintain a wide-range system on a purely cognatic basis; it is only a unilineal system that will permit the division of a society into separate organized kin-groups.

In a typological classification of unilineal systems an important place must be given to those systems, of which the Yakö are a good example, which recognize and attach importance to both matrilineal and patrilineal lineage relationships. This provides a special way of organizing a system of divided right by a cross-segmentation of the society.

XII

The view advanced [in this Introduction] is that to understand any kinship system it is necessary to carry out an analysis in terms of social structure and social function. The components of social structures are human beings, and a structure is an arrangement of persons in relationships institutionally defined and regulated. The social function of any feature of a system is its relation to the structure and its continuance and stability, not its relation to the biological needs of individuals. The analysis of any particular system cannot be effectively carried out except in the light of the knowledge that we obtain by the systematic comparison of diverse systems.

All the kinship systems of the world are the product of social evolution. An essential feature of evolution is diversification by divergent development, and therefore there is great diversity in the forms of kinship systems. Some idea of the diversity of African systems can be obtained from the sections of this volume. Comparison of diverse systems enables us to discover certain resemblances. Some of these are features which are confined to one ethnic region. An example in Africa is the important part played by cattle and their transfer in the system of marriage and kinship. This is a feature of the patrilineal cattle-keeping peoples of East and South Africa from the Sudan to the Transkei. It is illustrated in [*African Systems . . .*] in Professor Wilson's paper on the Nyakyusa. It would be valuable if some student could give us a systematic comparative study of the various customs of this kind. As an example of the kind of thing that is meant may be mentioned the custom in some parts of the Transkei that if a man drinks milk from the cattle of a lineage other than his own he may not thereafter marry a woman of that lineage; he is their kinsman through milk and cattle. In the same region the ceremony that completes a marriage is that in which the wife, who has usually borne at least one child, drinks for the first time the milk of her husband's herd.

There are other similarities of custom which, so far from being limited to one ethnic region, are widely distributed in parts of the world distant from one another. Customs of avoidance and joking between relatives by marriage are found in regions scattered all over the world. The custom of privileged familiarity of a sister's son towards his mother's brother is found in some peoples of Africa, Oceania, and North America. Then again the Swazi in South Africa and the Cherokee in North America both apply the term 'grandmother' (*ugogo* in Swazi) to all the women of the lineage or clan of certain grandparents (father's father and mother's father in the matrilineal Cherokee, father's mother and mother's mother in the patrilineal Swazi) and give some measure of preference to marriage with such a 'grandmother'. A general theory of kinship must be tested by the help it gives us in understanding or explaining these resemblances.

For a kinship system to exist, or to continue in existence, it must 'work' with at least some measure of effectiveness. It must provide an integration of persons in a set of relationships within which they can interact and co-operate without too many serious conflicts. Tensions and possibilities of conflict exist in all systems. Professor Fortes and Dr Richards have pointed out the tensions that exist in societies that approximate to mother-right. In systems approximating to father-right the tensions are different but exist none the less, as may be seen in the account of the Swazi. For a system to work efficiently it must provide methods of limiting, controlling, or resolving such conflicts or tensions. Dr Nadel, in his paper on the Nuba, contrasts the Nyaro system, which he regards as providing an effective social integration, with the Tullishi system, which functions less efficiently. The Tullishi, he thinks, have been less successful than the Nyaro in constructing a well-ordered system of social relations, and he looks for the reason.

Whether a kinship system functions well or not so well as a mode of social integration depends on the way it is constructed. Just as an architect in designing a building has to make a choice of structural principles which he will use, so, though in less deliberate fashion, in the construction of a kinship system there are a certain limited number of structural principles which can be used and combined in various ways. It is on the selection, method of use, and combination of these principles that the character of the structure depends. A structural analysis of a kinship system must therefore be in terms of structural principles and their application.

The unit of structure everywhere seems to be the group of full siblings—brothers and sisters. The group has its own internal structure by virtue of the distinction between the sexes and the order of birth. Its members, however, are of 'one flesh and blood', and every system makes some use of this solidarity between siblings. This means that everywhere it is felt that brothers and sisters ought to exhibit affection and ought to co-operate and interact without serious conflict. Some of the ways in which the solidarity and unity of the sibling group is utilized in building wider structures have been illustrated above.

Since in all societies the closest parental bond is that of children with their mother, the group of brothers and sisters with their mother constitutes a more extended unit of structure. This can be best seen in the polygynous families of patrilineal societies, and is illustrated in the accounts of the Zulu and Swazi. There the compound parental family consists of mother-children groups, each forming a separate 'hut' or 'house' (*indlu*), united to the man who is the father and husband.

[In this Introduction] it has been suggested that one of the most important questions to ask about a system is, in what way, if at all, it makes use of unilineal kinship as distinct from cognatic kinship. Unilineal kinship receives only a minimum of recognition, if even that, in the Lozi; matrilineal kinship is emphasized in the Ashanti, and patrilineal kinship in the Zulu and Nuer: both matrilineal and patrilineal kinship are made use of in the construction of the system of the Yakö. Between these four selected types there are many intermediate forms.

A further important feature of the social structure of any people is the way in which the kinship system is connected with the territorial arrangement of persons. In the past this has been often overlooked. Careful studies of this are now being made in Central Africa by the Rhodes-Livingstone Institute and the paper in [*African Systems* . . .] by Professor Evans-Pritchard is directed to a study of this aspect of the social structure of the Nuer. It is in the contact and co-operation of neighbours in a territorial group such as a village, or what Professor Schapera calls a ward, that relations of kinship have their most continuous influence on the social life. Professor Evans-Pritchard draws attention to the difference between the dyadic, person to person, relationships that every kinship system includes, and the group relationships that are established by a system of

281

lineages or clans. They are, of course, both included in what has been called here a kinship system, but the difference between them needs to be recognized.

In [*African Systems . . .*] it has not been possible to deal systematically with the relation of kinship systems to other parts of the social system, to religion, to political organization, and to economic life. This can, however, be studied in monographic studies of particular peoples. Professor Evans-Pritchard in his book on the Nuer, for example, has dealt with the part played by the system of lineages in the political organization of that people, and Dr Kuper in *An African Aristocracy* has shown how the kinship system is connected with the political organization of the Swazi.[52]

African societies are undergoing revolutionary changes, as the result of European administrations, missons, and economic factors. In the past the stability of social order in African societies has depended much more on the kinship system than on anything else. In the new conditions kinship systems cannot remain unaffected. The first changes are inevitably destructive of the existing system of obligations. The anthropological observer is able to discover new strains and tensions, new kinds of conflict, as Professor Fortes had done for the Ashanti and Professor Daryll Forde shows for the Yakö. How far the disruption of the existing social order will go, and in what direction reconstruction will be attempted or possible, it is at present impossible to judge. The sanctions provided by the kinship systems for the control of conduct are being weakened. For example, some of those sanctions were religious and cannot persist where missionary enterprise is successful. Judging by what is happening in some parts of Africa the new sanctions, of which the agents are the policeman and the priest or minister of the church, are proving much less effective than those of which the agents were kinsmen speaking with the authority of the ancestors behind them.

The process of change is inevitable. To a very limited extent it can be controlled by the colonial administration, and it is obvious that the effectiveness of any action taken by an administration is dependent on the knowledge they have at their disposal about the native society, its structure and institutions, and what is happening to it at the present time. A wise anthropologist will not try to tell an administrator what he ought to do; it is his special task to provide the scientifically collected and analysed knowledge that the administrator can use if he likes.

Notes

1 In Anglo-Saxon 'sibling' meant 'kinsman'.

2 W. H. R. Rivers, *The Todas,* Macmillan, 1906, p. 515.

3 'A system of notation for relationships', *Man,* 30, 1930, p. 93.

4 See M. J. Herskovits, *Dahomey,* New York, 1938, I, pp. 145 et seq.;
Northcote W. Thomas, *Anthropological Report on the Edo-speaking Peoples
of Nigeria,* 1910, part I, pp. 112 et seq. and *Anthropological Report on the
Ibo-speaking Peoples of Nigeria,* 1913, part I, p. 72.

5 Lafitau, *Moeurs des sauvages ameriquains,* Paris, 1724, vol. I, p. 552.

6 *The Early History of Institutions,* 1874, p. 214.

7 For an example of a terminology that is neither descriptive nor
classificatory see N. W. Thomas, *Anthropological Report on Sierra Leone,*
1916, part I, 'Law and Custom of the Timne'.

8 For a kinship terminology making use of both the descriptive and the
classificatory principles 'Double descent among the Yakö', by Daryll
Forde, [*African Systems . . .*].

9 An agreement between two families, whereby one promises to give a
daughter in marriage and the other undertakes to see that the marriage
payments are made, is a contract in the proper sense of the term. This
is a preliminary to the marriage, just as the Roman *sponsalia* or betrothal
was a preliminary promise or contract which was fulfilled in the *nuptiae.*

10 Sheldon Amos, *The Science of Law,* 1888, p. 87. See also Sir Frederick
Pollock, *First Book of Jurisprudence,* chap. iv.

11 'Sunt autem agnati per virilis sexus personas cognatione juncti' (Gaius);
'Agnati sunt a patre cognati' (Ulpian).

12 This account of the 'joints' of the sib is the one given in article 3 of the
first book of the *Sachsenspiegel.* I have used the Leipzig edition of 1545.
The statement about the 'nail kinsmen' is as follows: 'in dem siebenden
steht ein nagel und nicht ein glied darumb endet sich da die sip und
heisst ein nagel freund. Die sip endet sich in dem siebenden glied
erbe zu nemen'. This is explained in a Latin *nota:* 'gradus cognationis
finitur in septimo gradu, necesse est ergo in petitione haereditatis, q.
haeres et petitor articulet eum, vel se defuncto infra septem gradus
attigisse'.

13 The most readily accessible account in English of wergild payments is
Bertha S. Phillpotts, *Kindred and Clan,* Cambridge, 1913.

14 Tacitus, *Germania,* c. 20. 4: 'Sororum filius idem apud avunculum qui
ad patrem honor.'

15 A. C. Hollis, 'A note on the Masai system of relationship and other
matters connected therewith', *J. Roy. Anthrop. Inst.,* 40, 1910,
pp. 473–82. There are two misprints in the table facing p. 482. The
terms *e-sindani e-anyit* (wife's sister) and *ol-le-'sotwa* (her husband)
have been transposed.

16 The Masai are divided into five clans and each clan is subdivided into sub-clans. The sub-clan is the exogamous group, i.e. marriage is permitted within the clan but not within the sub-clan. A similar organization is found in tribes related to the Masai. The Kipsigis, for example, are divided into clans (*oret*) and the clan is subdivided into segments which Peristiany refers to by the native term *kot op chi* and calls a subdivision of the clan (Peristiany, *The Social Institutions of the Kipsigis,* Routledge, 1939). For the Nandi, Hollis tells us that 'second cousins, like cousins, are called brothers; more distant cousins are called *pick-ap-oret* (people of the family)'. This presumably refers to agnatic cousins only, and it would mean that the lineage proper (within which cousins are 'brothers') consists of the descendants of father's father's father. The Masai system may have been similar.

17 In the Kipsigis, for example, who belong to the same general area as the Masai and have a somewhat similar social organization. See Peristiany, op. cit.

18 *J. Roy. Anthrop. Inst.,* 71, 1942, p. 96.

19 Elizabeth Fisher Brown, 'Hehe grandmothers', *J. Roy. Anthrop. Inst.,* 65, 1935, pp. 83–96.

20 E. Dora Earthy, 'The role of the father's sister among the Valenge of Gazaland', *South African Journal of Science,* 22, 1925, pp. 526–9. Also in *Valenge Women,* Oxford University Press, 1933, pp. 14 et seq.

21 op. cit.

22 Sarat Chandra Roy, *The Oraons of Chota Nagpur,* Ranchi, 1915, pp. 352–5.

23 Meredith Sanderson, 'The relationship systems of the Wagonde and Wahenga tribes, Nyasaland', *J. Roy. Anthrop. Inst.,* 1923, pp. 448–59.

24 For an exposition of the theory see A. R. Radcliffe-Brown, 'The study of kinship systems', *J. Roy. Anthrop. Inst.,* 71, 1941, pp. 1–18.

25 For the Shangana-Tonga tribes see Henri Junod, *The Life of a South African Tribe,* Neuchâtel, 1913, and E. Dora Earthy, *Valenge Women.* For the Ndau, Franz Boas, 'Das Verwandtschaftsystem der Vandau', *Zeitschrift für Ethnologie,* 1923, pp. 41–51. For the Shona, B. H. Barnes, 'Relationships in Mashonaland', *Man,* 21, 1931, p. 210. Mr J. F. Holleman has kindly permitted me to see the manuscript of his very thorough analysis of the system of the Hera tribe of Mashonaland.

26 See A. R. Radcliffe-Brown, 'The mother's brother in South Africa', *South African Journal of Science,* 21, 1924, pp. 542–55, in which this analysis was first offered.

27 T. T. S. Hayley, *The Anatomy of Lango Religion and Groups,* Cambridge University Press, 1947, p. 40.

28 Quoted by Vinogradoff, *Outlines of Historical Jurisprudence,* 1, p. 252, from Liebermann, *Gesetze der Angelsachsen,* 1, p. 442. The 'wedding' was

the agreement or contract entered into by the kinsfolk of bride and bridegroom, equivalent to the Roman *sponsalia,* not the ceremony of handing over the bride (the Roman *traditio puellae*).

29 Belgian and some French writers make a similar misuse of the term 'dot', which is a woman's marriage portion of which the annual income is under her husband's control.

30 'Prestation' is defined in the *Oxford Dictionary* as 'the act of paying, in money or service, what is due by law or custom'. The prestations with which we are here concerned are all those gifts and payments of goods or services which are required by custom in the process of establishing a valid marriage.

31 R. P. G. Hulstaert, 'Le mariage des Nkundo', Inst. roy. colon. belge, *Mémoires,* 8, 1938, chap. ii.

32 This is the view of modern English law. If an unmarried woman is seduced, her father can recover damages for the loss of her 'services'; as though the only value attached to a daughter is as a servant.

33 P. Amaury Talbot, *The Peoples of Southern Nigeria,* Oxford University Press, 1926, vol. 3, pp. 437–40.

34 See Marcel Mauss, *The Gift,* Cohen & West, 1954.

35 H. Junod, op. cit., pp. 231 et seq.

36 E. J. and J. D. Krige, *The Realm of a Rain Queen,* Oxford University Press, 1943; J. D. Kridge, 'The significance of cattle exchanges in Lovedu social structure', *Africa,* 12 (4), 1939, pp. 393–424.

37 E. Dora Earthy, *Valenge Women.*

38 Hulstaert, op. cit., pp. 164 et seq.

39 John Roscoe, *The Baganda,* Macmillan, 1911, p. 129.

40 Werner, in *J. Afr. Soc.,* 13, 1914, p. 139.

41 J. F. Cunningham, *Uganda and Its Peoples,* Hutchinson, 1905, pp. 54, 331.

42 A. R. Radcliffe-Brown, 'On joking relationships', chapter 10 in this volume.

43 Ibid.; R. E. Moreau, 'The joking relationship (*Utani*) in Tanganyika', *Tanganyika Notes and Records,* 12, 1941, pp. 1–10, and 'Joking relationships in Tanganyika', *Africa,* 14(3), 1944, pp. 386–400.

44 After a lecture given more than thirty years ago in which this theory was explained, a member of the audience asked: 'Would it not be a good thing to introduce this custom (the avoidance of the wife's mother) amongst ourselves?' His question aroused a roar of laughter from the audience, which, I imagine, was what he aimed at.

45 E. Torday and T. Joyce, 'Notes on the ethnography of the BaHuana', *J. Roy. Anthrop. Inst.,* 36, 1906, p. 285.

46 Lindblom, *The Akamba,* which gives a good account of the relations between *athoni* (avoidance relatives).

47 M. Fortes, 'Kinship, Incest and Exogamy of the Northern Territories of

the Gold Coast', in *Custom is King,* ed. Dudley Buxton, Hutchinson, 1936; Hulstaert, op. cit.

48 There have been many accounts of the Nayars from the early fifteenth century to the present day. The *Report of the Malabar Marriage Commission* of 1894 is important in relation to Nayar marriage. More easily accessible is the article 'Nayars' in Hastings's *Encyclopaedia of Religion and Ethnics* and an article by K. M. Panikkar on 'Some aspects of Nayar life' in *J. Roy. Anthrop. Inst.,* 48, 1918, pp. 254–93.

49 See V. K. Raman Manon, 'Ancestor worship among the Nayars', *Man,* 20, 1920, p. 25.

50 A. Aiyappan, 'The meaning of the Tali rite', *Bulletin of the Rama Varna Research Institute,* 9(2), 1941, pp. 68–83.

51 See, for example, the correspondence in *Man,* March, April, October, November, December 1932 and August 1934.

52 E. E. Evans-Pritchard, *The Nuer,* Oxford University Press, 1940; Hilda Kuper, *An African Aristocracy,* Oxford University Press, 1949.

Bibliography

Published works of A. R. Radcliffe-Brown

(Articles followed by [MSA] appear in *Method in Social Anthropology* (1958); those followed by [S&F] appear in *Structure and Function* (1952, 1965).)

1909 Religion of the Andaman Islanders, *Folk-Lore*, 20, (3), 257-71.

1910 Puluga: a reply to Father Schmidt, *Man*, x, 17, 33-7.
Marriage and descent in North Australia, *Man*, x, 32, 55-7.

1911 Marriage and descent in North Australia, *Science of Man*, 13 (3), 63-4; (4), 81-2.

1912 Marriage and descent in North and Central Australia, *Man*, xii, 64, 123-4.
The distribution of native tribes in part of Western Australia, *Man*, xii, 75, 143-6.
Beliefs concerning childbirth in some Australian tribes, *Man*, xii, 96, 180-2.

1913 Australia, in W. Hutchinson (ed.), *Customs of the World: a Popular Account of the Manners, Rites, and Ceremonies of Men and Women in all Countries*, Hutchinson, vol. 1, pp. 139-98.
Three tribes of Western Australia, *Journal of the Royal Anthropological Institute*, 43, 143-94.
The distribution of native tribes in part of Western Australia, *Science of Man*, 14 (2), 34-5.

1914 Notes on the language of the Andaman Islands, *Anthropos*, 9, 36-52.
The definition of totemism, *Anthropos*, 9, 622-30.
Review of *The Family among the Australian Aborigines*, by B. Malinowski, *Man*, xiv, 16, 31-2.
The relationship system of the Dieri tribe, *Man*, xiv, 33, 53-6.

1916 Australian rafts, *Man*, xvi, 4, 8-9.

1918 Notes on the social organization of Australian tribes: part I, *Journal of the Royal Anthropological Institute*, 48, 222-53.

1922 *The Andaman Islanders*, Cambridge University Press.
Some problems of Bantu sociology, *Bantu Studies*, 1 (3), 38-46.

1923 Notes on the social organization of Australian tribes: part II, *Journal of the Royal Anthropological Institute*, 53, 424-47.
Methods of ethnology and social anthropology, *South African Journal of Science*, 20, 124-47. [MSA]

1924 The mother's brother in South Africa, *South African Journal of Science*, 21, 542-55. [*S&F*]

1925 Review of *Origin of Australian Beliefs*, by Lambert Ehrlich, *American Anthropologist*, n.s. 27, 161-3.

Reviews of *Atlas Africanus*, by Leo Frobenius and Ritter v. Wilm; *Das unbekannte Africa,* by Leo Frobenius; *Hadschra Maktuba,* by Leo Frobenius and Hugo Obermaier, *American Anthropologist,* n.s. 27, 325-9.

Culture areas of Africa, *American Anthropologist,* n.s. 27, 346-7.

Native dolls in the Transvaal Museum, *Annals of the Transvaal Museum*, 11 (2), 99-102.

1926 Introduction to *Among the Bantu Nomads*, by J. Tom Brown, Seeley Service & Co.

Father, mother, and child, *Man*, xxvi, 103, 159-61.

Arrangements of stones in Australia, *Man*, xxvi, 133, 204-5.

The rainbow-serpent myth in Australia, *Journal of the Royal Anthropological Institute*, 56, 19-25.

1927 The regulation of marriage in Ambrym, *Journal of the Royal Anthropological Institute*, 57, 343-8.

Australian Aborigines, Institute of Pacific Relations, General Session 2, Honolulu. Preliminary paper.

1928 (with William Warner and F. W. Burton) Some aspects of the aboriginal problem in Australia, *Australian Geographer*, 1 (1), 67-9.

1929 Age organization terminology, *Man*, xxix, 13, 21.

A further note on Ambrym, *Man*, xxix, 35, 50-3.

Bride price, earnest or indemnity, *Man*, xxix, 96, 131-2.

Bilateral descent, *Man*, xxix, 157, 199-200.

Notes on totemism in eastern Australia, *Journal of the Royal Anthropological Institute,* 59, 399-415.

Historical and functional interpretations of culture in relation to the practical application of anthropology to native peoples (abstract), *Proceedings of the Fourth Pacific Science Congress,* Java. [*MSA*]

The sociological theory of totemism, *Proceedings of the Fourth Pacific Science Congress,* Java. [*S&F*]

1930 Black Australia, *Australian Museum Magazine*, 4 (4), 133-8.

Editorial, *Oceania*, 1 (1), 1-4.

The rainbow-serpent myth in south-east Australia, *Oceania*, 1 (3), 342-7.

Review of *The Chronological Aspects of Certain Australian Social Institutions,* by D. S. Davidson, *Oceania*, 1 (3), 366-70.

The social organization of Australian tribes, *Oceania*, 1 (1-4), 1930-1, 34-63, 206-46, 322-41, 426-56; reprinted as *Oceania* Monographs, no. 1 (1931).

A system for notation of relationships, *Man*, xxx, 93, 121-2.

Former numbers and distribution of the Australian aborigines, *Official Yearbook of the Commonwealth of Australia*, no. 23, 671-96.

1931 The present position of anthropological studies, British Association for the Advancement of Science, *Report*, Section H, 141-71. [*MSA*]

Applied anthropology, Australian and New Zealand Association for the Advancement of Science, *Reports*, no. 20, 267-80.

1933 *The Andaman Islanders* (reprinted with a new Introduction and an Appendix on language), Cambridge University Press.

Law, primitive, *Encyclopedia of the Social Sciences*, vol. 9, New York, Macmillan, pp. 202-6. [*S&F*]

1934 Sanctions, social, *Encyclopedia of the Social Sciences*, vol. 13, New York, Macmillan, pp. 531-4. [*S&F*]

1935 On the concept of function in social science, *American Anthropologist*, n.s. 37, 394-402. [*S&F*]

Kinship terminologies in California, *American Anthropologist*, n.s. 37, 530-5.

Anthropology and Indian administration, *American Indian Life*, no. 26.

Patrilineal and matrilineal succession, *Iowa Law Review*, 20 (2), 286-303. [*S&F*]

Primitive law, Man, xxxv, 48, 47-8.

Review of *The Jealousy of the Gods and Criminal Law at Athens*, by Svend Ranulf, *American Journal of Sociology*, 40, (4).

1937 Australian social organization (summary communication), *Man*, xxxvii, 201, 178.

1938 Motherhood in Australia (letter to editor), *Man*, xxxviii, 14, 15-16.

1939 *Taboo* (Frazer Lecture), Cambridge University Press. [*S&F*]

1940 On joking relationships, *Africa*, 13 (3), 195-210. [*S&F*]

On social structure, *Journal of the Royal Anthropological Institute*, 70, 1-12. [*S&F*]

Preface to *African Political Systems*, ed. M. Fortes and E. E. Evans-Pritchard, Oxford University Press.

Introduction to *A Japanese Village: Suye Mura*, by John Embree, University of Chicago Press; Cambridge University Press.

1941 The study of kinship systems, *Journal of the Royal Anthropological Institute*, 71, 1-18. [*S&F*]

1942 Obituary of Sir James George Frazer, *Man*, xlii, 1, 1-2.

1944 The meaning and scope of social anthropology, *Nature*, no. 3904, 257-60. [*MSA*]

1945 Religion and society (Henry Myers Lecture), *Journal of the Royal Anthropological Institute*, 75, 33-43. [*S&F*]

1946 A note on functional anthropology, *Man*, xlvi, 30, 38-41.

1947 Evolution: social or cultural? *American Anthropologist*, 49 (1), 78-83.

Australian social organization, *American Anthropologist*, 49 (1), 151-4.

Review of *Society and Nature*, by Hans Kelsen, *Erasmus* (Amsterdam), 1 (1).

Review of *A Aculturação dos Alemães no Brasil*, by E. Williams, *Man*, xlvii, 95, 91.

1949 A further note on joking relationships, *Africa*, 19 (2), 133-40. [*S&F*]

Functionalism: a protest, *American Anthropologist*, 51 (2), 320-2.

White's view of a science of culture, *American Anthropologist*, 51 (3), 503-12.

1950 *African Systems of Kinship and Marriage* (ed., with C. D. Forde), Oxford Universtiy Press.

Introduction to *African Systems of Kinship and Marriage*.

1951 Murngin social organization, *American Anthropologist*, 53 (1), 37-55.

The comparative method in social anthropology (Huxley Memorial Lecture), *Journal of the Royal Anthropological Institute*, 81, 15-22. [*MSA*]

1952 *Structure and Function in Primitive Society: Essays and Addresses*, London, Cohen & West; New York, Free Press, 1965.

Introduction to ibid.

Foreword to *Religion and Society among the Coorgs of South India* by M. N. Srinivas, Asia Publishing House.

Historical note on British social anthropology, *American Anthropologist*, 54 (2), 275-7.

1953 Dravidian kinship terminology, *Man*, liii 169, 112.

1954 Australian local organization (letter to editor), *American Anthropologist*, 56 (1), 105-6.

Foreword to *Military Organization and Society*, by Stanislaw Andrzejewski, London, Routledge & Kegan Paul; California University Press, 1967.

1956 On Australian local organization (letter to editor), *American Anthropologist*, 58 (2), 363-7.

Primitive religion: notes on the lectures of Radcliffe-Brown, *Anthropology Tomorrow*, 4 (2), 3-41. [*The paper comprises notes taken by Sol Tax on a lecture course given in the University of Chicago by Radcliffe-Brown in the winter of 1932. The journal is a duplicated student publication.*]

1957 *A Natural Science of Society*, Chicago, Free Press.

1958 *Method in Social Anthropology: Selected Essays by A. R. Radcliffe-Brown* (ed. M. N. Srinivas), University of Chicago Press.

Social anthropology. [*MSA*]

1968 *Structure et fonction dans la société primitive* (translation of *Structure and Function in Primitive Society* by L. Martin), Paris, Éditions de Minuit.

Struttura e funzione mella società primitive (translation of ibid. by L. Conforti and G. Bertolini), Milan, Jaca Book.

Some critical and biographical sources on Radcliffe-Brown

Eggan, Fred (ed.), 1937, *Social Anthropology of North American Tribes*, University of Chicago Press (enlarged ed., 1955). [*A set of papers by Radcliffe-Brown's Chicago students, including a consideration of his theories, in historical perspective, by Sol Tax, and with an introduction by Robert Redfield.*]

Elkin, A. P., 1956, 'A. R. Radcliffe-Brown, 1880-1955', obituary in *Oceania*, 26 (4), 239-51. [*Particularly informative on his teaching and research in Australia.*]

Firth, Raymond, 1956, 'Alfred Reginald Radcliffe-Brown: 1881-1955'. Obituary in the *Proceedings of the British Academy*, 42, 287-302. [*The fullest account of his life.*]

Fortes, Meyer (ed.), 1949, *Social Structure: Studies Presented to A. R. Radcliffe-Brown*, Clarendon Press. [*Essays presented to Radcliffe-Brown on his retirement, and including an appreciation by the editor.*]

—— , 1955, 'Radcliffe-Brown's contributions to the study of social organization', *British Journal of Sociology*, 6 (1), 16-30.

—— , 1956, 'Alfred Reginald Radcliffe-Brown, F.B.A., 1881-1955: a memoir', *Man*, lvi, 172, 149-53.

—— , 1970, *Kinship and the Social Order*, Routledge & Kegan Paul. [*Chapter 4 is the fullest and most authoritative discussion of Radcliffe-Brown's kinship theories available.*]

Kuper, Adam, 1973, *Anthropologists and Anthropology: the British School 1922-1972*, Allen Lane (Peregrine paperback, 1975). [*Chapter 2 deals at length with Radcliffe-Brown's life and work.*]

—— , 1976, 'Radcliffe-Brown, Junod and the mother's brother in South Africa', *Man*, n.s. 11 (1), 111-15. [*Traces the points made by Junod and later Tsonga ethnographers against Radcliffe-Brown's famous analysis of the mother's brother among the Tsonga.*]

Lombard Jacques, 1972, *L'Anthropologie britannique contemporaine*, Paris, Presses Universitaires de France. [*Part II is an extended consideration of Radcliffe-Brown's theories.*]

Lowie, Robert H., 1937, *The History of Ethnological Theory*, New York, Farrar & Rinehart; London, Harrap, 1938. [*Contains a brief discussion of Radcliffe-Brown's theories, interesting as representing a contemporary, fairly critical, American viewpoint.*]

Needham, Rodney, 1974, *Remarks and Inventions: Skeptical Essays about Kinship*, London, Tavistock; New York, Barnes & Noble. [*Chapter 3 is an extended critical assault on Radcliffe-Brown's Australian studies, and on his scholarly integrity.*]

Two significant rejoinders have already been published. See F. Eggan's review (Aboriginal sins) in the *Times Litt. Supp.*, 13 December 1974, and H. Scheffler's note (Radcliffe-Brown and Daisy Bates) in *Man*, n.s. vol. 10 (2), 1975, 310-11.

Salter, Elizabeth, 1972, *Daisy Bates,* Angus & Robertson; Corgi, 1973., [*A biography of an Australian social worker and ethnographer with whom Radcliffe-Brown worked. It contains her view of their difficult relationship, and an accusation of plagiarism.*]

Singer, Milton, A neglected source of structuralism: Radcliffe-Brown, Russell and Whitehead. Paper presented at ASA conference, Oxford, 1973 (duplicated).

Stanner, W. E. H., 1968, 'Radcliffe-Brown, A. R.', *International Encyclopedia of the Social Sciences,* New York, Macmillan.

Watson, E. L. Grant 1946, *But to what Purpose: the Autobiography of a Contemporary,* Cresset Press. [*Contains a vivid description of Radcliffe-Brown at Cambridge, and engaged in fieldwork in Australia, by a friend.*]

White, Leslie A., 1966, *The Social Organisation of Ethnological Theory,* Houston, Rice University Studies. [*A critique of the 'Schools' of Boas and of Radcliffe-Brown from the point of view of an American cultural evolutionist.*]

Postcript

Two very interesting lectures were delivered after the compilation of this Bibliography, which both addressed themselves, critically, to the theories of Radcliffe-Brown. Edmund Leach's Radcliffe-Brown Lecture for 1976 has now been published: *Social Anthropology: a Natural Science of Society?* (the British Academy, 1976). Maurice Bloch's Malinowski Lecture, 'The Past and the Present in the Present', will appear in due course. It is worth contrasting what each states Radcliffe-Brown said with his own statements.

Index

adaptation, 18, 19, 44, 161
adoption, 190, 231
Aiyappan, A., 270, 286
ancestor worship, 22, 113-15, 120, 121, 125, 126, 217, 246, 270; defined, 113
Andaman islands, 1, 3, 6, 37, 43-4, 57, 59-60, 73-102, 107, 184, 274; medicine men in, 91-2
Anyula, 168
Aranda, 116, 156, 157, 159, 173; kinship terminology, 147-9; marriage rules, 148-50, 167-8, 169, 170; section system of, 153-6; 'type', 4, 143, 146-50, 151, 153-6, 165-9, (distribution, 150-1)
Aristotle, 273-4
Ashanti, 217, 259, 260-1, 275-6, 277, 281, 282
Australian aborigines, 2, 6, 7, 13, 26, 28, 29, 34, 37, 42, 90, 121-2, 176, 185; hordes, 131-3, 134, 157, 161, 173; kinship systems, 1, 117-18, 131-73, 176, 193, 218, 250-1, 257, 265-7; language, 133-4, 163; totemism, 55-68, 115-19, 126, 158-61; tribes, 132-4, 161; 'types of social organization', 4-5, 150; *see also* under tribal names
avoidance, 64, 142, 175-7, 184, 186, 248-53, 280
avunculate, *see* mother's brother

Bari, 222
Bateson, G., 40, 41
beliefs, 43-4, 73-5, 87, 103-5, 112-13, 125
Bemba, 177, 192, 233, 259, 276
bridewealth, 231, 236-46, 279
Boas, F., 25, 39, 53-4, 67, 68, 188, 284

change, 15, 17, 37, 68, 189; and European influence, 37-9, 275, 282
Cherokee, 182-3, 186, 188, 280
Chiga, 177
China, 65-6, 107-11, 114, 127, 193, 202, 261

Christianity, 105-7, 114, 122, 128, 204; and marriage rules, 236, 255-7, 265
clans, 34, 45, 46, 114, 175, 177, 178, 181-3, 186, 229, 230-4, 254, 261, 272, 282; in Australia, 157, 160, 170, 171-3; defined, 230
classification, 4, 5, 17, 31, 40, 143; *see also* comparison; typologies
cognatic kinship, 233, 261-2, 272, 274-5, 277-8, 281; defined, 190, 200-1; rare, 278; Teutonic, 202-6
comparison, 4, 5, 16, 44-5, 53-69, 279; Boas on, 53-4; indispensable, 31, 54, 174; unnecessary, 76, 97
Comte, A., 15-17, 24
conflict, 46, 48, 59, 61, 66, 78, 90, 101, 189, 250, 281
Confucius, 108-10, 125, 127
Coulanges, F. de, 12, 111-14, 126, 128
culture, 13, 19, 48, 50, 161; defined, 14-15, 24; not object of study, 26-7; and social structure, 40

descent, 190, 200; double, 275, 278, 281
diachrony, 14, 189
Dogon, 175
Durkheim, É.: and crime, 22; and R-B, 2-3, 5, 24; and religion, 101-2, 115-16, 118-19, 123, 126, 128

Earthy, E., 214, 284, 285
economics, 34, 47
Eggan, F., 1, 6, 187
Elkin, A., 171, 172
Embree, J., 30, 41
ethnography, 31, 43-4, 54, 68
ethnology, 27, 53, 54, 68, 74
Evans-Pritchard, E., 1, 28, 36, 41, 185, 188, 230, 273, 281, 282, 286
evolution, 17-19, 39-40, 51, 279
exchange, 47, 77, 84, 85, 184, 185
exogamy, 62-4, 231, 253-67
explanation, 67-8, 73-5, 189

293

Index

family, 20, 21, 131, 140, 175, 190-1, 212, 214, 264-7, 275, 281; basic unit of kinship structure, 191; types of, 191-2
father, 140, 143, 178-9, 190, 214, 272, 278
father-right, 23, 271-7, 280
Fiji, 23, 177, 182, 226-7
Forde, C. D., 232, 275, 282, 283
Fortes, M., 1, 7, 177, 188, 230, 259, 260-1, 275, 276, 280, 282, 285
Fortune, R., 120, 128
Frazer, J., 12, 53, 54, 101, 115
function, 7, 21-2, 37, 43-52, 279; of avunculate, 23-4; defined, 21-3, 36-7, 74, 189; of filial respect, 179; of religion, 22, 74-5, 79-80, 106-11, 114, 124, 161
functionalism, 25, 49-52

Galla, 230, 248, 249, 250, 252-3
Ganda, 218, 248
genealogical relations, 140-1, 172, 202
generations, 56, 66, 176, 178-80, 213, 215-21, 228-30, 249; combination of alternate, 179-80, 216-19, 221, 227-8
Gillen, F., 116, 138, 159, 168
Gluckman, M., 233, 258, 273, 275
Gregg, D., 49-52
Gusii, 63

Haida, 48, 55
Hehe, 217, 260
Henga, 218, 219
Herskovits, M., 283
history, 11, 12, 13, 39, 40, 53, 67-8, 117, 189; pseudo, 23, 24, 55, 205-6, 211, 267
Holleman, J., 225, 284
Hollis, A., 209, 224, 283
horde, 131-4, 157, 161, 173
Hsün Tsü, 107-10, 127
Huana, 213, 252
Hubert, H., 102, 115
Hulstaert, G., 228-9, 239, 285
Huron, 194

Ila, 233, 276
incest, 216, 248, 253-67
India, 114, 261-2
institutions, 3, 5, 13; defined, 20-1, 36, 51
Iroquois, 194, 195

joking relationships, 61-2, 64, 174-88, 219, 249-53, 280; between clans and tribes, 177-8; and contractual relations, 185-6; defined, 174; symmetrical and asymmetrical, 174
Junod, H., 181, 187, 226-7, 284, 285

Kamba, 253
Kamilaroi, 134
Kaonde, 219
Karadjeri, 150-1, 166
Kariera, 133, 134, 142, 156, 157, 159, 162-4, 168-9; distribution, 150; marriage rules, 143-5, 162-3; section system, 151-3, 155-6, 163; terminology, 144-9; 'type', 4, 143-7, 150, (discovered, 173)
Khasi, 268, 271
kinship systems, 23, 28, 46, 131-286; and affinity, 247; Australian, 1, 117-18, 131-73; and contractual relations, 198-9; defined, 16, 140, 190, 200; orders in, 192, 233-4; range, 141, 192-3, 210
kinship terminology, 141, 142, 183, 193, 219-22, 246; Australian, 141, 144-5, 147-9, 172-3; classificatory, 193-7, 211-15, 261, 266, 278, 280, 283, (and lineage, 206-9, 225-8); descriptive, 192, 283; Masai, 206-10; Omaha type, 222ff.
Kipsigi, 284
Kitara, 213, 222
Kongo, 113, 213
Kroeber, A., 61
Kumbaingeri, 150, 164, 166
Kuper, H., 282, 286

Labouret, H., 174, 177, 184, 185, 188
Lafitau, J. F., 194, 195
Lango, 231
language, 26, 32-3, 44; in Australia, 133-4, 163; and social structure, 33, 40
law, 35, 47, 104, 116, 122, 186; jural relations, 198-9
laws, social, 4, 16, 61, 68; Boas on, 53-4, 68
Lendu, 248
Lenge, 214
Lévi-Strauss, C., 1, 5, 7, 42
lineages, 23, 34, 113-14, 175, 181, 186, 201-2, 206-9, 230-4, 254, 261, 263, 272, 282; unity of, 225-8
Loisy, A., 105, 123-4, 126
Lovedu, 245, 260
Lowie, R., 25, 37
Lozi, 233, 258-9, 262-3, 275, 278, 281

Index